OXFORD WORL

COLLECT

PAUL VALÉRY was born in the M.
1871, second son of Fanni Grassi (from Trieste) and
Valerj (spelling later changed), a Corsican customs inspector. The family moved to nearby Montpellier in 1884 where Valéry attended the lycée before taking a degree in law at the university that now bears his name. From his teenage years, he began publishing verse but following a profound emotional and intellectual crisis in Genoa in October 1892, he abandoned this literary vocation. Resolving to master the sensibility and the mind, he undertook rational investigation and scientific research every morning for fifty years in his *Notebooks/ Cahiers*. In 1894, he settled permanently in Paris where he was introduced to the circle of Stéphane Mallarmé and became deeply involved in the literary and artistic milieu. Through Edgar Degas, he met Jeannie Gobillard (niece of Berthe Morisot) whom he married in 1900 and with whom he had three children. For the next twenty-two years, Valéry acted as personal secretary to the director of the Havas Agency. At the instigation of André Gide, he began reworking his youthful verse in 1912. This stirred him into a new surge of literary activity, resulting in the publication of *The Young Fate* (1917), the *Album of Early Verse* (1920) and *Charms* (1922) which brought him immediate fame. He was elected to the Académie française in 1927. Regarded as the pre-eminent French intellectual of the era, he lectured all over Europe, frequented high-society Paris salons and served on the International Committee on Intellectual Cooperation at the League of Nations from 1925–1940. During the Occupation, he lectured at the Collège de France, working on his unfinished play *Mon Faust*. He died on 20 July 1945 and, following a state funeral decreed by General de Gaulle, was buried in the cemetery by the sea at Sète.

PAUL RYAN is author of *Paul Valéry sous le signe de l'art et des artistes* (2019) and *Paul Valéry et le dessin* (2007), prefaced by Martine Rouart, Valéry's granddaughter. He has been a member of the Valéry group of the Institut des textes et manuscrits modernes (CNRS-École Normale Supérieure) for over twenty years and with whom he published numerous volumes of the series *Paul Valéry Cahiers 1894–1914* (Gallimard). He also worked as a translator of the series *Paul Valéry Notebooks* (Peter Lang) and participated in the digitization of the *Cahiers* with the Sorbonne University.

OXFORD WORLD'S CLASSICS

*For over 100 years Oxford World's Classics have brought
readers closer to the world's great literature. Now with over 700
titles—from the 4,000-year-old myths of Mesopotamia to the
twentieth century's greatest novels—the series makes available
lesser-known as well as celebrated writing.*

*The pocket-sized hardbacks of the early years contained
introductions by Virginia Woolf, T. S. Eliot, Graham Greene,
and other literary figures which enriched the experience of reading.
Today the series is recognized for its fine scholarship and
reliability in texts that span world literature, drama and poetry,
religion, philosophy, and politics. Each edition includes perceptive
commentary and essential background information to meet the
changing needs of readers.*

OXFORD WORLD'S CLASSICS

PAUL VALÉRY

Collected Verse

Translated with an Introduction and Notes by
PAUL RYAN

OXFORD
UNIVERSITY PRESS

OXFORD
UNIVERSITY PRESS

Great Clarendon Street, Oxford, OX2 6DP,
United Kingdom

Oxford University Press is a department of the University of Oxford.
It furthers the University's objective of excellence in research, scholarship,
and education by publishing worldwide. Oxford is a registered trade mark of
Oxford University Press in the UK and in certain other countries

Published in the United States of America by Oxford University Press
198 Madison Avenue, New York, NY 10016, United States of America

British Library Cataloguing in Publication Data
Data available

Library of Congress Control Number: 2023947648

ISBN 978-0-19-882032-1

Printed and bound in the UK by
Clays Ltd, Elcograf S.p.A.

MIX
Paper | Supporting
responsible forestry
FSC® C018072

For Fiona

ACKNOWLEDGEMENTS

MY sincere thanks to Luciana O'Flaherty for her support and patience, Judith Luna who first contacted me about this project, Kizzy Taylor-Richelieu, and colleagues at OUP.

I am deeply grateful to Michel Jarrety for his assistance in interpreting and clarifying various terms for me and whose Paul Valéry, *Œuvres* was so valuable for this project.

I thank my friend and colleague of the Valéry group in Paris, Micheline Hontebeyrie, who answered my very numerous queries, particularly on the finer points of diction, nuances in language, and Valéry's use of older meanings, as well as thorny semantic and interpretational issues in French, with her tremendous knowledge and insight which she so generously shared with me.

Most especially, I would like to express my deepest appreciation to my former professor and dear friend Robert Pickering for his time and effort in terms of guidance and inspiration but above all for his brilliant suggestions. I have benefited enormously from his expertise which he shared so generously and steadfastly with me. His input and influence here have been immeasurable and I thank him for his enduring loyalty.

To my wife Fiona, and my two sons Ronan, and Cillian, I offer my sincere thanks for their encouragement, understanding, and support.

CONTENTS

viii   *Contents*

INTRODUCTION

*A poem ought to be a feast for the Intellect. It cannot be any-
thing else. Feast: in other words a game, yet solemn; an image
of what we are not, of the state in which endeavours are merely
rhythmical, redeemed. We celebrate something by accomplish-
ing it or by representing it in its most pure and most beautiful
state. (...) Once the celebration is over, nothing should remain.
Ashes, trodden garlands.*

Paul Valéry[1]

Early Verse and Crisis

Much of Valéry's evolution and success can be ascribed to events and
forces of chance outside himself. Bemused by André Gide's observation that his life was 'calculated like a game of chess', Valéry stated in
a letter to the novelist Jean Voilier (pseudonym of Jeanne Loviton) that
everything was, more precisely, 'the work of others', mentioning in
particular the following personal landmarks: Pierre Louÿs who lured
him towards poetry; Joris-Karl Huysmans who steered him towards an
administrative career; André Lebey who secured him twenty-two
years' work with the Havas Agency; the combined efforts of Stéphane
Mallarmé, Edgar Degas, and the 'Mallarmé women' who matched
him up with his wife Jeannie (Berthe Morisot's niece); the publishing
company Gallimard whose persistent prodding gave rise to *The Young
Fate* (*La Jeune Parque*); and the statesman and diplomat Gabriel
Hanotaux who first mooted the idea of his election to the Académie
française. Had a conflation of these fortuitous circumstances not put
him back on the path of creative writing before the Great War, he
would probably be remembered as a minor Symbolist-inspired poet
who, in a creative flurry of late adolescence, composed a series of striking sonnets and then abruptly abandoned verse to pursue other intellectual and scientific interests. The equally unforeseen return to
writing poetry from around 1912, a key juncture after a twenty-year

[1] Paul Valéry, *Cahiers*, 29 vols., facsimile of the 261 original cahiers (Paris: CNRS,
1957–61), vi. 220. All further references to the *Cahiers* are from this edition unless otherwise stated and will be given in the text. All translations from French are my own.

hiatus, can be attributed to Gide whose persistent exhortations to revise his old verse brought about a resurgence of latent poetic energy. Little did Valéry imagine that his work on the poem, originally intended to be about forty lines long, would over the course of five long years expand to 512 verses to become *The Young Fate*, widely considered one of the greatest masterpieces of French poetry. In doing so, the erstwhile poet, then 46 years old, unwittingly tapped into a deep well from which emerged two other stunning poetic collections: *Album of Early Verse* (*Album de vers anciens*) and *Charms* (*Charmes*). By the mid-1920s, Valéry's output of poetry, prose, dialogues, prefaces, essays, and conferences had earned him international renown and he became a prominent public personage sought after by the foremost Parisian salons. His vast erudition, natural bonhomie, dazzling repartee, wit, and alacrity of mind put him at ease in the company of prime ministers, presidents (de Gaulle), pre-eminent scientists (Albert Einstein) and mathematicians, as well as artists of every hue from Degas to Salvador Dalí and Claude Monet to Henri Matisse.

It is important to recognize that Valéry practised verse at two distinct stages in his life, separated by a demarcation line that came in the form of a profound crisis at the age of 21, with both selves writing for different reasons and in radically altered personal circumstances. What is remarkable in the writer's chronology is both the brevity and intensity of the creative periods in question. Much of the early verse was concentrated in a period of approximately five years between 1887 and 1892 followed by a decade of intense poetic output beginning around 1912 and tapering off in the early 1920s. In his homage 'At the grave of Pierre Louÿs' in June 1925, Valéry acknowledged that he only felt inspired to write after his chance encounter thirty-five years earlier with Louÿs: 'My new friend insisted that I should take as a duty, and as a type of virtuous practice, what I had up to then undertaken for enjoyment but without allowing it to cause me pain.'[2] Aided by a dictionary of rhyme procured by his older brother Jules, Valéry began writing his very first verse in a black moleskin copybook whose cover bears the name and the coat of arms of his native port town of Sète in January 1884. This was a decisive year for the 13-year-old in which he discovered the poetry of Victor Hugo, Théophile Gautier, and Charles Baudelaire, and moved permanently with his family to

---

[2] Paul Valéry, *Œuvres*, ed. Michel Jarrety (Paris: Le Livre de Poche, 2016), i. 944.

nearby Montpellier in the autumn. At the start of the new school term in October 1885, he befriended Gustave Fourment (1869–1940), his earliest confidant and future senator of the department of the Var, to whom he sent and dedicated some of his first poems in 1887. Reflecting Valéry's Catholicism and interest in spiritual mysticism, many of these early sonnets are strongly imbued with liturgical symbolism and religious sentiment, as Fourment noted of 'Moonrise'. This artistic tendency was very much in the air at the time, particularly with the Symbolist poets who saw art as an esoteric form that could express the ineffable impressions and intuitions of man's inner existence through highly allusive language. Valéry envisaged bringing together his early verse in a volume called *Carmen mysticum* (later changed to *Chorus mysticus*), but the project never materialized. As one might expect, the early poetry is also naturally infused with the influence of the Mediterranean landscape of Sète which kindled the imagination of the young boy observing the *Mare Nostrum* from the busy quays and would equally inspire the poetic imagery of the later verse with its evocation of the resplendent expanse of sea.

Although Valéry wrote some sonnets during his years at the lycée, poetry still constituted an incipient interest alongside architecture and the study of ornament. His poetic creativity emerged properly in his first year at the University of Montpellier where he enrolled to study law in 1888, a subject choice based more on his older brother's career path than on a genuine vocation. It was in fact Jules who, having happened upon the poem 'Dream' in April 1889, sent it (unknown to Valéry) to the *Petite Revue du Midi* in Marseilles where it was published in August, the same month he discovered the work of Paul Verlaine and Mallarmé through reading Joris-Karl Huysmans's *A rebours*. While he felt great exhilaration at the sight of his name in print for the first time, Valéry admitted later in life that it induced a disquieting impression 'similar to that in dream where you are profoundly ashamed to find yourself stark naked in a living room' (*Cahiers*, xxvii. 684). Despite his initial reluctance to embark on a literary career, he began sending poems to various reviews. Fourment remained hitherto the sole critical reference for the young Valéry but a fortuitous encounter with the Parisian novelist and poet Pierre Louÿs (1870–1925) at the centenary of the University of Montpellier on 20 May 1890 proved to be an event of capital importance and led to a long friendship between the writers. Like Fourment, Louÿs constituted an

indispensable interlocutor for the budding poet, not least for his candour and criticism of what he saw as his new correspondent's sometimes slavish imitation of Hugo and Baudelaire. On 2 June, he sent his
first verse to Louÿs who suggested submitting them on his behalf to
reviews, but also exhorted him to send some poems to Mallarmé, then
the towering literary figure, friend of the Impressionists and defender
of Manet. On this prompt, Valéry established contact with the 'Master'
in October 1890, enclosing two poems with his letter:

Dear Master, A young man lost in the depths of the provinces, whom the
chance discovery in reviews of a few rare fragments has allowed to deci-
pher and love the secret splendour of your work, takes the liberty to write
to you. [. . .] Mr P. Louis has already spoken to you about him, and this has
prompted him to send you these lines and verses.[3]

A few days into Valéry's month-long stay in Paris in late September
of the following year, Louÿs, who was also the instigator of Valéry's
long-lasting and deeply rewarding intellectual friendship with Gide,
brought him to Mallarmé's apartment at the rue de Rome which
proved to be the pivotal encounter.

While it would be three more years before Valéry permanently
exchanged the provincial isolation of Montpellier for Paris, he under-
went in the meantime an intensely prolific phase in his development,
publishing many of the poems later included in the *Album of Early
Verse* in literary reviews such as *La Conque*, *Le Centaure*, *L'Ermitage*,
La Plume, and *La Syrinx* (the last founded in Aix-en-Provence by
Joachim Gasquet, poet of the Félibrige and a friend of Paul Cézanne).
The favoured poetic form of the young Valéry was the sonnet which,
introduced to France in the Renaissance era by Mellin de Saint-
Gelais and Clément Marot, had fallen out of favour until the
Romantic era in the early nineteenth century and later again by the
Parnassian poets such as Verlaine. What appealed to him most of all
was the structure of this 'finite and *brief* system' (*Cahiers*, ix. 650)
within which each component has a separate function yet is unified
with the others by the form of entity:

Glory evermore to he who devised the sonnet. However, while many
beautiful sonnets have been written, the most beautiful has yet to be
written; it will be one whose four sections will each carry out a function which is progressive and quite distinct from that of the others, yet

---

[3] Paul Valéry, *Lettres à quelques-uns* (Paris: Gallimard, 1952), 28.

the differences will be fully justified by the *life* of the discourse as a whole. (*Cahiers*, viii. 774)

However, just as he was integrating into Mallarmé's circle, Valéry experienced a growing disenchantment which led him to disavow all forms of idealism and the belief in the exalted and transcendental power of poetry, in particular the Mallarméan Symbolist ideal with its attendant obscurity and linguistic modishness. The trigger that precipitated the abandonment of poetry as well as a complete reappraisal of his being came in the guise of an unrequited and obsessive passion for Sylvia de Rovira (1852–1930) or 'Madame de R——', whom he first saw in Montpellier in 1889. The affective turmoil came to a head during a stay in Genoa in October 1892, a month after graduating in law, when, in the course of a violent thunderstorm, he underwent an existential and spiritual crisis which he viewed as a veritable revolution of self and a crisis of his feminine Other. Out of this vulnerability emerged the clinical-analytic defence which Valéry instituted under the name of the 'System' in the *Notebooks* (*Cahiers*). The 'Night in Genoa', as it became known, is in essence the dramatization of the crisis of the mind which would find its poetic embodiment in the dramatic monologue *The Young Fate* in 1917.

Having finally settled in Paris in March 1894 where he took up a post as redactor at the Ministry of War, Valéry continued to frequent Mallarmé's famous Tuesday gatherings for a number of years where he brushed shoulders with the literary and intellectual elite of fin-de-siècle Paris, such as the Symbolist poet Henri de Régnier (1864–1936) and José-Maria de Heredia (1842–1905). Soon after first seeing Valéry at Mallarmé's funeral in 1898, Julie Manet (daughter of Berthe Morisot, niece of Édouard Manet, and pupil of Pierre-Auguste Renoir) and her two first cousins Jeannie and Paule Gobillard invited him to attend their Thursday evening gatherings held at 40 rue de Villejust. Two years after the jointly celebrated marriage of Valéry and Jeannie and of Julie Manet and Ernest Rouart in 1900, both couples moved into renovated apartments on different floors of Berthe's erstwhile residence where they would spend the rest of their lives surrounded by the art of Manet and the Impressionists. Valéry became personal secretary to Édouard Lebey, director of the Havas Agency, a post he occupied until Lebey's death in 1922 and which allowed him to devote time to his own private research. Liberated from the falsehoods of literature, vague sentiment, and other 'idols', Valéry turned his attention to 'exact sciences', closely studying the work of Maxwell, Faraday, de Broglie, Poincaré, Carnot, Riemann, and Willard Gibbs, and later Jean Perrin, Émile Borel (with whom he became close friends), and Einstein who attended the writer's conferences. Adopting the rigorous model of mathematics and physics, Valéry devised an intellectual method or System which, akin to Descartes's 'tabula rasa', sought to enquire into every conceivable subject. The model was the polymath Leonardo da Vinci, the paradigm of the Universal man, whose notebooks served as a template for the *Cahiers* which, after half a century, totalled over 26,000 pages. Now detached from the exigencies of publishers, he devoted himself steadfastly every morning before dawn to this project intended solely for his own purposes and in which he found his true intellectual stimulation. The scale and breadth of the corpus of writing are so vertiginous that Valéry the analyst, theoretician, and aphorist has largely foreshadowed Valéry the poet.

The Return: Poems and Passion

Pressed by Gide and Gaston Gallimard from 1911 to revise the verse of his youth, Valéry, who had eschewed publication during the so-called 'period of silence', embarked on a process that marked a slow transition to his great creative phase. While redrafting a selection of poems composed principally between 1889 and 1892 and published in various journals and magazines, Valéry was invariably struck by the strangeness of revisiting work written by his 'ex-self' under the sign of his eminent Symbolist predecessors in an era long since past; in a notebook entry he remarked: 'It's an odd sensation seeing these collected poems which I wrote at very different periods of my life and widely separated from each other, subject to varying impressions, but always in the same spirit—Exercises' (*Cahiers*, ix. 526). Having embarked on this path, he found himself unexpectedly drawn to a new 'exercise', *The Young Fate*, which, although initially conceived as a valedictory work, would take in effect five years (1912–17) to complete. Much of it was composed against the traumatic backdrop of the war, which he recalled years later in his notebook:

5 a.m. All of a sudden, I am reminded of the time when, around this time of the day, I would resume work on my *Jeune Parque*, and feel very alone,

with this solitary work for the solitary soul, while people were killing each other at the front, out of obedience and out of dread, subjected to an artificial kind of fatality, and while my mind, absorbed in poetic nothings, kept an anxious vigil for the morning *communiqué*. (*Cahiers*, xvi. 189).

This description runs counter to the perception which subsequently emerged of Valéry the poet removed from the brutal reality of war. In effect poetry became a refuge from the personal and political anxiety occasioned by the cataclysm observed from Paris while Jeannie and the children spent the summer at Berthe Morisot's country residence at Le Mesnil which Julie Manet had inherited.

Even though the long and anguished gestation of *The Young Fate* consumed most of his time during the war years, Valéry had not lost sight of the original request from Gide to publish his early verse. He turned his attention almost immediately to the poems 'Aurore' and 'Palme', as if to recompense himself for the energy expended on the long poem. At the end of his life, he wrote that being so preoccupied by *The Young Fate* roused him to pursue simultaneously other projects (notably the Socratic dialogues), which yielded a fruitful exchange of ideas between the different subjects. In tandem with the ongoing major revisions of the early sonnets, he began working on some new poems with the intention of publishing them in a single collection. Nourished by the creative energy unleashed by the composition of *The Young Fate*, Valéry soon realized that the future *Album of Early Verse* could not accommodate the growing number of pieces, leading him thus to reserve the new verse for a separate collection which he began compiling in a new copybook entitled *Charms*. The painstaking genesis and evolution of the two projects remained inextricably interwoven between 1917 and late 1920 to such an extent that some of the poems featured for a time on both lists before being eventually assigned to one or other of the collections, if not eliminated. The first edition of the *Album* which appeared in December 1920 comprised sixteen pieces, later augmented to twenty-one for the definitive edition. Half of the poems had originally been published in reviews between 1890 and 1892, and in many instances lightly retouched, but in some cases so radically redrafted that they constitute in effect new works.

With the *Album* now in print, Valéry set about completing *Charms*. However, this new period of creative fervour coincided with his encounter in June 1920 with the writer Catherine Pozzi (1882–1934).

Born into an aristocratic family and daughter of an eminent surgeon, she was a member of the tout-Paris literary and intellectual milieu which he was now actively frequenting. Valéry was immediately struck by her immense erudition and self-taught intellectual curiosity, but also by her passion for science and letters. The tormenting highs and lows of the passionate and tempestuous relationship plunged him into a crisis in 1921 which the contemporary notebooks and his abundant correspondence with Pozzi evince. Rekindling a latent metaphysical and existential anguish, the encounter served as a painful reminder of the founding youthful crisis of 1892 which had caused him to abandon the practice of poetry and to put in place 'desperate defensive measures' (*Cahiers*, xxii. 842) against the ravages of extreme sensitivity provoked in him by 'Mme de R———'. In his mind, both events, set almost thirty years apart, were resonant, as he states in this recapitulative note: 'If I view myself historically two astounding events in my secret life stand out. A coup d'état in '92 and something immense, boundless, immeasurable, in 1920. I tossed the thunderbolt upon what I was in '92. Twenty-eight years later, it fell on me—from your lips' (*Cahiers*, viii. 762). The impact of the affair on Valéry's personal, emotional, and intellectual being cannot be underestimated. It imparted a powerful inflection to the self-referential analysis which he wrote under numerous code names for Pozzi in the rubric 'Eros' of the *Notebooks* but equally to the verse and other contemporaneous literary projects, such as the dialogue *The Soul and Dance* (*L'Âme et la danse*). Although the poems of *Charms* were largely conceived prior to 1920, the vicissitudes of the relationship left their mark on the tonality of 'The Footsteps', 'Poetry', and 'Secret Ode', while others, such as the 'Fragments of Narcissus', were redrafted in light of the encounter. Despite the passionate and intensely intellectual reciprocities between the two kindred spirits, their liaison was beset by various irreconcilable differences, chiefly his refusal to leave Jeannie but also Pozzi's mystico-spiritual and religious proclivity that conflicted with his rationalism and sceptical rigour, jealousies regarding other acquaintances, and Valéry's new-found fame.

By the time *Charms* was published in 1922, the relationship had already foundered, even if it were not definitively renounced for another six years. While still labouring over the 'Fragments of Narcissus' which caused him immense frustration, Valéry made a final push in the spring to pull the collection together, continuously reviewing and updating the proposed table of contents, eliminating some poems, redrafting others, and adding new ones, some of which first appeared in separate editions: 'The Graveyard by the Sea' in August 1920, 'Sketch of a Serpent' the following year, and 'Serpent' in 1922. After two missed deadlines, principally occasioned by difficult personal and emotional circumstances attendant on its compilation, along with the death of his employer Édouard Lebey in February 1922, *Charms* finally went to print four months later. The collection is striking for the range of poetic form, comprising sonnets, odes, elegies, and longer verse. Its themes and symbols are equally varied, with reflections on mortality, time, dawn, the sea, the tree, the serpent, fruit, architecture, poetry, as well as love and desire expressed through mythological figures such as Narcissus and the Pythia. Moreover, the highly polished poems of *Charms* present a wide array of metrical schemes (from pentasyllable lines to dodecasyllabic alexandrines), unlike the *Album* where the preponderant metric form is the classical alexandrine.

Theory and Legacy

In the intensely prolific period following the publication of *The Young Fate*, Valéry became, almost overnight, the darling of the most prestigious Parisian salons hosted mostly by affluent foreign women such as Anna de Noailles, the Princesse de Polignac (née Winnaretta Singer, daughter of the sewing machine magnate Isaac), Mme Lucien Mühlfeld, Renée de Brimont, Florence Blumenthal, Mme Émile Halphen, and Martine de Béhague. Deprived of a steady salary since the death of Lebey and being, as he put it, 'up for sale or for rent'[4], Valéry was grateful for the generous benefaction that these admiring patrons of the arts offered him. His exceptional social and political connections with the leading figures of the day secured him various positions on committees or in institutions that helped supplement a precarious income now largely dependent on sales of essays or deluxe editions of his literary work. Within a few months of the publication of *Charms*, he was invited to give a lecture in London to a literary audience that included Virginia Woolf, Arnold Bennett,

[4] *Cahiers*, viii, 511 (This quotation appears in the original notebook (Cahier ccc) at the Bibliothèque nationale).

George Moore, Aldous Huxley, and Vita Sackville West. Valéry had
not been to England since the spring of 1896 where he worked as
a translator for Cecil Rhodes's chartered company. The mining magnate and founder of the De Beers diamond firm, who had helped
establish British dominion of southern and central Africa through his
British South Africa Company, had resigned in January as prime minister of the Cape Colony. In an essay, 'My Early Days in England',
written for the *Bookman's Journal* in December 1925, Valéry fondly
recalled this stay in London and his encounters with Aubrey
Beardsley, Edmund Gosse, George Meredith, and Joseph Conrad.
A very complimentary article on *The Young Fate* by John Middleton
Murry in the *Times Literary Supplement* in August 1917 renewed
Valéry's connections with the country which deeply fascinated him
and which he would visit on numerous occasions in the interwar years
for conferences in London, Cambridge, and Oxford where he was
conferred an honorary doctorate in 1931.

Unsurprisingly, Valéry's enviable reputation as a great poet, man of
letters, and intellectual attracted a considerable amount of criticism
and reproach. He was condemned (often unjustly) for past misjudge-
ments and his dubious stance on political issues (such as not support-
ing Dreyfus); his misrepresentations of Freudian[5] theory (dream
narrative and the unconscious) and his distrust of Surrealism's
exploration of the same domain; his deep aversion to the novel as
a literary form; his dismissal of Marcel Proust's notion of sleep,
dream, and memory's connection to the past; his rejection of Henri
Bergson's[6] conception of duration as a continuum or indivisible
movement; and his rejection of traditional philosophy. Nor was Valéry
without his detractors in the domain of poetry. These were mostly
peers who saw in *The Young Fate* a classical work noted for its complexity and formal beauty from a bygone era, written in a mode no
longer practised and thus at variance with the modern artistic aesthetic. The self-imposition of strict metrical and formal constraints

---

[5] Describing himself as 'the least Freudian of men' (*Lettres à quelques-uns*, 225), Valéry
was more interested in the mechanisms and structures of consciousness than in interpreting its meanings.

[6] Valéry enjoyed a warm relationship with Bergson, despite their intellectual differences, and paid fulsome tribute to the Jewish philosopher (notwithstanding the context
of the Occupation) in his funeral oration in 1941. He particularly cherished Bergson's
remark: 'What V[aléry] has done had to be attempted' (*Cahiers*, xxiv. 762).

constituted the antithesis of prevailing avant-garde radicalism. Having built on the multifarious artistic precedents of the Belle Époque, modernism sought a realignment of art with the reality of a society profoundly altered and scarred by the experience of war and one which would reflect its new cultural and social values. In an age attuned to Dada and (soon) Surrealism in which experimental free verse flourished, there was thus something anachronistic about Valéry's neoclassical formalism. Following the publication of *The Young Fate* in 1917, he became for a time a source of fascination for the Surrealists André Breton and Philippe Soupault who regularly visited his apartment. However, he soon incurred their displeasure for his disparagement of revolt, inspiration, and incompletion as well as his conception of the poem as a calculated and fictive construct of the intellect. Notwithstanding his connections with the modernists or the avant-garde artists who frequented the Salon d'automne, Valéry's aesthetic was much more attuned to an earlier era. Educated in the classics, yet an avid reader in his teenage years of the Romantic, Decadent, and Symbolist writers of the nineteenth century, he absorbed the notion of poetic creation promulgated by Edgar Allan Poe whose work was immensely important to him (as it had been for Baudelaire, Huysmans, and Mallarmé). For other critics, Valéry's work recalled all too transparently the last, notably 'Hérodiade' and 'L'Après-midi d'un faune', whose poetics and formalism, as he stated, were quite distinct from his own:

While Mallarmé's two poems ['Hérodiade' and 'Après-midi d'un faune'] are fashioned from a weave stitched to form, with a subject whose sole condition consists in making itself known [. . .] *La Jeune Parque*, which, strictly speaking, has no subject, stems from the objective to define or designate a knowledge of the living being, which is not just about recognizing—but must be learnt. This, allied to the conditions of form, gives the poem its very major complexities. (*Cahiers*, xxiv. 117)

In view of their close relationship, it is understandable that he would be perceived as the true disciple of Mallarmé, yet being defined as such irked him. Nurtured in the fin-de-siècle cradle of Symbolism which he described as 'a tendency to turn the cultivation of the arts into a veritable religion' (*Cahiers*, vi. 881), Valéry did indeed owe a debt to its leading figure whose art excited in him 'boundless admiration' and to which he devoted numerous essays. However, feeling

cast down in 1892 by the impossibility of equalling the artistic ambi-
tions and the unique perfection of the poetry of Mallarmé and
Rimbaud, Valéry had long since abandoned the Symbolist aesthetic
and what he viewed as the vanity of its idealism.

In reality, Mallarmé was one of several writers from a wider poetic
tradition who at different times exerted an influence on Valéry, beginning with Hugo and Baudelaire, followed later by Racine whose work
he rediscovered when writing *The Young Fate*, but also including that
of Petrarch, Euripides, and Vergil whose *Bucolics* he translated
between 1942 and 1944. Classicism is manifestly visible in the
Socratic dialogues *Eupalinos* and *L'Âme et la danse* that Valéry published in 1920–1 (between the *Album* and *Charms*), as well as in
frequent references to the mythology (Narcissus, Orpheus, Pindar,
Zeno) of classical antiquity. Perceived as a classical poet by critics and
contemporaries such as T. S. Eliot who placed him firmly in the classical renaissance of early twentieth-century France, Valéry was slightly
bemused by the designation and anxious to avoid being placed under
some 'ism'. He affirmed in the *Notebooks* that he only ever wrote for
himself, not with any public in mind, and that his principal motivation was the exercise of the intellect. In the privacy of these pages,
the self-reflecting Valéry equally gives echo to the criticism occasioned by his anti-literary conception of literature and to perceptions
attributed to him by some critics who saw him as obscure, dry, excessively theoretical, pessimistic (indeed nihilist), lacking sensitivity and
substance, prone to sterility and to archaisms, with a narrow attach-
ment to form.

Although he professed to know little about Hellenism or Greek
culture, Valéry's artistic sensibility was deeply informed by his early
interest in architecture and aesthetic principles that were espoused
and assimilated by artists of the neoclassical era whom he admired,
such as Lorraine, Poussin, and Ingres. In fact, a key to understanding
his own conception of writing can be found in his remarks pertaining
to the artistic method of Degas who, like Wagner and Mallarmé, represented the embodiment of the supremely conscious artist. His relationship with Degas, notoriously irascible and dismissive of the
'literary set'[7] yet remarkably sympathetic and warm to Valéry, endured
until the painter's death in 1917. A disciple of Ingres whose maxims

[7] Paul Valéry, *Œuvres*, ed. Jarrety, ii. 570.

he would quote to Valéry, Degas bridged the gap between academic art and the nascent modernism of the late nineteenth century which it sought to undermine. Valéry, who identified with the classical ideal of simplicity, harmony, and the pre-eminence of the line, was above all captivated by the painter's painstaking draughtsmanship and his conception of a drawing or a painting as an exercise that could be endlessly reworked and modified, as he stated in his monograph *Degas Dance Drawing* (*Degas Danse Dessin*, 1936):

The work for Degas was the product of an unlimited number of studies, and then a *series of operations*. I truly believe he thought that a work could never be regarded as *finished*, and that he could not imagine that an artist could look at one of his paintings after an interval without sensing the urge to take it back and re-work it.[8]

Valéry, who left numerous projects unfinished, had certainly much in common with this conception of artistic creation. That he managed to complete what he did was a veritable achievement. He stated that his works resulted from more complicated conditions than those of other writers and were not products of a desire to create but often occasioned or generated by a kind of duty imposed by circumstances on a mind which did not like that method. Literature per se never much interested Valéry who was more instinctively engaged with the challenge of devising or writing 'models of thought [. . .] programmes for some imagination or for establishing some connection. Psychological stage shows, ways of representing some system or other' (*Cahiers*, iv. 784). He affirms numerous times in the *Notebooks* that his 'works' were those that he had not actually accomplished: 'A poem is, for me, a *state* in a sequence of elaborations. Those I have published are, in my view, productions ended by external circumstances. And had I kept them, I would have transformed them indefinitely' (*Cahiers*, xxviii. 435). It was precisely the acts and exercises of the mind involved in composition, or *poietics*, which preoccupied Valéry who stated that his goal, unlike the more conventional ambition of a writer, was not 'to act on other people, so much as on myself—*Myself*—insofar as it can be treated as though it were a work . . . of the mind' (*Cahiers*, xviii. 703). It was the crisis of 1892 that caused this seismic shift in how he understood the function of writing from being a public-oriented

---

[8] Paul Valéry, *Œuvres*, ed. Jarrety, ii. 540.

art to a self-directing exercise. While the form of the poem was Mallarmé's sole obsession, Valéry viewed verse as a particular application of the power of the mind. His primary motivation lay not in the idea of creating a finite and beautiful object but in the combinatory potential that the work in progress instigated. Despite their very polished form, Valéry considered the poems of *Charms* as a series of formal and prosodic experiments. A poem was an accidental construction, in other words an artificial end point of a mental development which resulted in one possible state in a process of indefinite reworking: 'I can understand, in my case, how the same subject matter and virtually the same words could be endlessly reworked, and occupy an entire lifetime' (*Cahiers*, viii. 657). Finishing a work was more likely to be contingent on factors like chance, accident, the clamouring of a publisher, the advent of another poem, or simply lassitude. This conception necessarily challenged the teleology of the literary work that can be explained with reference to some end or purpose. The quest for perfection entailed the practice of obsessively redrafting and modifying the poems, which often caused him to miss publication deadlines. Without the compulsion of the latter, Valéry confessed that he would not have finished anything of significance. Publication was the necessary yet accidental conclusion of a development in which he struggled with not just the arbitrary nature of writing but also, as he often stated, the sheer tedium of it. The actual crafting of a poem—in other words, fashioning an idea into verse through a well-wrought use of words (which he expressed under the Greek term *poïein*[9]: to make)—interested him more than the finished object given up to public consumption. This overarching principle is affirmed in several of his essays on aesthetics and poetics as well as in the *Notebooks*. That Valéry devoted a separate classification—one of the thirty-one comprising the gargantuan corpus of private reflections—to the domain of *poietics* is indicative of its importance within his 'System'.

Valéry's conception is in effect more attuned to the seventeenth-century principles of formal mastery, rigour, and control which made his work a foremost exemplar of 'pure poetry'[10]. This doctrine was articulated by Poe in his seminal essay 'The Poetic Principle' in 1850 and widely discussed by writers from Baudelaire (who translated the text), Mallarmé, and George Moore to Eliot and the Jesuit Abbé Henri Bremond (1865–1933). Taken in a general sense, pure poetry can be defined as that which does not have a didactic intention or seek to convey an ostensible semantic narrative, but focuses instead on exploring the musicality of language and the relationship of words and sounds. In his essay on Baudelaire whom he described as Romantic in origin but fundamentally classical, Valéry discusses at length the pre-eminence of Poe for the author of *The Flowers of Evil*, but also his continued importance for an entire generation of late nineteenth-century poets including Mallarmé, Rimbaud, and Verlaine. It is noteworthy that in his first letter to Mallarmé in October 1890, Valéry describes himself as being 'profoundly enthused by the smart doctrines of the great Edgar Allan Poe', adding that the name alone is revelatory of his own 'Poetics'. T. S. Eliot's essay 'From Poe to Valéry' serves as a reminder of the conceptual evolution and lineage of *poésie pure* in which these writers found validation for their belief that, as Baudelaire famously wrote, 'a poem should have nothing but itself in view'[11]. As an autotelic construct, the poem thus creates its own necessity and has no outward purpose or limiting objective: 'I am unable to separate my conception of poetry from that of perfected forms— self-sustaining, whose sound and psychic effects are in correspondence, in some way "indefinitely"' (*Cahiers*, xxv. 698). Following in Valéry's footsteps, Eliot was similarly dismissive of the notion of the poem as a vehicle for meaning or content, seeing it as an impersonal entity with its own immanent values which are wholly independent of the author. In Mallarmé's art of subtle suggestion, the voice of the poet disappears and the initiative is handed to language itself. He attained exquisitely evocative verse by combining words in novel ways and emancipating them from rhetoric and their conventional referential function to the point that the meaning supplanted form and medium. The spiritual writer Abbé Bremond famously relaunched the debate in France following his important lecture *La Poésie pure* at the Institut de France on 24 October 1925 in which he established the connection between mysticism and poetry whose aspiration should be the condition of prayer. Rejecting this dimension, Valéry posited that a pure poem remained an elusive ideal and unattainable in anything longer than one line; in his essay 'Pure Poetry' published in 1928—one of

---

[11] Baudelaire, *Œuvres complètes*, ii (Paris: Gallimard, ed. Claude Pichois, 1976) 333.

many he wrote on aesthetics, art, and literary theory in the interwar years—he defined it thus:

> If the poet succeeded in creating works where no element of prose would appear, poems where musical continuity would never be disrupted, where relations of meaning would themselves be constantly identical to harmonic relations, *where the transmutation of thoughts from one to the other would be of greater importance than any thought*, where the play of figures would contain the reality of the subject—then one could talk of *pure poetry*.[12]

He later remarked to Jean de Latour that lines 48 to 55 of the 'Fragments of Narcissus' were the finest he had ever composed and representative of this principle since 'they are [. . .] absolutely devoid of ideas and attain thereby this degree of purity which constitutes precisely what I call *pure poetry*'[13].

Valéry argues that poetic language draws attention to language itself and, using as an analogy the distinction between prose and poetry or that between walking and dancing, has as its sole objective the creation of an '*état poétique*' or '*poetic state*'[14]. As action that is non-utilitarian and non-purpose-oriented, dance exists in and for itself, expending energy within its own self-contained system of resonance and, akin to a flame, eventually consuming itself. Like all works of art, a poem has the creation of this state as its condition; in other words, it must intensify and gratify desire. Beauty is thus the creation of a longing for renewal of the same, as opposed to a longing for the new, which makes the work inexhaustible and self-perpetuating. Valéry states that the aim of poetry is to generate this state of expectation and resolution at every instant, thereby creating resonance in which 'things commune with the treasures of innermost energy' (*Cahiers*, ix. 802). Music, 'the most powerful (non-chemical) engine for stirring pure possibility' (*Cahiers*, xix. 893), achieves this much more effortlessly than poetry, hence his deep envy of its resources and particularly those employed by Wagner in his music dramas (operas whose actions are not interrupted by formal song divisions and characterized by an integrative use of leitmotifs). Valéry reminds us that Baudelaire played an important role in promoting Wagnerism in France, notably following his famous review of the performance of

---

[12] Valéry, *Œuvres*, ed. Jarrety, i. 1713.
[13] Jean de Latour, *Examen de Valéry* (Paris: Gallimard, 1935) 159.
[14] Paul Valéry, *Œuvres*, ed. Jarrety, iii. 827.

Tannhäuser and the uproar surrounding it in Paris in 1861. It was through the poet, who found in Wagner's 'magical power of suggestion' the articulation of his own conception of synaesthetic correspondences, that Mallarmé was drawn to the interchange between the two art forms. As passionate advocates of Wagner's art, both endeavoured to develop a musicalized language that could match the richness of sound, and thus ensure that poetry would not be overhauled in the hierarchy of the arts. In his essay on Baudelaire whom he believed to be one of the first French writers 'to be passionately interested in music', Valéry quotes Mallarmé's definition of Symbolism as an aesthetic objective, common to a group of writers, which consisted in ' "taking back from Music what rightfully belonged to them" '[15]. Mallarmé, who was essentially concerned with the *sound* and the musical nature of words, sought to attain a state of resonance not only by combining them in new ways, but also by expunging these linguistic signs of their conventional association and denotative reference. Endowed with new and unexpected evocative energy, this purified poetic language could rouse the emotions and express more powerfully the complexity of human sensibility through emphasis on sound and suggestion. Using analogy as its medium, it sought to depict not the object but the sensorial response it engenders, and thereby distil or transmute its essence.

Valéry later acknowledged that he and his Symbolist predecessors dreamed of 'drawing from language almost the same effects that purely sound sensation generates on our nervous system'[16]. Wagner's impact on the young Valéry was even more profound. It added to the despondency he felt in 1892 when he realized the impossibility of matching the sublime art of either the composer, whom he placed in the same bracket as Leonardo and Poe, or of Mallarmé, who took intellectuality to its supreme degree:

Nothing made me despair more than Wagner's music [. . .] Isn't that the supreme aim of the artist—*To Despair!* [. . .] He caused me a different type of despair than Mallarmé—The latter more directly, because his craft was more intelligible to me—But then again M[allarmé] himself was driven to despair by W[agner]. (*Cahiers*, xxiv. 564)

[15] Valéry, *Œuvres*, ed. Jarrety, i. 759.
[16] Valéry, *Œuvres*, ed. Jarrety, i. 759. See also in 'Propos sur la poésie': 1739.

Valéry's deeply held admiration for Wagner's 'attempt to represent
the whole sentient being' (*Cahiers*, iv. 207) through music never
waned and he continued to find, at a theoretical or ideal level at least,
confirmation and fulfilment of his own artistic quest for a musico-
poetic language: 'what is immeasurable in his music is the recording
by timbres and combinations of the various *levels* of consciousness-
sensibility and of the psychophysical modulations bonding them
similar to Riemannian intersections' (*Cahiers*, xviii. 78). For Valéry,
the force of music lay precisely in modulation which allows the
smooth transition from one key signature to a closely related one by
way of a pivot chord common to both. The device became the principal tenet of his compositional technique, a continuum which he integrated as a gliding of ideas and images as well as in the musical
succession of syllables and verse[17], emerging as both the central motif
and mode of expression in *The Young Fate* which he described as 'a
literally boundless quest for what could be achieved in poetry analogous
to what is called "modulation" in music'[18]. As the formal embodiment of this effortless system of substitutions of parts, the great poem
charts the fundamental moments and experiential phenomena of the
living being, through the physiological states and mental phases that
were the subject of intellectual and scientific analysis in his private
Notebooks: dream, awakening, consciousness, time, and language, as
well as emotions such as desire, fear, shame, and sorrow symbolized
and embodied by the most fundamental image of all: the tear.

Valéry repeatedly states that his obsession with form and changes
of tone overrode any concern for the subject or meaning which he
considered a shadow show. It was form and rhythmic pattern, not the
motif, which engendered both *The Young Fate* and 'The Graveyard
by the Sea', as he later elucidated in the essay 'On the Subject of
"The Graveyard by the Sea"' ('Au sujet du *Cimetière marin*'). One
must of course caution against reading too much into such absolute
affirmations concerning the pre-eminence of form in relation to
content and acknowledge that the poems do indeed reveal central
themes and preoccupations. A more appropriate representation of the
formal–semantic dialectic lies perhaps in the following metaphor:

[17] Valéry had already endeavoured to represent the mind's complex functioning, particularly regarding the transition to sleep and dream, in one of his earliest prose works,
the unfinished *Agathe* from 1898.
[18] Valéry, *Œuvres*, ed. Jarrety, iii. 789.

'Thought should be hidden in verse like the nutritional value in a fruit. It is food, but it appears as pure delight. All you perceive is the pleasure, but you are getting nourishment' (*Cahiers*, viii. 309). Valéry remarked that he never applied or devoted himself to external phenomena, such as a landscape, a character, or a scene, which he saw as the domain of the novel—a form he profoundly disliked. A work of art has as its duty to eliminate the sensation of the arbitrary or the feeling that something could be replaced or modified—which he viewed as the natural flaw of fiction—and thereby create its own necessity. His subjects and models were never anything but internal in nature, intellectual objects in accordance with his mental propensities which shunned external links. In a fundamental divergence from Mallarmé, Valéry foregrounds and accentuates the exploration of mental processes, such as consciousness, self-awareness, inner voice or discourse, modulation of thought, sleep, and memory. In keeping with the rationale and intellectual purpose underpinning the System of the *Notebooks*, he conceived poetic creation as an exploration of the possibilities of the psyche and the art of composition as an 'exercise' (*Cahiers*, ix. 526) that reveals its mechanism in action.

Valéry's intellectualism gave rise to a perception among some critics that he wrote poetry lacking emotion and dedicated to formal perfection which has overshadowed the elemental and sensual aspects of his verse. It is more apposite to view his poetic work, particularly the accomplishment of maturity, as an amalgam of intellectual eloquence and highly lyrical and richly textured language consisting of internal rhymes, sounds, cadences, and strikingly blended patterns of alliteration and assonances. Poetry for Valéry was of course mostly concerned with the harmonic power and suggestive potential of words through which he sought to attain '*enchantment* and the edification of the *state of enchantment*' (*Cahiers*, xxi. 478). As the extensive analysis of prosody in the *Notebooks* evinces, harmonics lie at the very heart of his verse. Akin to the technique in music where the fundamental pitch causes composite frequencies or overtones to sound, it allows combinations and associations of meaning of words. This resonance emanates from the constant interplay of sound and sense, generating what Valéry called a '*singing state*' (*Cahiers*, xv. 875)—a fundamental tenet of his poetics—which he likened to the image of a pendulum oscillating between both poles:

Poetry is—the *singing* state—(resounding—resonating—rebounding) of the *function which speaks* [. . .] The vibrating singing state—as though the internal dictionary, the table of potential signs were . . . *tautened* and the relations between words had altered their reciprocal tension. The inter-change of sound and sense having become reciprocal, of equal value. (*Cahiers*, xi. 744)

It is not surprising that Racine and Rimbaud, whose influence over him was scarcely less profound than that of Mallarmé, emerge as prized models for the musicality of their poetry. Moreover, it is worth recalling Valéry's deep involvement in musical life, from his regular attendance with his wife Jeannie (a talented pianist who studied under the composer Raoul Pugno) at concerts, opera, and Diaghilev's Ballets Russes to actual or proposed musical collaborations with friends like Claude Debussy, Arthur Honegger, Maurice Ravel, Germaine Tailleferre, Sergei Prokofiev, and Igor Stravinsky.

During the interwar years Valéry turned his attention to other genres of expression. He composed four dramatic dialogues, two melodramas set to music by Honneger with choreography by Ida Rubinstein, the libretto *Cantata of Narcissus* (*Cantate du Narcisse*) written in the style of Gluck to music composed by Tailleferre in 1938, as well as his late unfinished play *Mon Faust*. Even if he pri-vately worked on the cycle of prose poems entitled *Alphabet*, begun in 1925 but published posthumously, *Charms* turned out to be his last major poetic work. Unlike the published poetry which is universal in nature and avoids self-reference, much of the later verse, scattered across his correspondence, constitutes occasional pieces written for close friends and for mistresses. From the early adolescent quatrain for Mme de R——, it was through poetry that Valéry expressed the emotional crisis of his amorous encounters with Catherine Pozzi, Renée Vautier, Émilie Noulet, and particularly Mme Jeanne Voilier for whom he wrote over 130 improvised love poems between 1937 and 1945.[19] That he found himself composing such verse so late in his life surprised no one more than himself, as he noted in 1939:

It is odd that the poems I am capable of writing now are dedicated only to Eros—setting Sun—Stranger still that the idea of writing poetry *out of love, about love* did not cross my mind between the ages of 15 and 30—It

---

[19] These poems were posthumously published under the titles *Corona* and *Coronilla*.

would have stunned me—not having recognized any direct relationship between art and the amorous self. (*Cahiers*, xxi. 909)

Although he abandoned verse in 1892 as a reaction against anxious obsession, idolatry, literary vanity, and in particular 'mental suffering— (Mme de R[ovira])' (*Cahiers*, xxii. 204), there is a certain irony in the fact that it constituted the medium through which he expressed the surfeit of the very same passion in later life.

In fact, Valéry felt this acute estrangement from his verse very soon after the publication of *Charms* which brought the period of great creativity to a close. Upon seeing a poem composed from that era in 1928, he reflected in his notebook:

A poem I wrote, appearing by pure chance before my eyes—I feel very detached from *what crafted* it [. . .] It is very distant from the main road of my mind. It's because I composed it during a specialized phase in verse—and even at a specific moment of this mental period. I consider it a curiosity. A game of my nature. It is an *external creation*. (*Cahiers*, xviii. 907)

If the time he devoted to composing verse proved, in the end, to be as brief as his renown was immense, it was precisely the latter which occasioned such a radical change in his circumstances. Valéry was quickly overtaken by other cultural, political, and literary engagements which brought him into contact with the eminent intellectuals, philosophers, scientists, writers, and artists of the era by way of his appointment as president of the PEN Club and to the Council of National Museums, but more importantly to the Committee for Arts and Letters of the International Institute of Intellectual Cooperation (a predecessor of UNESCO) under the League of Nations which counted among its notable members Einstein, Bergson, Marie Curie, Thomas Mann, and the physicist Hendrik Lorentz. Elected to the Académie française in 1927 and nominated for the Nobel Prize in twelve different years, he was now widely recognized as the de facto French ambassador of letters as well as the unofficial poet laureate.

However, Valéry found himself increasingly torn between the dictates of public life with its attendant travel for lectures around Europe and the desire for the privacy of contemplation and research in the *Notebooks* to which he gave primacy over all aspects of his very considerable intellectual output. He termed the latter his '*natural* work' (*Cahiers*, xxii. 462) which he distinguished from his '*artificial* work' that included verse. While 'poet' is the label most commonly ascribed to him, he stated that it occupied 'a moderate place' (*Cahiers*, xxvii. 37) in a multifarious and prolific writing career. It is not surprising thus that he felt outside any specific designation of genre or art form and indeed deeply estranged from the idea of literature itself. Not long after the publication of *Charms*, Valéry was well aware of the dichotomy between the public perception and the personal reality, as this note from 1925 attests:

Several critics have wondered if I was a 'great poet', a 'great writer'. But they have not asked themselves if I had the desire, the intention of being so [. . .] In short if literature was my—primary—goal. Their judgement is based on probability. Their error is a natural one. But I am merely what I seem to be out of circumstance. My character does not direct me towards the public, towards effect, but only towards what interests me at any particular moment—and usually, in short, towards the exercise of the intellect. (*Cahiers*, x. 785)

One must, of course, put in context such self-effacement and candour, typical of the self-analytical introspection of the *Notebooks*. For contemporaries, colleagues, and the literary world, Valéry was indeed the 'great poet', despite himself.

NOTE ON THE TEXT AND TRANSLATION

THOUGH one of the greatest poets of the twentieth century, Valéry has not been translated very often into English. While the three major works (*The Young Fate*, *Album of Early Verse*, and *Charms*) and the poem 'The Graveyard by the Sea' have been published in separate bilingual editions, no complete anthology of his verse has appeared since David Paul's *Poems* in 1971 (*Collected Works* series, Princeton University Press). One reason for the dearth of translations may be the challenge in linguistic, interpretational, and intellectual terms that such an endeavour poses. This was understood very early by Rainer Maria Rilke who, having translated *Charmes* into German in 1925, a project begun four years earlier, concluded that *La Jeune Parque* was virtually 'untranslatable'. Despite the daunting challenges, the great lyric poet was inspired to make these great works accessible to a German-language audience. He was a deep admirer of Valéry about whom he wrote: 'I was waiting, my whole work was waiting. One day I read Paul Valéry and I knew my waiting was over.'[1] A century later, Valéry has fallen somewhat out of public consciousness, particularly in the English-speaking world.

This volume brings together all the poems of youth, *The Young Fate*, *Album of Early Verse*, and *Charms*; the later occasional poems, quatrains, and dedications; as well as a selection of unpublished poems from his voluminous correspondence. Since *Poems* by David Paul, the early poetry has remained overlooked. Octave Nadal (1904–85), professor at the Sorbonne, estimated that there are more than two hundred pieces in prose and verse, written during the period 1887–90, when Valéry was aged between 16 and 19. I have ordered the early poems according to the chronology of their composition, as does Michel Jarrety with the French originals in his *Œuvres*, as well as indicating to which of Valéry's correspondents (Fourment, Louÿs, or Gide) he sent them for comment or opinion. Most of Valéry's early verse was sent to Gide and Louÿs in the early letters of their abundant correspondence (André Gide, Pierre Louÿs, and Paul Valéry, *Correspondances à trois voix, 1888–1920*, ed. Peter Fawcett and Pascal

[1] Monique Saint-Hélier, À Rilke pour Noël (Chandelier, Berne, 1927), p. 21.

Mercier (Paris: Gallimard, 2004)), to which I refer throughout. In addition, I use here the augmented edition of the correspondence between Valéry and Gide by Peter Fawcett (André Gide and Paul Valéry, *Correspondance 1890–1942* (Paris: Gallimard, 2009)) which has replaced the early volume by Robert Mallet in which a couple of Valéry's early sonnets ('Bathyllus of Lesbos...' and 'Reflections on the Approach of Midnight') were first published.

For the French originals, I have used the excellent edition (Livre de Poche) by Michel Jarrety who favours the later versions of the poems, as well as Jean Hytier's *Œuvres* (Gallimard, Pléiade). The changes that Valéry made between the early and subsequent versions are mostly negligible, and nearly always concern punctuation, capitalization, or italics. I have chosen what I deem to be the most suitable version for the reader. As a complement to the later verse from the mid-1920s to the 1940s, I have included a sample of previously untranslated poems from Valéry's correspondence to Catherine Pozzi, Renée Vautier, and André Lebey. While less polished than those of the great works, they offer insight into the consuming and intimate passions of maturity.

I have favoured a more literal fidelity to the original with a translation that preserves the integrity of structure while upholding where possible the rhythm, alliteration, patterns of metre, and richness of diction. Many recent translations of Valéry's poems have been less than accurate or faithful to the original texts, offering versions that deviate markedly from the original conception for the sake of forging rhymes, and thereby leading to infelicities, solecisms, and misinterpretations. In many instances, I have eschewed this temptation to replace a French sonority or rhyme with a contrived English equivalent. Valéry's verse is so singularly marked by his individual intellectual and philosophical system that any translation must give precedence to the notions underpinning it. I have, on occasion, added punctuation signs for clarity or fluency and made small changes in syntax, principally concerning subject/object and verb order, to create more natural-sounding English. Valéry's particular lexicon, often classical in nature, has required me in various contexts to go beyond a simple translation and to interpret the term or expression for the reader in order to avoid a vague or meaningless equivalent in English. My overarching concern has been to capture the beautiful lyricism of poetry in all its rich and varied complexity, and thereby renew interest with a new generation of readers less familiar with the writer.

SELECT BIBLIOGRAPHY

Editions

Valéry, Paul, *Cahiers*, 29 vols. (facsimile edn. of the 261 original cahiers) (Paris: CNRS, 1957–61).

Valéry, Paul, *Cahiers*, 2 vols., ed. Judith Robinson (Paris: Gallimard, Bibliothèque de la Pléiade, 1973–4).

Valéry, Paul, *Cahiers 1894–1914*, 13 vols. (integral edn.), ed. Nicole Celeyrette-Pietri and Robert Pickering (Paris: Gallimard, 1987–2015).

Valéry, Paul, *Cahiers/Notebooks*, 5 vols., ed. Brian Stimpson, assoc. eds. Paul Gifford and Robert Pickering (Frankfurt am Main: Peter Lang, 2000–10).

Valéry, Paul, *Œuvres*, 2 vols., ed. Jean Hytier (Paris: Gallimard, Bibliothèque de la Pléiade, 1957–60).

Valéry, Paul, *Œuvres*, 3 vols., ed. Michel Jarrety (Paris: Le Livre de Poche, 2016).

Valéry, Paul, *Douze poèmes*, ed. Octave Nadal (Paris: Bibliophile du Palais, 1959).

The following also include texts of some of Valéry's poems:

Cahiers Paul Valéry 1 – Poétique et poésie. Introduction de Jean Levaillant. (Paris: Gallimard, 1975).

Bever, Adolphe Van, and Léautaud, Paul (eds.), *Poètes d'aujourd'hui, 1880–1900* (Paris: Société du Mercure de France, 1900).

Mondor, Henri, *Précocité de Valéry* (Paris: Grasset, 1957).

Mondor, Henri, *Les Premiers Temps d'une amitié: André Gide et Paul Valéry* (Monaco: Éditions du Rocher, 1947).

Walzer, Pierre-Olivier, *La Poésie de Valéry* (Geneva: Cailler, 1953).

Letters

Gide, André, Louÿs, Pierre, and Valéry, Paul, *Correspondances à trois voix, 1888–1920*, ed. Peter Fawcett and Pascal Mercier (Paris: Gallimard, 2004).

Gide, André, and Valéry, Paul, *Correspondance 1890–1942*, ed. Robert Mallet (Paris: Gallimard, 1955); augmented edn. Peter Fawcett (2009). References are to the 2009 augmented edn. unless otherwise stated.

Pozzi, Catherine, and Valéry, Paul, *La Flamme et la cendre: Correspondance* (Paris: Gallimard, 2006).

Valéry, Paul, *Lettres à quelques-uns* (Paris: Gallimard, 1952).

Valéry, Paul, and Fourment, Gustave, *Correspondance 1887–1933*, ed. Octave Nadal (Paris: Gallimard, 1957).

Valéry, Paul and Fontainas, André, *Correspondance 1893-1945*, ed. Anna Lo Giudice (Paris: Éditions du Félin, 2002).

Critical Studies

Crow, Christine, *Paul Valéry: Consciousness and Nature* (Cambridge: Cambridge University Press, 1972).

Crow, Christine, *Paul Valéry and the Poetry of Voice* (Cambridge: Cambridge University Press, 1982).

Franklin, Ursula, *The Rhetoric of Valéry's Prose 'Aubades'* (Toronto: University of Toronto Press, 1979).

Gifford, Paul, *Paul Valery, le dialogue des choses divines* (Paris: Corti, 1989).

Gifford, Paul, *Paul Valéry: Charmes* (Glasgow: Introductory Guides to French Literature, 1995).

Gifford, Paul, and Stimpson, Brian (eds.), *Reading Paul Valéry: Universe in Mind* (Cambridge: Cambridge University Press, 1998).

Ince, Walter, *The Poetic Theory of Paul Valéry: Inspiration and Technique* (Leicester: Leicester University Press, 1961).

Lawler, James, *The Poet as Analyst: Essays on Paul Valéry* (Berkeley and Los Angeles: University of California Press, 1974).

Paul Valéry vivant (Marseille: Cahiers du Sud, 1946).

Paul Valéry, l'intime, l'universel (Marseille: Actes Sud, 1995).

Rouart-Valéry, Agathe, *Paul Valéry* (Paris: Gallimard, 1966).

Stimpson, Brian, *Paul Valéry and Music: A Study of the Techniques of Composition in Valéry's Poetry* (Cambridge: Cambridge University Press, 1984).

A CHRONOLOGY OF PAUL VALÉRY

1871 (30 October) birth of Ambroise Paul Jules Valéry, henceforth known as Paul, in the Mediterranean port town of Sète, second son of Fanni Grassi (from Trieste) and Barthélemy Valerj (from Corsica).

1878 After two years at the Dominican school, Valéry moves to the Collège de Sète.

1884 Writes his first verse and reads Victor Hugo, Gérard de Nerval, and Charles Baudelaire; (September) the family move to nearby Montpellier where Valéry enters the lycée; meeting with Gustave Fourment.

1886 Family moves to 4 rue Urbain in Montpellier; regular visits to the Musée Fabre and the municipal library.

1887 (14 March) death of Valéry's father.

1888 Obtains his baccalaureate and enrols in the Faculty of Law at the University of Montpellier.

1889 Publication of his first poem 'Rêve'; reads Joris-Karl Huysmans and Stéphane Mallarmé; (November) begins twelve months of compulsory military service which interrupts his law studies.

1890 Valéry makes the acquaintance of Pierre Louÿs (May) and André Gide (December) beginning lifelong friendships.

1891 (September–October) during a visit to Paris, visits Huysmans and is introduced by Louÿs to Mallarmé; his friend and neighbour Pierre Féline introduces Valéry to mathematics and Richard Wagner; reads Edgar Allan Poe.

1892 Graduates with a degree in law; (October) stays in Genoa, where on the night of 4–5 October a storm triggers an affective crisis and intellectual awakening (famously known as the 'Crisis in Genoa'), following which he takes the decision to abandon poetry.

1893 Beginning of scientific reading, particularly on thermodynamics; befriends Belgian poet André Fontainas and Symbolist writer Marcel Schwob.

1894 (3 March) Valéry moves permanently to Paris; he begins writing the *Cahiers*, the notebooks kept daily from early dawn for the following fifty years and which eventually total 26,000 pages; introduced by Louÿs to Claude Debussy; (June) visit to London where he meets Charles Whibley, Ernest Henley, George Meredith, Aubrey Beardsley, and Lord Kelvin.

1895   Invitation to the first of many dinners by Henri Rouart, industrialist, painter, and major art collector; meeting with André Lebey, poet and future Socialist politician; (May) passes the exam for post as redactor in the Ministry of War, which he does not take up until 1897; (15 August) publication of *Introduction à la Méthode de Léonard de Vinci*.

1896   Introduced to Edgar Degas; spends three weeks in London working for the British South Africa Company of mining magnate, imperialist, and founder of De Beers, Cecil Rhodes; frequents Mallarmé's salon; publication of *La Soirée avec Monsieur Teste*.

1897   Publication of the essay 'La Conquête allemande' in the *New Review*, requested by poet William Ernest Henley.

1898   (14 July) last visit to the country residence of Mallarmé who dies suddenly on 9 September, which deeply saddens Valéry; (22 December) introduced to Jeannie Gobillard, niece of Berthe Morisot, who lives with her first cousin Julie Manet (daughter of Morisot and Eugène Manet, brother of Édouard) at 40 rue de Villejust (16th arrondissement).

1899   (December) engagement to Jeannie Gobillard.

1900   (31 May) marriage to Jeannie Gobillard in a joint ceremony in which Julie Manet marries Ernest Rouart, son of Henri Rouart; honeymoon in the Low Countries; (31 July) becomes personal secretary to Édouard Lebey, administrator of the Havas Agency and uncle of André.

1902   Paul and Jeannie move into the third-floor apartment at 40 rue de Villejust, living below the apartment of Ernest Rouart and Julie Manet who inherited the building from her mother Berthe Morisot; while Jeannie spends each summer up to 1943 in the summer residence of Morisot, Valéry remains in Paris where he frequently dines with Degas.

1903   (14 August) birth of Claude Valéry; visits the Salon d'automne and the Salon des indépendants.

1906   (7 March) birth of second child Agathe; regular visits to Huysmans and Degas.

1907   Befriends artists Maurice Denis, José-Maria Sert, and Aristide Maillol; (15 May) attends funeral of Huysmans; first attempt to classify the *Cahiers*.

1908   Introduced to Claude Monet.

1911   Introduced to Arnold Bennett.

1912   Gide and Gaston Gallimard encourage Valéry to revise his early poems; meets Saint-John Perse; begins writing *La Jeune Parque*, which takes five years.

1914 First visit from André Breton whom Valéry advises and encourages; (July) with the outbreak of war, the family moves to the Pyrenees.

1916 (17 July) birth of François Valéry, third and last child.

1917 (30 April) publication of *La Jeune Parque* (Gallimard); begins frequenting the salon of Mme Mühlfeld, and the bookshops of Adrienne Monnier (La Maison des Amis des Livres) and Sylvia Beach (Shakespeare & Company); (29 September) attends the funeral of Degas.

1918 Begins working on *Charmes*; first contact with Jean Paulhan, future owner of the *Nouvelle Revue française* (*NRF*).

1919 Befriends Jean Giraudoux, Jean Cocteau, Paul Morand, Anna de Noailles; visits the affluent Princesse de Polignac, patron of artists.

1920 Publication of the long poem 'Le Cimetière marin' by the *NRF*; (June) meets Catherine Pozzi, marking the beginning of an often tempestuous eight-year relationship; makes the acquaintance of Marie Laurencin, Surrealist writers, and James Joyce; (December) publication of the *Album de vers anciens*.

1921 Publication of the dialogues *Eupalinos* and *L'Âme et la danse*; Pablo Picasso creates a lithographic portrait of Valéry for *La Jeune Parque*.

1922 (14 February) death of Édouard Lebey, leaving Valéry without a steady income; beginning of period of conferences in France and around Europe; publication of *Charmes*; (October) visit to London and meeting with Bennett, Aldous Huxley, and Joseph Conrad.

1923 (February) portrait painted by Jacques-Émile Blanche; Valéry frequents the salon of Noémi Révelin (grandmother of Roland Barthes) where he meets mathematician Émile Borel and physicist Jean Perrin.

1924 Publication of *Variété*; beginning of friendship with Prince Pierre of Monaco; (15 March) meets Marshal Ferdinand Foch at the home of Edmée de la Rochefoucauld; conferences in Brussels, Geneva, Milan, Rome (where he meets Mussolini), Madrid, and Barcelona; (23 August) Perrin introduces Valéry to Paul Langevin.

1925 (14 February) first meeting of the National Committee of International Intellectual Cooperation under the auspices of the League of Nations; first of many visits to the residence 'La Polynésie' in Hyères on the Mediterranean; meets Edith Wharton and Dorothy Bussy; attends the PEN Club banquet with Joyce, Thomas Mann, and Luigi Pirandello; visits to Rainer Maria Rilke, Monet, Nadia Boulanger, and Henri Bergson; (7 June) funeral of Louÿs; elected member of the Commission of Arts and Letters, League of Nations; (19 November) elected to the Académie française; (21 November) marriage of Claude Valéry; conferences in Belgium and Holland.

1926 Becomes president of the French PEN Club; conferences in Czechoslovakia, Austria, and Switzerland.

1927 (18 May) death of Valéry's mother; (16 July) marriage of Agathe to Paul Rouart (grandson of Henri); conferences in Oxford and Cambridge.

1928 Break-up with Pozzi; (23 February) dines with Henri Poincaré and Léon Bérard and is invited by Borel to speak at the French committee of the Coopération européenne; collaborates with Ida Rubinstein and Arthur Honegger on the melodrama *Amphion*.

1929 Introduced to mathematician Vito Volterra, Victoria Ocampo, and Orega y Gasset; (20 June) Valéry receives Marshal Pétain at the Académie française; (9–12 November) attends Einstein's conference at the Sorbonne; meets the physicist at the home of Borel and at a conference by Louis de Broglie, recent Nobel Laureate in Physics; Valéry brings Einstein to Bergson's house on the rue Piccini.

1931 Valéry becomes vice-president of the French committee for International Cooperation, along with Marie Curie; conferences in Copenhagen (where he meets Neil Bohr) and Stockholm; decorated by Pétain with *Commandeur de la Légion d'honneur*; (23 June) first performance of *Amphion* at the Paris Opéra; awarded a *doctor honoris causa* by Oxford University; publication of *Pièces sur l'art* and *Regards sur le monde actuel*; poses for sculptress Renée Vautier (1898–1991) whom he woos but his passionate feelings remain unreciprocated.

1932 Nominated to the National Council of Museums; conferences in Austria, Switzerland, and Spain; writes Preface to the Manet retrospective in Paris.

1933 (8 June) meets Eamon de Valera, president of Ireland in Paris; (July) becomes administrator of the Centre Universitaire Méditerranéen in Nice; conferences in Rome.

1934 Presentation at the Paris Opéra of the melodrama *Sémiramis* by Valéry, written for Ida Rubinstein and set to music by Honegger; (November) in London, attends a series of conferences at King's College, and meets Prime Minister Ramsay MacDonald and Austen Chamberlain; (3 December) death of Catherine Pozzi.

1935 Relationship with historian and critic Émilie Noulet (1892–1978).

1936 Publication of the monograph *Degas Danse Dessin*; conferences in Algiers, Tunis, Geneva, Belgium, Bucharest, and Warsaw; Valéry becomes president of the Committee of Arts and Letters (International Commission for Intellectual Cooperation).

1937 Valéry is elected to the chair of poetics at the Collège de France.

1938 (29 March) death of his brother Jules (professor of law in Montpellier); (June) meets Salvador Dalí, dinner at the Élysée Palace with Prime Minister Lebrun and the Queen of Belgium; beginning of his relationship with writer and publisher Jean Voilier, pseudonym for Jeanne Loviton (1903–96).

1939 Production of the *Cantate du Narcisse* with music by Germaine Tailleferre; Valéry frequents Igor Stravinsky and Nadia Boulanger.

1940 (April) nominated to the Hungarian Academy of Sciences; (May) Valéry family leaves Paris for Dinard with the invasion of France imminent.

1941 Publication of *Tel Quel* and *Études pour 'Mon Faust'* (later called *Mon Faust*).

1942 Publication of *Mauvaises pensées et autres*; death of Ernest Rouart.

1943 Valéry suffers from recurrent bronchitis; publication of *Dialogue de l'arbre*; (October) exhibition of Valéry's lithographs in Paris.

1944 (26 August) attends the celebrations of the Liberation of Paris; (4 September) invited to dinner by de Gaulle.

1945 (20 July) death of Valéry at home in the rue de Villejust; de Gaulle declares a state funeral which he attends on 25 July at the Trocadéro; (27 July) burial in Sète in the graveyard of 'Le Cimetière marin'.

1946 The rue de Villejust is renamed rue Paul Valéry.

COLLECTED VERSE

VERS DE JEUNESSE 1887–1892

Testament de Vénitienne

La pompe sereine de la lune, Scelle le bonheur du repos
Gœthe, Le Second Faust

Le jour où je mourrai, courez à ma gondole
Emplissez-la d'œillets, de roses, de jasmins
Couchez-moi sur ces fleurs, croisez mes pâles mains,
Laissez mes yeux ouverts comme ceux d'une idole...

Déposez sur mon front aussi pur que le lait   5
Un diadème vert de feuilles enlacées,
Mettez un long baiser sur mes lèvres glacées,
Et recouvrez mon corps d'un crêpe violet.

Quand vous aurez fini cette tâche importune,
Oh ! regardez-moi bien blanche au milieu des fleurs...   10
Regardez, regardez... puis sans soupirs, sans pleurs,
Poussez-moi dans la mer un soir de pleine lune

...La gondole s'en va... s'en va parmi les flots !
Chantez ! là-bas ! chantez. Je vous entends encore
Oh ! les douces chansons que l'espace dévore...   15
Que les accords sont lents !... Vos chants sont des sanglots.

Adieu ! moi je m'en vais froide et morte sur l'onde
L'eau me berce et la lune argente ma beauté
La gondole s'avance et puis l'immensité
M'entoure lentement, bleuissante et profonde.   20

Pessimisme d'une heure

Il est une douleur sans nom, sans but, sans cause
Qui vient je ne sais d'où, je ne sais trop pourquoi,
Aux heures sans travail, sans désir et sans foi
Où le dégoût amer enfielle toute chose.

EARLY POEMS 1887–1892

A Venetian Woman's Last Will

The serene pomp of the moon, Seals the happiness of rest
Goethe, *Faust*, Part II

The day I die, hurry to my gondola
Fill it with carnations, roses, and jasmine
Lay me down upon these flowers, fold my pale hands,
Leave my eyes open like those of an idol...

Place upon my brow so milky-white
A green diadem of leaves entwined,
Plant a long kiss upon my icy lips
And swathe my body in violet crêpe.

When you have finished this tiresome task,
Oh, behold me so white amidst the flowers...
Behold, behold... then without sighs, without tears,
Thrust me out to sea on an evening lit by the full moon

...The gondola sets sail... off amid the waves!
Sing, over yonder, sing. I hear you still
Oh, the sweet songs engulfed by the expanse...
How languorous their harmony!... Your chants sound of sobs.

Farewell! I set forth cold and lifeless upon the sea
The waters lull me and the moon silvers my beauty
The gondola moves on and then the boundless realm
Gradually enshrouds me, growing ever deeper and blue.

An Hour's Gloom

There is a sorrow without name, purpose, or cause
Welling up from I know not where, or I know not why,
In the hours barren of work, of desire, and of faith
Where sharp disgust embitters all.

Rien ne nous fait penser, rien ne nous intéresse,   5
On a l'esprit fixé sur un maudit point noir.
Tout est sombre : dedans, dehors, le jour, le soir,
C'est un effondrement dans un puits de tristesse.

C'est surtout vers la nuit, quand s'allume la lampe.
Cet ennui fond sur nous, aussi prompt qu'un vautour.   10
Le découragement nous guette au coin du jour,
Quand s'élève du sol l'obscurité qui rampe.

Ce n'est pas celui-là qui mène à la rivière
C'est un mauvais moment à passer, voilà tout.
Il nous fait ressortir la joie, ce dégoût   15
Comme l'obscurité fait aimer la lumière.

La voix des choses

À Monsieur G.F.
C'est ainsi que se font les vers !

Si vous le voulez revenons en ville !
Mais on est si bien sur ce vieux rempart...
L'on ne parle pas !... C'est fort inutile
Et l'on se comprend bien mieux qu'autre part !...

Oui. L'on se comprend sans vaines paroles.   5
Et sans dissiper par le bruit des voix
Le charme divin des idées folles,
Près du flot battant, une rose aux doigts...

La matière parle et l'homme l'écoute
La vague murmure et la brise geint,   10
La cloche bourdonne et le vent, sans doute,
Ou bien quelque esprit, dans la nuit se plaint...

Et l'Homme, attentif aux phrases troublantes
Des ondes, des bois, des clochers lointains...
Laisse s'évader des Choses troublantes...   15
...Et ce sont des vers aux sons argentins.

Nothing prompts thought, nothing concerns us,
The mind is fixed on a cursed black point.
Gloom reigns within and without, day and night,
All plunges into the sorrowful depths.

It is above all towards night, when the lamp is lit.
This weariness swoops down on us, as swift as a vulture.
Discouragement stalks us as daylight ebbs away,
When from the ground the creeping gloom rises.

It is not the former that leads to the river
It is a painful moment to be endured, and no more.
This disgust brings out joy in us,
Just as the darkness makes us relish light.

The Voice of Things

For M.G.F.
Thus verse is made!

If you wish, let us go back to town!
But life is so sweet here upon this old rampart...
Let there be no communion between us! It is so pointless
And we understand each other much better than anywhere else!...

Yes. We understand each other without empty words.
And without the sound of voices dispelling
The divine charm of trifling things
By the beating waves, a rose in the hand...

Matter speaks and man listens
The wave murmurs and the breeze whines,
The clock chimes and no doubt the wind
Or some spirit laments in the night...

And Man, attentive to the unsettling words
Of the waters, the woods, and the distant bells...
Allows troubling Things to steal away...
...And these are verses of silvery sounds.

Rêve

Je rêve un port splendide et calme, où la nature
S'endort entre la rive et le flot infini,
Près de palais portant des dômes d'or bruni
Près des vaisseaux couvrant de drapeaux leur mâture.

Vers le large horizon où vont les matelots   5
Les cloches d'argent fin jettent leurs chants étranges.
L'enivrante senteur des vins et des oranges
Se mêle à la senteur enivrante des flots...

Une lente chanson monte vers les étoiles,
Douce comme un soupir, triste comme un adieu.   10
Sur l'horizon la lune ouvre son œil de feu
Et jette ses rayons parmi les lourdes voiles.

Brune à la lèvre rose et couverte de fards,
La fille, l'œil luisant comme une girandole,
Sur la hanche roulant ainsi qu'une gondole,   15
Hideusement s'en va sous les falots blafards.

Et moi, mélancolique amant de l'onde sombre,
Ami des grands vaisseaux noirs et silencieux,
J'erre dans la fraîcheur du vent délicieux
Qui fait trembler dans l'eau des lumières sans nombre.   20

Élévation de la lune

L'ombre venait, les fleurs s'ouvraient, rêvait mon Âme,
Et le vent endormi taisait son hurlement.
La Nuit tombait, la Nuit douce comme une femme
Subtile et violette épiscopalement !

Les Étoiles semblaient des cierges funéraires   5
Comme dans une église allumée dans les soirs ;
Et semant des parfums, les lys Thuriféraires
Balançaient doucement leurs frêles encensoirs.

Une prière en moi montait ainsi qu'une onde
Et dans l'immensité bleuissante et profonde   10
Les astres recueillis baissaient leurs chastes yeux !...

Dream

I dream a splendid and peaceful port* where nature
Slumbers between the shore and the boundless waters,
Near palaces bearing domes of burnished gold,
Near ships bedecking their masts with flags.

Out towards the wide horizon where sailors venture
Bells of fine silver pitch their strange songs.
The dizzying scent of wines and oranges
Blends with the waves' heady scent...

A restful song rises towards the stars,
Soft as a sigh, sorrowful as a farewell.
On the horizon the moon opens her fiery eye
Darting her beams among the ponderous sails.

Brown with rosy lips and coated with make-up,
The lady of the night, her eye glistening like a candelabra,
Swaying on her hips as though a gondola,
Slinks off beneath the pale lanterns.*

And I, lamenting lover of the sombre sea,
Companion of great, black silent ships,
Amble in the fresh delightful breeze
Setting countless lights shimmering upon the water.

Moonrise

The shadows drew in, flowers opened, dreamed my Soul
And the howling sleepy wind fell silent.
Night descended, Night, tender like a woman,
Pontifical, subtle, and violet!

The Stars gleamed like funeral candles
In a church at night;
And lily-white Thurifiers,* sending forth sweet smells,
Gently swayed their frail censers.

A prayer within me surged like a wave
And in the blue and deepening expanse,
The assembled Stars lowered their chaste eyes!...

Alors, *Elle* apparut ! hostie immense et blonde
Puis elle étincela, se détachant du Monde
Car d'invisibles doigts l'élevaient vers les Cieux !...

Solitude

Loin du monde, je vis tout seul comme un ermite
Enfermé dans mon cœur mieux que dans un tombeau.
Je raffine mon goût du Bizarre et du Beau,
Dans la sérénité d'un Rêve sans limite.

Car mon esprit, avec un Art toujours nouveau,   5
Sait s'illusionner—quand un désir l'irrite.
L'hallucination merveilleuse l'habite
Et je jouis sans fin de mon propre Cerveau...

Je méprise les sens, les vices, et la Femme,
Moi qui puis évoquer dans le fond de mon âme   10
La Lumière... le Son, la Multiple Beauté !

Moi qui puis combiner des Voluptés étranges
Moi dont le Rêve peut fuir dans l'Immensité
Plus haut que les Vautours, les Astres et les Anges !...

La marche impériale

Sous l'arche triomphale où flottaient les bannières,
Des clairons éclataient dans la gloire du soir,
Et le soleil mourant, gigantesque ostensoir,
Ondoyait sur les fers luisants et les crinières,

Un cri montait dans la vapeur des encensoirs,   5
Les rois vaincus hurlant sous les coups des lanières,
Et des chars écrasaient des fleurs dans les ornières,
Et de grands chevaux blancs se cabraient sous des noirs !

Les images des Dieux passaient mystérieuses,
Dans le recueillement et le ruissellement   10
Des armes, des métaux, des pierres précieuses ;

Et puis—l'empereur d'or, beau solennellement !...
Des veuves sanglotaient alors dans le silence !
Mais lui, resplendissait, appuyé sur sa lance.

Then, *She* appeared! immense white host,*
Next she sparkled, detaching herself from the World
For invisible fingers raised her towards the Heavens!...

Solitude

Far from this world, I live alone like a hermit
More cut off in my heart than in a tomb.
I refine my taste for the Bizarre and the Beautiful,
In the quietude of a boundless Dream.

For my mind, with an Art eternally renewed,
Knows how to delude itself—when stirred by desire.
It is possessed by wondrous hallucination,
And I take endless delight in my own Brain...

I scorn the senses, vices, and Women,
I who, deep within my soul, can evoke
Light... Sound, Beauty in every form!

I who can bring together strange, sensual Pleasures
I whose Dream can take flight into the immense Expanse
Higher than Vultures, Stars, and Angels!...

The Imperial March

Beneath the triumphant arch where banners fluttered,
Bugles resounded in the glory of evening,
And the sinking sun, massive monstrance,
Danced upon the glistening irons and the plumes.

A cry rose up in the vapours of the censer,
The vanquished kings yelling to the crack of the lashes,
And chariots crushed flowers in the potholes,
And great white horses reared up beneath black ones!

Mysterious images of Gods slipped by,
In the meditation and the glistening
Of arms, metal, and gems;

And then appeared the emperor of gold, so solemnly handsome!...
Widows began to sob in the silence!
Yet he stood there resplendent, leaning on his spear.

Les chats blancs

À Albert Dugrip

Dans l'or clair du soleil, étirant leurs vertèbres,
—Blancs comme neige—on voit des chats efféminés,
Closant leurs yeux jaloux des intimes ténèbres,
Dormir—dans la tiédeur des poils illuminés.

Leur fourrure a l'éclat des glaciers baignés d'aube.   5
Dessous elle, leur corps, frêle, nerveux et fin,
A des frissonnements de fille dans sa robe,
Et leur beauté s'affine en des langueurs sans fin !

Sans doute ! ils ont jadis animé de leur Âme
La chair d'un philosophe ou celle d'une femme,   10
Car, depuis, leur candeur éclatante et sans prix

Ayant l'orgueil confus d'une grande première
Les aristocratise en un calme mépris,
Indifférents à tout ce qui n'est pas *Lumière* !

Repas

Le saltimbanque et sa femelle,
À l'ombre de l'âne broutant,
Vident sous le ciel éclatant
Une déplorable gamelle.

Mais la nature peu cruelle   5
Pour le fol et joyeux passant
Met un soleil éblouissant
Dans le fer blanc de l'écuelle,

Fait fondre un rubis dans le vin
Inspirateur du vieux devin   10
Faiseur de tours, mangeur de flamme,

Et verse, pleine de bonté,
Une rasade de gaieté
Dans la tristesse de son âme.

The White Cats

For Albert Dugrip

Beneath the sun's bright gold, languidly stretching
Their snow-white backs, behold the voluptuous cats,
Closing their eyes envious of their inner gloom,
Cosily slumbering in their warm gleaming fur.

Their coats glow like dazzling glaciers bathed in dawn—
Beneath them, frail, nervous, and gracile bodies
Quiver like a girl in her dress,
Refining their beauty in languor unending!

Their Soul no doubt once stirred
A philosopher's flesh or that of a woman,
For, since then, their radiant and precious whiteness

Possessing the confused pride of a *grande première*
Ennobles them in serene scorn
Indifferent to all but *Light*!

Meal

The travelling performer and his female companion,
Shadowed by the grazing donkey,
Empty a wretched bowl
Beneath the blazing sky.

But nature, not too harsh
On the mad and joyful passer-by,
Lays a glaring sun
In the white tinplate bowl,

Melts a ruby in the wine
Inspiring the old soothsayer
Conjurer, fire-eater,

And, brimming with kindness, pours
A glassful of gaiety
Into the sorrow of his soul.

Mirabilia sæcula

Il fut un âge où tout était grand dans le monde
Les livres amusaient les plèbes et les rois
La guerre engloutissait les races comme une onde
Et les vainqueurs clouaient les vaincus sur des croix.

Les peuples enfantaient d'ardents visionnaires   5
Et descendaient de monts lointains au son du cor
Des Césars entourés de leurs légionnaires
Passaient dans l'or des soirs couverts d'armures d'or !

L'encens fumait. Le sang ruisselait dans les fêtes.
Les tonnerres roulaient dans l'horreur des tempêtes.   10
Sous l'arc en ciel planaient les aigles des grands Dieux

Jusqu'à l'heure où montant dans l'aube symbolique
Le doux christianisme éployé dans les Cieux
Surgit dans l'ombre immense, oiseau mélancolique.

L'église

Parmi l'Immensité pesante du Saint lieu
Dans l'ombre inexprimable, effrayante, dorée,
Solennelle, se sent la présence de Dieu
Dans le recueillement de la chose adorée.

L'obscurité confond les pourpres et les ors   5
Et les lampes d'argent, gardiennes des Reliques
Et dans ce sombre éclat plane sur ces trésors
L'âpre mysticité des dogmes catholiques.

Le Grand Christ, constellé de pleurs en diamants
Et de rubis saignants, coulant du coup de lance,   10
Là-haut semble rêver fermant ses yeux aimants
Dans ce vague parfum d'encens et de silence !

La Vierge byzantine et de massif argent
Demeure hiératique en sa chape orfroisie
Fixant ses yeux de perle aux Cieux, comme songeant   15
Aux Azurs lumineux et lointaines de l'Asie.

Mirabilia Sæcula

There was an age when everything was rosy in the world
Books entertained plebeians and kings
War engulfed races like a wave
And the vanquishers nailed the vanquished to the cross.

Races begot zealous prophets
And descended from far-off mountains to the sound of the horn
Caesars surrounded by their legionaries
Passed into the golden evening arrayed in gilded armour!

Incense burned. Blood flowed in the festival.
Thunder rumbled in the petrifying storms.
Eagles of the great Gods glided beneath the rainbow.

Up to the hour when, soaring in the symbolic dawn,
Gentle Christianity, spread out in the Heavens,
A melancholy bird loomed up in the immense shadow.

The Church

Amid the ponderous Vastness of the Holy site
In the ineffable shadow, frightening, gilded,
Solemn, the presence of God glows
In the reverent meditation of the thing adored.

The darkness blends the purples and golds
And the silver lamps, custodians of the Relics;
Above these treasures shrouded in the shadowy glare
Hovers the harsh mysticism of Catholic dogmas.

The Great Christ, speckled with teary diamonds
And with bleeding rubies, trickling from the spear wound,
Seems to dream upon high, closing his loving eyes
In the delicate fragrance of incense and silence!

The Byzantine Virgin, wrought of solid silver
Remains hieratic in her orphrey-adorned cope
Casting her pearly eyes heavenward, as though dreaming
Of the far-off and resplendent blues of Asia.

Le divin adultère

(SCÈNE ANTIQUE, AN 30 APRÈS J.C.)

L'Époux triste, médite en sa douleur profonde
Des larmes ont roulé sur sa Tunique d'or
Car l'Épouse est rêveuse, et tandis qu'elle dort
Murmure un nom d'amant caressant comme l'Onde,

'Ô compagne des jours lointains de Volupté,   5
Colombe de mon cœur amoureux envolée,
Sèche mes pleurs ! Donne à mon âme désolée
Le bon pain et le vin rose de ta Beauté !'

Mais *Elle*, repoussant la prière charnelle
Dit d'une voix où tremble une ardeur éternelle :   10
'J'adore un Jeune Dieu venu de l'Orient !'

Puis elle se rendort—puis il la contemple
Toute pâle, suivant un songe et souriant :
'*Jésus* ! Mon doux *Jésus* ! Ouvrez-moi votre Temple !...'

Conseil d'ami

À Albert Dugrip

Verse en un pur cristal un or fauve et sucré.
Allume un feu ; songe un doux songe et fuis le Monde.
Ferme ta porte à toute amante, brune ou blonde.
Ouvre un livre à la pure extase consacré.

Délicieusement imagine et calcule   5
Que Rien peut–être, hormis ton Rêve, n'est Réel...
Caresse ton vieux chat, et regarde le ciel
Dans ses yeux, verts miroirs du rose Crépuscule.

Puis, écoutant parler l'intérieure Voix,
Évoque le Passé. Sommeille, lis ou bois,   10
Et n'ayant nul chagrin, car tu n'as nulle envie

Sens à travers tes jours paisibles mais divers
À travers les printemps, les étés, les hivers
Paresseusement fuir le fleuve de ta Vie !

The Divine Adulterer

(ANCIENT SCENE, AD 30)

The sorrowful Husband, meditates in the depths of despair
Tears trickled down his golden Tunic
For his Spouse is dreaming and, in her slumber,
Whispers the name of a lover affectionate like the Waters.

'O companion of those days of Delight long past,
Dove of my loving heart that took flight,
Dry my tears! Offer my saddened soul
The nice bread and the rosy wine of your Beauty!'

But *She*, spurning the carnal plea,
Utters in a voice quavering with eternal ardour:
'I adore a Young God who has come from the East!'

Then she falls back to sleep—and then he gazes at her,
All pale, on the trail of some dream and smiling:
'*Jesus!* My sweet *Jesus*! Open your Temple to me!...'

Friend's Advice

For Albert Dugrip

Pour a tawny honeyed gold into pure crystal.
Light a fire; dream a sweet dream and flee the World.
Close your door to every lover, both dark and fair.
Open a book devoted to pure ecstasy.

Joyfully imagine and suppose that
Nothing is Real, save perhaps your Dream...
Lovingly caress your old cat, and ponder Heaven
In his eyes, green mirrors of the rosy Gloaming.

Then, listening to the inner Voice whisper,
Recall the Past. Slumber, read, or drink,
And now free from sorrow, for desire has departed,

Feel through your peaceful yet changing days
Through spring, summer, and winter
How languidly the river of your Life flows by!

Le cygne

Au rire du soleil posé sur une branche
Et sous sa plume un flot limpide se plissant
Le Cygne file en plein saphir carène blanche
Et l'eau miroir le fait deux fois éblouissant.

Neige sur l'onde ! un souffle insensible le pousse   5
Comme un vaisseau fantôme enfui parmi l'azur
Puis il va s'échouer sur la rive de mousse
Et dort dans la lumière idéalement pur !

Vase de chasteté symbolique et splendide
Ayant d'un monde vil oublié le Destin   10
Ô Cygne immaculé tu fuis dans le matin

Baiser de la lueur sur ton aile candide
Vers la Rive céleste où dans l'Éternité
Se confondent l'Amour et la Virginité.

La mer

Du zénith le soleil trouant l'azur éclate
Au miroir de la mer orbiculaire et bleu
Les flèches d'or, tombant du haut du ciel en feu,
S'enfoncent pesamment dans l'onde calme et plate.

Et la houle odorante au large se dilate   5
Sinueuse s'allonge et puis se dresse un peu
Comme un serpent sacré sous l'œil fixe d'un Dieu.
Le jour baisse. Le flot s'infuse, s'écarlate.

Dans l'océan d'émaux translucides fondu
L'astre, mourant oiseau qui plonge, est descendu   10
Et l'or du soir se perd dans l'Éternelle tombe.

Une vague s'élève à peine et puis retombe
Cependant que s'étend la belle au crêpe sombre
La Nuit mystérieuse avec ses yeux sans nombre.

The Swan

To the sun's smile gilding a bough and
Upon a limpid stream rippled by a feather
The Swan's white hull glides in sapphire
Made all the more dazzling by the glassy waters.

Snow upon the water! some imperceptible breath moves it
Like a phantom vessel that set sail for the wide blue yonder
Then it will run aground upon the foamy shore
And slumber in the perfectly pure light!

Vase of splendid and symbolic chastity
Having forgotten Destiny in a vile world
O immaculate Swan you set forth in the morning

To kiss the glow beneath your pure white wing
Towards the celestial Shore where
Love and Virginity blend in Eternity.

The Sea

From its zenith, the sun piercing the brilliant expanse
Blazes in the limpid blue sea,
As gilded arrows, shooting from the fiery heavens,
Drop ponderously into the still, lustrous waters.

And the scented swell on the high sea dilates,
Stretches its sinuous curve and then faintly rises
Like a sacred serpent beneath a God's fixed gaze.
Daylight draws in. The tide becomes suffused with crimson.

Melting into the shimmering, enamel-hued ocean
The sun, like a dying bird plummets, has set and
Twilight's gold spills into the Eternal tomb.

A wave scarcely rises and then falls again
Whilst the darkly etched being beauteous spreads
Mysterious Night with her boundless eyes.

Renaissance spirituelle

Christ ! quand tu régnais, les Poètes
Méprisant ta simplicité
Vers le Passé tournaient leurs têtes
Et préféraient l'Antiquité.

Ils aimaient les temples de neige   5
Épanouis au bord des Cieux
Qu'un bosquet de cyprès protège
Ils aimaient la beauté des Dieux,

Les déesses d'or cuirassées
Les Faunes aux rires lointains   10
Les nymphes roses enlacées
Dans la lumière des matins.

Ils chantaient la fureur d'Hercule
Les combats, les lueurs des fers
Sous les émaux du crépuscule   15
Et Phœbé souriant aux mers !...

Mais ô Jésus ! ta croix chancelle
Sur les autels et dans les cœurs
Et l'aube dernière étincelle
Sur tes dogmes jadis vainqueurs !   20

Ton vieil édifice s'écroule
Et la science t'a chassé
Des âmes vaines de la foule
Ainsi qu'une erreur du Passé !

—C'est maintenant, Maître des maîtres,   25
Que nous venons, nous, t'adorer
Et c'est nous qui serons tes Prêtres
Car tes prêtres vont t'ignorer.

C'est la grande mélancolie
Des Dieux autrefois vénérés   30
Que l'on méprise et qu'on oublie
Par qui nous sommes attirés.

Spiritual Renaissance

Christ! when you reigned, Poets
Scorning your simplicity
Turned their minds to the Past
And cherished Antiquity.

They idolized the snowy temples
Flourishing on the edge of Heaven
Shielded by a copse of cypresses
They worshipped the beauty of the Gods,

The golden-armoured goddesses*
The Fauns'* distant laughter
The rosy nymphs entwined
In the first flush of morning.

They sang the rage of Hercules
Battles, gleaming swords
Beneath twilight's glaze
And Phoebe* smiling at the seas!...

But O Jesus! your cross is tottering
On the altars and in hearts
And the last dawn is gleaming
On the once triumphant dogmas!

Your old edifice is collapsing
And science has chased you
From the crowd's shallow souls
Just like an error of Yesteryear!

—It's now, Master of masters,
That we come to adore you
And it is we who shall be your Priests
For your priests will ignore you.

It is the great gloom
Of the once venerated Gods
Now despised and forgotten
Who attract us.

Comme aux chapelles encensées
Aux temps de ta Divinité
Monteront nos douces pensées   35
Vers ta bonne Sérénité.

Nous sommes bien peu sur la route
De ton cœur mais tous éprouvés
Tous ayant traversé le Doute
Tous fils prodigues retrouvés.   40

Nous avons supporté la plainte
De la chair en notre saison
Et nous avons brisé sans crainte
L'affreux scalpel de la Raison

Et nous sommes prêts car nous sommes   45
Ardents de t'aimer ô mon Christ
Et nous remercions les Hommes
—Les ingrats, de t'avoir proscrit.

Nos esprits t'élèvent un temple
Bâti de Rêve et de Beauté   50
Et celui-là seul le contemple
Qui dans son âme l'a porté.

Chaque jour nous viendrons nous-mêmes
L'orner et t'entourer ô Roi !
Des lumières de notre Foi   55
Et des encens de nos poèmes.

Port du midi

Le bateau, sur l'eau, se balance,
Et la houle, avec nonchalance,
Jusqu'au bout des mâts peints en blanc,
Fait courir son frisson tremblant.

C'est midi. Des vaisseaux brûlants   5
Et de l'onde en feu, des relents
S'élèvent—chaude pestilence—
Qui règnent dans le lourd silence.

As in the incensed chapels
In the time of your Divinity
Our kind thoughts will soar
Towards your good Serenity.

We are too seldom on the path
Of your heart but all steadfast
All having doubted
All prodigal sons found once again.

We have endured the call
Of the flesh in our time
And we have fearlessly broken
Reason's dreadful scalpel

And we are ready for we are
Zealous in our love for you O Christ
And we give thanks to Men
—The ungrateful, for having banished you.

Our minds erect a temple to you
Built of Dream and Beauty
And only he who carried it in his soul
May contemplate it.

Each day we shall come ourselves to
Adorn it and to surround you O King!
With the light of our Faith
And the incense of our poems.

Southern Port

The boat sways upon the water,
And the swell languidly
Sends its shimmering quiver
To the tops of the white-painted masts.

It is noon. From the sweltering vessels
And the glaring waves a foul smell
Rises—a warm pestilence—
Lingering over the heavy silence.

Car, les cales, les bois moisis
Répandent des parfums étranges.
Sur l'eau cuisent des peaux d'oranges.   10

Azurés, dorés, cramoisis
Étoilés ou portant des Lunes,
Des drapeaux dorment dans les hunes.

Le navire

Ayant des mers fendu cent ans le bleu miroir,
—L'impassible miroir aux vagues musicales,—
Le Vaisseau, vieux coureur d'innombrables escales,
Revient dormir au Port dont il partit, un Soir,

Parfum d'un mort chéri que garde son tiroir,   5
L'odeur des flots enfuis hante les sombres cales.
Le sucre, le tabac, les houles tropicales
Imprègnent le ponton silencieux et noir.

...Revenant de l'Amour lointain—ainsi mon Âme
Conserve la senteur des rêves d'autrefois,   10
Et ne peut oublier une certaine *Voix*,

Et ne peut oublier un certain nom de femme...
Mais quel *Navire* a-t-il sur l'Océan laissé
Sa trace—et sa Mémoire à travers le Passé ?...

Fleur mystique

Lys mystique ! Elle avait la ferveur des Élus !
Et Vierge ! Elle adorait les pieds calmes des Vierges ;
Sous l'étincellement des métaux et des cierges,
Sa voix douce tintait comme un doux Angélus.

Une couleur de lune ondulait sous son voile.   5
Et dans sa chair, semblaient fuir les reflets nacrés
Du petit jour, luisant sur les vases sacrés,
Aux messes du matin, vers la dernière étoile.

Ses yeux étaient plus clairs que des astres naissants !
Indicible parfum de cires et d'encens,   10
Son vêtement sentait l'antique sacristie !

For the hulls and the humid wood
Spread strange odours.
Upon the water, orange peel cooks.

Blue-tinged, gilded, crimson
Star-spangled or emblazoned with Moons,
Flags slumber in the topmasts.

The Ship

Having cleaved for years the crystalline blue sea
—Soulless mirror rising and falling in melodious cadence,—
The Vessel, old voyager of many a port of call,
Returns to drop anchor in the Port whence, one Evening, she set forth.

Scent of a dear departed one stowed in a drawer,
The fragrance of the waves behind lingers in the sombre holds.
Sugar, tobacco, tropical swells
Permeate the silent black hulk.

...Returning from distant Love—thus my Soul
Preserves the scent of dreams of old.
And cannot forget a certain *Voice*,

And a certain woman's name...
But what *Ship* has left its trace on the
Ocean—and its Memory through the Past?...

Mystical Flower

Mystical lily! Blessed with the fervour of the Elect!
And She, this Virgin, worshipped the gentle feet of Virgins;
Beneath the glimmer of metals and candles,
Her sweet voice chimed like a mellow Angelus*.

Silvery moonlight shimmered beneath her veil,
And, in her flesh, pearly glints of dawn
Seemed to evanesce, gleaming on the sacred vases
At morning mass, as the last star declines.

Her eyes were brighter than dawning stars!
Inexpressible scent of wax and incense,
Her garment smelled of the ancient sacristy!

Et c'est en la voyant que le regret me vint
De n'être pas le Christ de ce rêve divin,
Car son visage pâle était comme une Hostie !

Pour la nuit

Oh ! quelle chair d'odeur fine aromatisée
Où de l'huile blonde a mis sa molle senteur,
Est plus douce que la Nuit au souffle chanteur,
Et sa brise parmi les roses tamisée ?

Quel féminin baiser plus léger que le sien ?   5
Et ses yeux, ses yeux d'or immortels, quelle Femme
Peut égaler ses regards noirs avec leur flamme
Et quelle Voix vaudrait ce vent musicien ?...

Adieu donc ! toi qui m'attendais ! L'heure est trop bonne !
À l'amour immatériel je m'abandonne   10
Que me promet ce Soir calme et ce bord de l'eau.

Car, j'aime cette grève où mon ombre s'allonge
Et cette Nuit ! Et cette lune au blanc halo
Et puis la murmurante et triste Mer qui songe !...

Tu sais ?...

Oh ! combien de soirs ensemble hantés
Amis nous ont faits ! amis pour toujours !
Et combien de vers ensemble chantés
Au pied de tu sais quelles vieilles tours.

La lune a mêlé nos ombres, la nuit.   5
Nos ombres mystérieuses de songeurs,
De songeurs fuyant l'Éternel Ennui
Fuyant par les nuits les ennuis rongeurs !

...Frère ! Sois cette lune qui ruisselle
Le large sceau d'or à jamais qui scelle   10
Nos âmes, et nos splendides désirs...

Mon Rêve et tes Pensers métaphysiques
S'aiment ! Et nous enlaçons nos plaisirs
Comme le soir—tu sais ?—de ces belles musiques !...

And seeing her sorrow came over me
At not being the Christ of this divine dream,
For her pale face glowed like a Host!

For Night

Oh! what flesh of sweet-scented perfume
Where white oil has infused its soft fragrance,
Is more tempting than Night's melodious breath,
And its breeze sifted through the roses?

What woman's kiss can be softer than hers?
And her eyes, her immortal golden eyes, what Woman
Can match her dark eyes with their flame
And what Voice could match this melodious wind?...

Farewell, then! You who were waiting for me! The hour is perfect!
I give myself up to immaterial love,
Promised to me by this Evening and the water's edge.

For I adore this strand where my shadow lengthens
And this Night! And this moon with its silvered halo
And then the murmuring sorrowful Sea, adrift in dream!...

Do You Recall?

Ah! how many haunted evenings spent together
Made us friends! friends forever!
And how many verses sung together,
You recall, at the foot of old towers.

The moon blended our shadows by night,
Our mysterious shadows of dreamers,
Dreamers fleeing the Eternal Ennui*
Fleeing gnawing worries through the night!

...Brother! Let this moon streaming down
Be the great golden seal that forever bonds
Our souls, and our glowing desires...

My Dream and your metaphysical Meditations
Love one another! And we entwine our pleasures
Like on those evenings—do you recall?—lulled by sweet music!...

Viol

BRONZE DU MUSÉE SECRET

Dans le métal sonore et rare de Corinthe,
Un artiste ancien a figé savamment
Le païen rêve—si troublant et si charmant
D'une coupable et triste et trop exquise étreinte.

Belle et chaude !—une Femme agace un mince enfant   5
Ignorant de l'Amour, qui repousse la lèvre
Et les tétins vers lui dardés, brûlants de fièvre
Et les regards chargés d'un désir triomphant...

...Millénaire ! le viol de bronze se consomme !
Le petit inquiet, sous le brasier charnel   10
Se tord et ne veut pas, horreur ! devenir homme...

Mais Elle le contient ! qui d'un geste éternel
Impose la splendeur de ses chairs odieuses
Et lui cherche le sexe avec des mains joyeuses !...

Le jeune prêtre

Sous les calmes cyprès d'un jardin clérical
Va le jeune homme noir, aux yeux lents et magiques.
Lassé de l'exégèse et des chants liturgiques
Il savoure le bleu repos dominical.

L'air est plein de parfums et de cloches sonnantes !   5
Mais le séminariste évoque dans son cœur
Oublieux du latin murmuré dans le chœur
Un rêve de bataille et d'armes frissonnantes.

Et—se dressent ses mains faites pour l'ostensoir,
Cherchant un glaive lourd ! car il lui semble voir   10
Au couchant ruisseler le sang doré des anges !

Là-haut ! il veut nageant dans le Ciel clair et vert,
Parmi les Séraphins bardés de feux étranges,
Au son du cor, choquer du fer contre l'Enfer !...

Rape

BRONZE OF THE SECRET MUSEUM

In the resonant and rare metal of Corinth,*
An ancient artist skilfully cast
The pagan dream—so unsettling and so enchanting
Of a guilty, sorrowful, and all too exquisite embrace.

Beauteous and warm!—a Woman lures a slender child
Ignorant of Love, rebuffing the mouth
And the breasts thrust towards him, feverishly aflame
And the gaze smouldering with triumphant desire...

...Millennium! the rape in bronze is consummated!
The worried child, beneath the carnal brazier
Writhes horror-struck, loath to enter manhood...

But She holds him! she who in an eternal gesture
Bears the splendour of her vile flesh down upon him
And gropes for his member with exultant hands!...

The Young Priest

Beneath the calm cypresses of a clerical garden
The young man robed in black moves by, his eyes slow and magical.
Wearied of exegesis and liturgical chants
He savours the blue Sunday repose.

The air teems with scents and the sound of bells!
But forgetful of the Latin intoned in the choir
The seminarian hears in his heart
The clamour of battle and thrilling arms

And, cupped for the monstrance, his hands are raised,
Seeking a ponderous sword! for he seems to glimpse in the sunset
The gilded blood of angels streaming down!

Up above! soaring in the bright-green Heavens,
Among the Seraphim clad with eerie fires,
He longs, at the sound of the horn, to clash swords with Hell!...

Myriam

Parmi les cailloux blancs, Myriam, des fontaines
Sous l'ombre mauve du platane où l'eau s'endort
Tu rêvais, Syrienne, au pâle masque d'or,
Et tes yeux s'allumaient de lumières lointaines...

Et tu laissais tomber la Nuit tout en songeant,   5
Nazaréenne !... Des larmes tendres et lentes
Te venaient sans savoir pourquoi, perles brûlantes,
Tes regards se noyaient dans la source d'argent.

Cependant s'apaisaient les Choses.
                                   Émeraude
Le lampyre rôdait en feu dans l'herbe chaude.   10
Des puits morts la voix des mornes crapauds montait

Sonore et creuse vers le ciel plein d'hirondelles.
Et toi ! tu rêvais, tu rêvais ! Ton cœur battait
Au bruit des norias, Myriam, et des ailes !...

Luxurieuse au bain

L'eau se trouble—amoureusement—de Roses vagues
Riantes parmi la mousse et le marbre pur,
Car une chair, illuminant l'humide azur
Vient d'y plonger, avec des ronds d'heureuses vagues !...

...Ô baigneuse !... de ton rire c'est le secret !...   5
Aux caresses de l'eau, tes mûrs désirs s'apaisent
Tu chéris la clarté fraîche et ces fleurs qui baisent
Tes seins de perle, tes bras clairs, ton corps nacré.

Et tu te pâmes dans les lueurs ! Dédaigneuse
Des amantes et des jeunes gens ! Ô baigneuse !   10
Toi, qui, dans la piscine, attends l'heure où soudain

Les bûchers s'allument, rouges, sur le ciel vide
Ta nudité s'enflamme et tu nages splendide
Dans la riche lumière impudique du bain !...

Myriam

Amid the white pebbles, Myriam, fountains
Beneath the plane tree's mauve shade where water slumbers,
You were dreaming, Syrian in a light gold mask,
And your eyes gleaming with distant lights...

And while dreaming you allowed Night to fall,
Nazarene!... Tender and slow tears
Welled up without you knowing why, blazing pearls,
Your glances drowning in the silvery spring.

Yet Things were lulled to silence.
                                    The emerald
Glow-worm crawled, afire in the warm grass.
From dead pits the voice of gloomy toads rose

Resonant and hollow towards the sky teeming with swallows.
And you were dreaming, dreaming! Your heart was beating
To the hum, Myriam, of waterwheels and wings!...

Voluptuous Bather

The water becomes languorously troubled by shadowy Roses
Laughing amongst the iridescent bubbling and the pure marble,
For a body illumining the moist blue sheen
Has just dived in, sending forth ripples of exultant waves!...

...O bather!... this is the secret of your laughter!...
Your sensual desires are appeased by the water's caresses
You cherish the fresh clarity and these flowers kissing
Your pearly breasts, your fair arms, your lustrous body.

And you swoon in the glimmer! Scornful
Of lovers and the young! O bather!
You who in the pool await the hour where suddenly

The pyres are ablaze, glowing red beneath the empty sky
Your nudity enflames and splendidly you bathe,
Immersed in the rich immodest light!...

Ultime pensée du pauvre poète

À Paul Verlaine

Autrefois maman me gâtait ! Les songes roses
Que je songeais en mon lit blanc et doux, le soir,
Je croyais que c'étaient des promesses d'avoir
Les meilleures toujours et les plus belles choses !...

Maintenant je suis seul, poète, et peu gâté,   5
J'erre par la cité terrible et je frisonne,
Sur ce trottoir humide et lumineux, personne
Ne viendra me bercer lorsque j'aurai chanté !...

Maman ! maman ! Reviens d'en haut, toi qui consoles !
Verser les baumes des baisers et des paroles   10
Par qui la Mère sait en souriant guérir !...

Lors le poète pauvre et dolent, dans les charmes
Du souvenir s'apaise et veut, grisé de larmes,
Comme un léger parfum s'évapore, mourir !...

Splendor

À Karl Boès

Sois belle purement comme un vase sacré,
Tel un ciboire d'or encensé sous un dôme,
Et garde ta splendeur comme un trésor secret
Très loin du baiser fauve et flétrisseur de l'homme !

Car, c'est Toi le vivant et le rare Cristal   5
Longtemps élaboré par les antiques races,
L'Émeraude limpide et sainte, le Graal !
Que veillent les guerriers aux mystiques cuirasses !

Oh !... Sois de marbre ! sois d'un métal froid et clair,
Et, parmi la résine aromale brûlée,   10
Brille lointaine et pâle, ô Reine Immaculée !

The Wretched Poet's Last Thought

For Paul Verlaine

Long ago mummy spoiled me! I believed those rose-wreathed
Dreams that came to me at night in my soft white bed
Offered the promise of
The best and the most beautiful things!...

Now I am the solitary poet, and rather deprived,
I wander the streets of the forbidding city and shudder.
On the damp and glassy footpath, no one
Will come to lull me when I sing!...

Mummy! mummy! Come down from on high, you the comforter!
Bestow on me the balm of words and kisses
With which Mother tenderly knows how to heal!...

Then the poor and mournful poet, cast under memory's spell,
Is soothed and, brimming with tears, yearns to die
Just as a delicate perfume evaporates!...

Splendor

For Karl Boès

May you be pure and beauteous like a sacred vase,
Like an incensed golden ciborium* beneath a dome,
And safeguard your splendour like a secret treasure
Far from man's wild and withering kiss!

For You are the rare living Crystal
Long crafted by ancient races,
The limpid and holy Emerald, the Grail!
Watched over by warriors in mystical armour!

Ah!... May you be of marble! of cold and lustrous metal,
And, through a veil of fragrant incense,
Cast your soft, faint glow, O Immaculate Queen!

N'es-tu pas le Calice adorable de Chair
Où l'artiste—blanc prêtre à la magique phrase—
Boit à long traits le vin suprême de l'Extase ?

Sur l'eau

Fuir ! sur un fleuve calme et si calme et si lent
Dans l'ivoire incrusté d'argent d'un canot frêle
Qui sur l'eau glisse comme un rêve,—vague et blanc !
Fuir ! avec elle fuir l'heure sous son ombrelle !

Sous les feuilles frôler les riches nénuphars,   5
Au fil du songe, avec une lenteur suave,
Et boire l'oubli tendre en ces parfums épars
Vaporisés par le doux vent—tel un esclave !...

Puis—le calme et le calme et les magiques ronds
Que font les perles qui tombent des avirons   10
Et ce pétale fin qui tournoie et qui file !...

Puis, ses Yeux dans les miens cherchant le vrai miroir
De son visage pâle aux baisers difficiles
Où passent des rougeurs délicates—ce Soir...

Basilique

Le Vase d'or contient le Signe et le Secret
L'Âme du prêtre sait. Le Cœur du Prêtre scelle.
Et le métal fondu de flamme et d'étincelle
Enferme le Mystère ineffable et sacré.

Le pur Soleil tisseur de nimbes impalpables   5
Tremble à travers les fleurs de verre et sur l'Autel
Vient glorieusement baiser le vieux missel
Où resplendit le Verbe indulgent aux Coupables.

Sept cierges, fiers et clairs, magnifiques pistils
Symboles des vertus liliales ardentes   10
Érigent la lueur de leurs cires ferventes.

Et seule, blanche, veuve entre ces feux subtils,
Lune mystique en un Soleil rouge sertie
Pâlit dans l'Ostensoir le disque de l'Hostie !

Are you not the venerated Chalice of Flesh
Where the white-robed priest, blessed with magical words,
Imbibes in great gulps Ecstasy's supreme wine?

On the Water

Set sail! upon a peaceful river, so languid and slow
On the silver-coated ivory of a frail boat
Gliding across the water like a dream—vague and white!
Set sail! Sail away from the hour with her beneath the parasol!

Brush against the resplendent water lilies beneath the leaves,
Dream's lulling and smooth glide,
And drink tender oblivion in these diffuse scents
Vaporized by the gentle wind—like a slave!...

Then—the calm, the calm and the enchanting rings
Spreading from the purled droplets of the oars
And this supple petal twirling and gliding off!...

Then, her Eyes seeking in mine the true mirror
Of her pallid face with awkward kisses
Where delicate blushes evanesce—this Evening...

Basilica

The golden Vase contains the Sign and the Secret
The priest's Soul knows. The Priest's Heart seals.
And the molten metal of flame and spark
Locks in the ineffable and sacred Mystery.

The pure Sun weaver of impalpable halos
Quivers through glass flowers and upon the Altar
Gloriously places its lips upon the old missal
Where the indulgent Verb to the Guilty is gleaming.

Seven candles, proud and radiant, magnificent pistils
Symbols of ardent and lily-white virtues
Erect the glow of their fervent wax.

And standing alone, white and widow-like amid these delicate flames,
Like a mystical moon set in a red Sun
The disc of the Host turns pale in the Monstrance!

L'enchemisée

Oh ! demeure, muette et blanche, en ce sourire
Avec cette aube fine, Ô pâle enchemisée,
Et ces perles tirant tes oreilles de cire,
Tels des calices lourds des gouttes de rosée !

Droite ! Tu resplendis ! tenant la lampe fauve   5
Si liliale—Ô fleur d'ombre tiède sertie
Par le seuil odorant et vague de l'alcôve
Que tu sembles en son corporal, une hostie !...

Oh ! demeure ! Fais-moi songer. Toi dont s'élève
Le frais souffle du linge et des chairs précieuses   10
Comme un appel vers le mourir et vers le Rêve...

Et tardons jusqu'à l'aube, autel de mes Tendresses
Où ma lèvre ouvrira des Roses furieuses
Le rite délicat et joyeux des caresses.

Petit sonnet

Elle est si frêle et si parfumée
Qu'elle a le charme fin des bijoux.
J'aime à souffler dans ses cheveux roux,
Ses cheveux comme de la fumée !

Un baiser—le plus lent—le plus doux !—   5
La ferait pâlir la bien-aimée :
Elle serait comme une fleur fermée
Avec des gouttes dans ses yeux fous !

D'un rayon de lune elle est coiffée !
Elle se vêt, comme les sultans,   10
D'odorants, pâles, légers rubans...

Et son cœur bat sous ses seins de fée
—Deux blancs camélias clos encore—
Comme une petite montre d'or...

Fair Maiden in a Nightdress

Oh! remain silent and fair, with your smile bathed
By this tender dawn, O pale maiden veiled in a nightdress,
And these pearls dangling from your waxen ears,
Like chalices bearing ponderous dewdrops!

How resplendent you are, standing tall! holding the tawny lamp
So lily-like—O flower set with warm shade
Whose smooth and wafting scent glides by the alcove's dim threshold—
That you seem a monstrance in its altar-cloth!...

Oh! remain! Make me dream. You from whom
The scented breath of linen and precious flesh wafts
Like a call to death and to Dream...

And until dawn, altar of my Tenderness
Where my mouth will open vibrant Roses,
Let us put off the delicate and joyous ritual of the caress.

Small Sonnet

So frail and so sweet-scented
She exudes the delicate charm of jewels.
I love to breathe in her red hair,
Her hair wispy like smoke!

The slowest, softest kiss
Would make the loved one turn pale:
She would resemble a closed flower
With droplets welling up in her wild eyes!

She wears a moonbeam!
She dresses like sultans
In scented, pale and light ribbons....

And her heart beats under her fairy breasts
—Two while camellias as yet unopened—
Like a little golden watch...

Ensemble

À Pierre Louÿs

Je vous salue, ô frère exquis !... ô Mien !
Ensemble venons quand le jour mourra
Écouter le vieux chant grégorien !
Pénitente, une cloche tintera.

Comme un couvercle de tombeau, le soir   5
Bandera nos yeux, ouvrant notre cœur
Et nous marcherons, tenant l'encensoir
Dans la Nuit silencieuse du chœur.

Ô combien seuls devant Dieu ! combien seuls
Cherchant les purs et nocturnes linceuls   10
Où bruit la parole auguste d'or...

Marchons vers la Lampe des Bien-Aimés,
Prions, ô frère ! puis, les yeux fermés
Embrassons-nous devant le Saint Thrésor.

La suave agonie

Pourquoi tes Yeux sont si grands, ce soir ?...
Et, dans ces flammes de soleil mortes,
Toi qui vas mourir, que veux-tu voir ?

Pourquoi ces baisers purs vers le soir ?
Pourquoi de ta main pâle tu portes   5
Lentement, des sourires secrets,

Comme des fleurs vaguement données
À des vierges aux regards sacrés,
Qui dans l'air passent couronnées ?...

Toi, qui verras *ailleurs* le Matin,   10
Ô ma chère agonisante, admire,
Parmi ces brouillards tendres de myrrhe,

Les Salutaires Voix d'or lointain...

Together

For Pierre Louÿs

I greet you, O exquisite brother!... O Mine!
Let us come together when the day is ebbing
To listen to the old Gregorian chant!
A penitent bell will be pealing.

Like a lid of a tomb, evening
Will blindfold our eyes, opening our heart
And softly we shall tread, the thurible in hand,
In the silent Night of the choir.

O how alone before God! How alone
Seeking the pure nocturnal shrouds
Where the august golden word murmurs...

Let us walk towards the Lamp of the Beloved,
Let us pray, O brother, and then with eyes closed
Let us kiss before the Holy Treasure.

Appeasing Death Throes

Why are your Eyes so large this evening?...
And in these lifeless flames of sun,
What do you hope to see, you who are dying?

Why these pure kisses towards evening?
Why upon your pallid hand do you
Slowly bear secret smiles,

Like flowers delicately offered
To crowned virgins with sacred gazes
Gliding by in the air?...

You who shall see Morning *elsewhere*,
Marvel, my beloved one in your death throes,
Amid these gentle mists of myrrh,

At the Salutary Voices of faraway gold...

Cimetière

Ô fleurs obscures des sépulcres, vos parfums
Montent vers le soleil immobile des tombes...
En moi, battent de l'aile, Éternelles colombes
Les blancs désirs du calme où dorment les défunts.

Car les poètes morts me soufflent les Paroles   5
Les rêves plus subtils qui hantent les tombeaux
Rêves sans fin ! lents et secrets, toujours plus beaux
Encens des vagues Nuits souterraines et molles.

...Les funèbres jardins sont tendres, et les fleurs
Y sont fraîches de l'eau douloureuse des pleurs   10
Et je sens que parmi vos corolles vermeilles

Ô fleurs obscures ! fleurs de pressentiment,
Légères de la Vie, ivres confusément,
Les Âmes valsent comme un essaim blond d'abeilles.

Celle qui sort de l'onde

La voici ! fleur antique et d'écume fumante,
La nymphe magnifique et joyeuse, la chair
Que parfume l'esprit vagabond de la mer,
Celle qu'une eau légère encore diamante !

Elle apparaît ! dans le frisson de ses bras blancs   5
Les seins tremblent ! mouillés à leurs pointes fleuries
D'océaniques et d'humides pierreries.
Des larmes de soleil ruissellent sur ses flancs.

Les graviers d'or, qu'arrose sa marche gracile,
Croulent sous ses pieds fins, et la grève facile   10
Garde les frais baisers de ses pieds enfantins.

Le doux golfe a laissé dans ses yeux fous et vagues
Où luit le souvenir des gouffres argentins
L'eau riante, et la danse infidèle des vagues.

Cemetery

O dark blossoms of the tomb, your sweet scents
Waft up to the still sun of the graves...
Within me, Eternal doves helplessly flounder,
White yearnings for the calm where the dead are sleeping.

For departed poets whisper Words to me,
The most subtle dreams haunting the tombs
Dreams without end! gentle and secret, ever more beauteous
Incense of subterranean Nights, so shadowy and soft.

...The mournful gardens are tender and the flowers there
Blossom with the painful trickle of tears
And amidst your vermillion corollas

O obscure flowers! flowers of portent, I feel
The Souls, lightened of Life in their dizzy bewilderment,
Waltz like a vibrant swarm of bees.

Being Beauteous Emerging from the Sea

Here she comes! ancient flower in a foamy mist,
The magnificent and joyous nymph, her flesh
Perfumed by the roaming spirit of the sea,
Bathed by the water's sparkling diamonds!

She appears! her fair arms trembling,
Her breasts quivering! moist at their tips
Adorned with glistening gems from the sea.
Tears of the sun trickle down her sides.

The golden gravel, sprinkled by her graceful tread,
Folds beneath her delicate footsteps, and the tranquil shore
Keeps the fresh kisses of her childish feet.

The gentle gulf has left in her wild and glassy eyes,
Wherein the memory of silvery depths gleams,
The frolicking water and the waves' treacherous dance.

Vierge incertaine

Toi qui verses, les nuits tendres, sur tes pieds blancs
Des larmes de statue oubliée et brisée,
Telle une douloureuse et mystique rosée,
Par qui se courbent les doux calices tremblants,

J'irai, ce soir, vers l'eau taciturne où bleuissent   5
De pâles fleurs, dans la triste mare d'azur,
Cueillir pour tes doigts longs l'iris antique et pur
Que les pleurs amoureux de la fontaine emplissent.

Ainsi je t'aimerai dans ton droit vêtement,
Tes yeux morts dans les miens arrêtés longuement,   10
Avec ma fleur en tes mains vagues d'innocence ;

Nous resterons longtemps muets, d'ombre voilés,
Et je t'adorerai sous ces bois violets
Où de pudiques lys grandissent en silence...

A Alcide Blavet

Tu rappelles ces grands enfants frais et naïfs
D'abeilles amoureux et de légers dytiques
Dont la flûte attirait aux lisières antiques
Les nymphes en amour qui s'enlaçaient aux ifs.

Tu leur ravis quelqu'un de ces hymnes furtifs   5
Sur leurs lèvres, mêlés au miel aromatique.
Mais tu surpris aussi le sourire érotique
Donc s'éclairait le bas de leurs masques pensifs !

...Et c'est pourquoi, mon tendre Alcide, quand tu chantes,
Sur tes lèvres souvent des lèvres de Bacchantes   10
Nous dérobent tes vers—pour ton baiser sucré.

La dryade que nul poète n'effarouche
A traversé, parfois, le soir, le bois sacré
Et de sa lèvre d'or, elle a scellé ta bouche !

Uncertain Virgin

You who, during nights so tender, shed upon your pale feet
Tears of a shattered and long-forgotten statue,
Just as soft quivering calices bend
Beneath a torturous and mystical dew.

This evening, I shall go to the still water where
Pale flowers turn blue in the sorrowful azure pool,
To pick for your long fingers the pure and ancient iris
Which the fountain's loving sobs will fill...

Thus I shall love you in your strait-laced garment,
Your lifeless eyes long fixed on mine,
With the flower of my hesitant innocence in your hands;

Veiled by shadows, we shall long remain hushed,
And I shall adore you beneath these violet woods
Where modest lilies silently grow...

To Alcide Blavet

You remind me of those grown-up children fresh and naïve
Lovers of bees and lithe diving beetles
Whose flute-playing drew to the edge of ancient forests
Smitten nymphs entwined around the yews.

You purloined one of their furtive hymns
Blended with sweet-scented honey upon their lips.
Yet you also startled the sensual smile
Which illumined the bottom of their pensive masks!

...And that is why, my gentle Alcide, when you sing,
Upon your lips often those of Bacchantes*
Steal your verse from us—for your honeyed kiss.

The dryad whom no poet can frighten
At times stole across the sacred wood at evening
And sealed your mouth with her golden lip!

Retour des conquistadors

Le soir victorieux dans les vagues s'allume,
Et, sur l'eau vierge, ainsi que des rires hautains,
Et les clairons messagers des fastueux destins
Émerveillent la guivre éparse dans la brume.

Car, de sa voile immense ouvrant la mer qui fume,   5
Le navire se cabre, écrasé du butin,
Sur l'orbe du soleil chimérique et lointain
Et soulève, éperdu, l'éblouissante écume !

Vois ! Sur la proue en flamme, un grand Conquistador
Vers Palos triomphale élève un lingot d'or   10
Dont l'éclat se souvient de l'héroïque grève !

Et, gloire de nos yeux, alors irradia
Le pur métal mûri dans les grottes du Rêve,
L'or fabuleux que tu ravis, Heredia !...

'Vers l'Orient marche la mer...'

Vers l'Orient marche la mer...

Puis elle est neigeuse,
De blancs tores s'y baignent, des corps amers,
Des corps ailés se posaient sur la mer
Sur les épaules d'une mer   5
Neigeuse.

Le pur soleil descendait dans le sel d'écume
Comme si des dieux respiraient ma chair
Et du ciel a bu le bon bain qui fume
Sans quitter le ciel, le bain de la mer   10
Des corps ailés se posent sur ce soleil
Sur les poses de ce soleil
Dans le sel d'écume.

Vers l'Orient marche la mer limpide
À millions, millions de lames et de fleurs vides   15
Les nus peuples allaient murmurant, montrant
Du soleil et du feu ou leurs épaules claires

Return of the Conquistadors

The victorious evening glows resplendently in the waves,
And, upon the virgin waters, to peals of haughty laughter,
The harbinger buglers of lavish destinies
Fill with wonder the wyvern* enshrouded in mist.

For, from its boundless sail opening the steaming sea,
The ship, burdened with its plunder, rears up
On the orb of the far-off mythical sun
And frantically lifts the shimmering foam!

Look! Upon the flaming bow, a great Conquistador
Holds up towards triumphant Palos* a gold ingot
Whose gleam recalls the heroic shore!

And then, praise be our eyes, the pure metal
Seasoned in Dream's caves illuminated
The dazzling gold that you purloined, Heredia!...*

'To the East Sweeps the Sea...'

To the East sweeps the sea...

Soon it is flecked with white horses
Pale torsos there bathing, bitter bodies,
Winged bodies coming to rest upon the sea
Upon the shoulders of a
White-crested sea.

The pure sun was sinking into the briny foam
As though the gods were inhaling my flesh
And the sky drank the fine steaming bath
Without leaving the sky, or the sea where they bathe
Winged bodies come to rest upon this sun
Upon this sun's playful radiance
In the briny foam.

To the East sweeps the limpid sea
Myriads, myriads of waves and hollow flowers
The naked set forth, murmuring, displaying
Sun and fire flickering on their lustrous shoulders

Qui portaient vers le jour naissant
Le balancement de séraphiques galères
Ailes salines, voix fidèles, vol pur   20
Vers là où la mer manque, où tangue un seul azur.

Sur le minuit futur

À minuit sur la montagne calme !
la mer comme un souffle dans des palmes
la mer comme une veuve, à mi-voix
pleure la morte Lune et les bois...

les harpes légères du silence   5
sur le minuit s'écoutent languir.
Il n'y a plus d'heures ni d'espérances
Les fleurs sont mortes sans un soupir.

Toi ! le seul qui vis, Ô Cœur solitaire,
Et sur la montagne et sur la terre   10
Tu dors ! et la mer t'appelle en vain...

Peut-être sans éveil tu reposes...
tu rêves qu'il n'y a plus de demain
Comme il n'y a plus de lune et de roses !

Votre portrait

Hermès ! sous ces vêtements sombres et légers
Dieu jeune, et dieu svelte, et doucement farouche
Dont les longs cheveux sont les voiles mensongers
Des purs secrets gardés en l'ombre de la Bouche !

Ô vos Yeux éternels dans la flamme perdus   5
Dans la flamme et les soleils fauves sur les vagues !
Ô vos mains ! par qui les saluts sont épandus
Où dort la pierre et l'or sacerdotal des bagues.

Bathylle de Lesbos...

Bathylle de Lesbos que frise un doigt servile
A de sa jupe iris... déconcerté

Bearing towards daybreak
Angel–like galleys gently swaying
Briny wings, faithful voices, pure flight
To where the sea is no more, to where only the blue horizon shimmers.

Reflections on the Approach of Midnight

At midnight upon the mountain so still!
the sea like a breath in the palms
the sea like a widow, in hushed tones
laments the lifeless Moon and the woods...

the lingering harps of silence
can be heard languishing at midnight.
Hours and hope are no more
The flowers have wilted without a sigh.

You! the sole living being, O solitary Heart
And upon the mountain and upon the land
You slumber! while the sea calls out to you in vain...

Perhaps you rest without waking...
you dream there will be no tomorrow
Just as there will be no moon or roses!

Your Portrait

Hermes! beneath those clothes so gloomy and light
Young god, lissom and mildly fierce
Whose tumbling locks hang like the deceitful veils
Of the deepest secrets concealed in your Mouth's shadow!

O your immortal Eyes shadowed by the flame
By the flame and the fawn suns dancing upon the waves!
O your hands! from which greetings pour forth
Where the stone and the gold of holy rings lie slumbering.

Bathyllus of Lesbos...

Bathyllus of Lesbos moved by a meek finger
Disturbed on her rainbow skirt

Tel pli trop peu naïf dans le miroir tenté
Et le voile qu'amuse le beau geste habile.

Voici son rire en l'air éventer le flambeau,	5
Gai de voir sous la tresse obscure qui le cingle
Éclose la beauté par la rose et l'épingle
Du pied bleu de saphirs au sein gelé dans l'eau.

Le Poète sourit, Bathylle, dans ton ombre
Et dévore à mi-mot des grappes dans ton ombre	10
Sa lyre, en noble bois d'ébène pur, se tait.

Car, vibrante ! aux échos des étoffes profondes
À tes amants magnifiques elle chantait
Orphée antique mort par tes mains furibondes !

Intermède

Ô SOIRÉE à peine frivole
D'une mince lune sur l'eau
Qu'hallucine sans qu'il s'envole
Le noir silence d'un oiseau.

La plume d'ombre un peu lointaine	5
Du cygne funèbre qui dort
Charmant tombeau sur la fontaine
Anciennement pleine d'or

Se mire à l'eau sainte et lucide
Qu'égratigne un souffle enchanté	10
Frôlant un souvenir limpide
Dans son exil diamanté.

Le deuil d'une dame nocturne
Éprise de larmes, ce soir,
Ne serait-ce la taciturne	15
Ténèbre où gît le cygne noir ?

Naïve ! qui ne dissimule
Sous l'aile triste un doux éclair
De plume, érotique scrupule
Comme un jupon deviné clair.	20

A crease too naïvely attempted in the mirror
And the veil with which her slender fingers play.

Here is her laughter tearing asunder the torch held aloft,
Filled with delight to see beneath the obscure plait whipping it
Beauty blossoming forth by the rose and the pin,
From her sapphire-blue foot to her icy breast in the water.

In your shadow, Bathyllus, the poet smiles
And subtly devours grape clusters in your shadow
His lyre, wrought of ebony noble and pure, falls silent.

For, resounding with deep mysteries
It sang to your splendid lovers
Ancient Orpheus slain by your enraged hands!

Interlude

O EVENING scarcely pregnant with frivolity
With a slender moon upon the water
Held spellbound by a bird's dark silence
Without it taking wing.

The shadowed and distant feather
Of the mournful slumbering swan
Charming tomb on the fountain
Once brimming with gold

Is mirrored in the limpid and holy water
Rippled by an enchanted breath
Brushing against a clear memory
In its sparkling exile.

The lament of a woman of night
Smitten with tears, this evening
Might it be the hushed darkness
Where the black swan lies buried?

Truly naïve is she who does not conceal
Beneath the sorrowful wing a gentle flutter
Of a feather, a sensual scruple
Glimpsed like a gossamer petticoat.

Arion

Inter delphinas Arion

Le luth luit sur le monstre élu pour un tel astre
Plus haut que le sourire adoré des oiseaux
Qu'amuse la beauté des larmes du désastre
À la figure sidérale du héros

Dont la main d'or, dans la splendeur du soir, délivre   5
Par le luth où scintille un vol pur de sa chair
L'eau vagabonde, peau d'azur claire et nue, ivre
Au jeu de la mortelle écume de la mer.

Des papillons neufs naissent vers des fleurs futures,
Doux dans les boucles d'onde, ô fines chevelures   10
Qu'une profonde enfant démêle du cristal...

Mais la lèvre du dieu par le silence insulte
Toute épaule limpide éparse au flot natal,
Vénus !... et nul beau cri dans le ciel ne se sculpte !

Merci

Comme pour prédire un sort pur
À qui des nudités s'amuse,
Penchant sa vérité camuse
Et sa barbe d'automne sur

L'ornemental pré qu'il effeuille   5
Un Faune, épars au calme esprit
Du paysage et qui sourit
De son ironie haute, cueille

La gerbe ! heureuse de se voir
Surprise au détour du dimanche   10
Pour, rieuse, odorante et blanche,
Être au gré de ce geste noir

Offerte en signe de malice
À qui s'amuse de Narcisse.

Arion

Arion among the dolphins*

The lute gleams on the monster chosen for some star
High above the birds' cherished smile
Entranced by the tragedy's beautiful tears
Trickling down the starry-faced hero

Whose golden hand in the splendour of evening sets free
With a caress of his sparkling fingers upon the lute
The gently gliding water, as pure as clear blue skin,
Intoxicated by the gambol of the sea's mortal foam.

New butterflies are born near flowers yet to be,
Soft in the sea's tresses, O fine hair
Untangled from crystal by a pensive child...

Yet the lip of the god insults by its silence
Any limpid shoulder scattered upon the native tide,
Venus!... and no beauteous cry can be sculpted in the sky!

Thank You

As though to foretell a pure fate
For anyone poking fun at nakedness,
Leaning his pug-nosed candour
And his autumn beard upon

The adorned meadow he strips of leaves
A Faun, spread in the landscape's
Tranquil soul and smiling
With haughty irony, plucks

The sheaf, happy to be taken by
Surprise on Sunday,
To be offered, joyous, fragrant, and white,
At the whim of this dark gesture,

As a sign of malice
To anyone mocking Narcissus.

Ballet

Sur tes lèvres, sommeil d'or où l'ombreuse bouche
Bâille (pour mieux se taire à tout le bête azur),
Sens-tu, tel un vil astre indifférent, la mouche
Transparente tourner autour du mot très pur

Que tu ne diras pas—fleur, diamant ou pierre   5
Ou rose jeune encor dans un vierge jardin
Une nudité fraîche sous une paupière
Balancée, amusée hors du chaos mondain.

Cette minute ailée éparpille un sonore
Vol d'étincelle au vent solaire pour briller   10
Sur tes dents, sur tes hauts fruits de chair, sur l'aurore

Des cheveux où j'eus peur à la voir scintiller
Petit feu naturel d'un sidéral insecte
Né sous le souffle d'or qui tes songes humecte.

Moi à Paris

Ô ! Tu diligemment vagues
Parmi ton semblable et tu
Exposes si n'extravagues
Et si même un pur mais tu

Son de flûte humaine émue   5
Dans la ville où tu t'en vas
Voir sur les ponts si remue
Moins d'ivresse que rêvas

Tu ? jadis dans cette blême
Tête où s'esquive du feu   10
Née en solitaire emblème
Pour savoir si c'est un Dieu

Qui se mire les narines
Dans l'eau de gauche, vitrines !

Ballet

Upon your lips, golden slumber where the shadowed mouth
Yawns (better to fall silent to the stark blue sky),
You can feel, like a vile and indifferent star, the
Translucent fly hovering around the word so pure

Which you will not utter—flower, diamond or stone
Or rose still young in a virgin garden
A cool nudity beneath an eyelid
Balanced and contented beyond the worldly chaos.

This winged moment casts a myriad resonant
Sparks to the solar wind so they may glisten
On your teeth, on your mounts of fleshy fruits, on the dawn

Of the tresses where I feared to see it sparkle
Small natural flame of a starry insect
Born upon the gilded breath moistening your dreams.

Me in Paris

O! hastily you roam
Amid your like and you
Reveal unless you rant and rave
And even if a pure yet hushed

Sound of a sorrowful human flute
In the city where you set out to see
If less heady pleasure than you once
Imagined stirs upon the bridges?

Once within this pale
Head where fire steals away
Born as a solitary emblem
To know if it be a God

Whose nostrils are reflected in the
Left Bank waters, glistening shop windows!

LA JEUNE PARQUE

À André Gide
Depuis bien des années
J'avais laissé l'art des vers ;
Essayant de m'y astreindre encore,
J'ai fait cet exercice
Que je te dédie.
1917

> Le Ciel a-t-il formé cet amas de merveilles
> Pour la demeure d'un serpent ?
> P. Corneille

Qui pleure là, sinon le vent simple, à cette heure
Seule avec diamants extrêmes ?... Mais qui pleure,
Si proche de moi-même au moment de pleurer ?

Cette main, sur mes traits qu'elle rêve effleurer,
Distraitement docile à quelque fin profonde,   5
Attend de ma faiblesse une larme qui fonde,
Et que de mes destins lentement divisé,
Le plus pur en silence éclaire un cœur brisé.
La houle me murmure une ombre de reproche,
Ou retire ici-bas, dans ses gorges de roche,   10
Comme chose déçue et bue amèrement,
Une rumeur de plainte et de resserrement...
Que fais-tu, hérissée, et cette main glacée,
Et quel frémissement d'une feuille effacée
Persiste parmi vous, îles de mon sein nu ?...   15
Je scintille, liée à ce ciel inconnu...
L'immense grappe brille à ma soif de désastres.

Tout-puissants étrangers, inévitables astres
Qui daignez faire luire au lointain temporel
Je ne sais quoi de pur et de surnaturel ;   20
Vous qui dans les mortels plongez jusques aux larmes
Ces souverains éclats, ces invincibles armes,
Et les élancements de votre éternité,

THE YOUNG FATE

For André Gide
For many years
I had given up the art of verse;
while trying to apply myself to it again,
I undertook this exercise,
which I dedicate to you.
1917

> Did Heaven create this mass of marvels
> To be a serpent's lair?*
> P. Corneille

Who weeps there, if not simply the wind, at this hour
Alone with the remotest diamonds?... But who weeps,
So close to myself at the moment of weeping?

This hand, dreaming it touches my features,
Idly obedient to some deep purpose,
Awaits a tear to melt from my weakness
And, slowly separated from my destinies,
For the purest to illumine in silence a broken heart.
The swell murmurs its mild reproach,
Or draws into its rocky gorges here below,
Like some disenchanted thing drunk in all its bitterness,
An anxious and low moaning...
What brings you here, your hair tousled and this icy hand,
And what shivering of a faded leaf
Still lingers among you, isles of my naked breast?...
I sparkle, bound to this unknown sky...
The immense cluster glistens on my thirst for disasters.

Omnipotent strangers, inescapable stars
Deigning to light up in time's distant reaches
Something mysterious and pure;
You who plunge into mortals, to the deep spring of tears,
These supreme splinters, these invincible weapons,
And the darting rays of your eternity.

Je suis seule avec vous, tremblante, ayant quitté
Ma couche ; et sur l'écueil mordu par la merveille,   25
J'interroge mon cœur quelle douleur l'éveille,
Quel crime par moi-même ou sur moi consommé ?...
...Ou si le mal me suit d'un songe refermé,
Quand (au velours du souffle envolé l'or des lampes)
J'ai de mes bras épais environné mes tempes,   30
Et longtemps de mon âme attendu les éclairs ?
Toute ? Mais toute à moi, maîtresse de mes chairs,
Durcissant d'un frisson leur étrange étendue,
Et dans mes doux liens, à mon sang suspendue,
Je me voyais me voir, sinueuse, et dorais   35
De regards en regards, mes profondes forêts.

J'y suivais un serpent qui venait de me mordre.

Quel repli de désirs, sa traîne !... Quel désordre
De trésors s'arrachant à mon avidité,
Et quelle sombre soif de la limpidité !   40

Ô ruse !... À la lueur de la douleur laissée
Je me sentis connue encor plus que blessée...
Au plus traître de l'âme une pointe me naît ;
Le poison, mon poison, m'éclaire et se connaît :
Il colore une vierge à soi-même enlacée,   45
Jalouse... Mais de qui, jalouse et menacée ?
Et quel silence parle à mon seul possesseur ?

Dieux ! Dans ma lourde plaie une secrète sœur
Brûle, qui se préfère à l'extrême attentive.

Va ! je n'ai plus besoin de ta race naïve,   50
Cher Serpent... Je m'enlace, être vertigineux !
Cesse de me prêter ce mélange de nœuds
Ni ta fidélité qui me fuit et devine...
Mon âme y peut suffire, ornement de ruine !
Elle sait, sur mon ombre égarant ses tourments,   55
De mon sein, dans les nuits, mordre les rocs charmants ;
Elle y suce longtemps le lait des rêveries...
Laisse donc défaillir ce bras de pierreries
Qui menace d'amour mon sort spirituel...
Tu ne peux rien sur moi qui ne soit moins cruel,   60

I am alone with you, quivering, having abandoned
My bed; and upon the reef worn by wonder,
I ask my heart what pain rouses it,
What crime committed by or against me?...
...Or if the pain of a dream now sealed shadows me,
When (the lamps' gold borne away by a velvety breath)
I enfolded my temples with my firm arms,
And long awaited the thunderbolts of my soul?
All? Yes, all of me, mistress of my flesh,
Hardening its strange expanse with a shudder,
And in my soft bonds, suspended on my blood,
I saw me seeing myself, sinuous, and gilding*
My innermost forests, glance after glance.

I trailed there a serpent that had just bitten me.

What a coil of desires, his train!... What a tangle
Of treasures snatched from my greed,
And what a dark yearning for clarity!

O trickery!... Languishing in the pain's afterglow
I felt more known than wounded...
In my soul's treacherous core, a sting is begotten;
The poison, my poison, enlightens me and reveals its potency:
It brings a flush to a virgin entwining herself,
Jealous... But of whom and by whom threatened?
And what silence speaks to my sole possessor?

Heavens! In my grievous wound a secret sister burns
Who loves herself more than this other, attentive to the extreme.

Be off! I no longer need your naïve race,
Dear Serpent!... I curl up, vertiginous being!
Lend me no more these mingled knots
Nor your faithfulness which flees and sees through me...
My soul, this ornament of ruin, may suffice instead!
With its torments straying across my shadows, it can
Suck my breast's bewitching rocks at night;
There it long draws the plenteous milk of dreams...
So let this bejewelled arm, which threatens
My spiritual fate with love, flag and yield...
Nothing you do to me could be less cruel,

Moins désirable... Apaise alors, calme ces ondes,
Rappelle ces remous, ces promesses immondes...
Ma surprise s'abrège, et mes yeux sont ouverts.
Je n'attendais pas moins de mes riches déserts
Qu'un tel enfantement de fureur et de tresse :   65
Leurs fonds passionnés brillent de sécheresse
Si loin que je m'avance et m'altère pour voir
De mes enfers pensifs les confins sans espoir...
Je sais... Ma lassitude est parfois un théâtre.
L'esprit n'est pas si pur que jamais idolâtre   70
Sa fougue solitaire aux élans de flambeau
Ne fasse fuir les murs de son morne tombeau.
Tout peut naître ici-bas d'une attente infinie.
L'ombre même le cède à certaine agonie,
L'âme avare s'entr'ouvre, et du monstre s'émeut   75
Qui se tord sur le pas d'une porte de feu...
Mais, pour capricieux et prompt que tu paraisses,
Reptile, ô vifs détours tout courus de caresses,
Si proche impatience et si lourde langueur,
Qu'es-tu, près de ma nuit d'éternelle longueur ?   80
Tu regardais dormir ma belle négligence...
Mais avec mes périls, je suis d'intelligence,
Plus versatile, ô Thyrse, et plus perfide qu'eux.
Fuis-moi ! Du noir retour reprends le fil visqueux !
Va chercher des yeux clos pour tes danses massives.   85
Coule vers d'autres lits tes robes successives,
Couve sur d'autres cœurs les germes de leur mal,
Et que dans les anneaux de ton rêve animal
Halète jusqu'au jour l'innocence anxieuse !...
Moi, je veille. Je sors, pâle et prodigieuse,   90
Toute humide des pleurs que je n'ai point versés,
D'une absence aux contours de mortelle bercés
Par soi seule... Et brisant une tombe sereine,
Je m'accoude inquiète et pourtant souveraine,
Tant de mes visions parmi la nuit et l'œil,   95
Les moindres mouvements consultant mon orgueil.

Mais je tremblais de perdre une douleur divine !
Je baisais sur ma main cette morsure fine,

Less desirable... So appease, calm these waters,
Call back these eddies, these vile promises...
My surprise is cut short, and my eyes are opened.
I expected no less of my bounteous deserts
Than such an outpouring of fury and tresses:
Their barren depths burn ever more brightly
The further I advance, thirsting to see
The despairing confines of my mind's inferno...
I know... My weariness is at times a spectacle.
My mind is not so pure that, never idolatrous,
Its solitary fervour glowing like a torch
Cannot banish the walls of its mournful tomb.
Here below, all may spring from infinite waiting.
Even darkness yields to certain agony,
The greedy soul is half open, and takes fright at the monster
Writhing on the threshold of a fiery gate...
Yet, however capricious and hasty you may seem,
Reptile, O spirited coils all rippling with caresses,
So quick to impatience and so weary with languor,
What are you, next to my eternally long night?
You were watching my abandon tenderly slumber...
But, I am in league with my perils,
More versatile, O Thyrsus, and more treacherous than they.*
Be gone! Resume the viscid trail of your shadowy retreat!
Go seek other closed eyes for your lumbering dances.
Slither your shedding skins towards other beds,
Brood on other hearts the seeds of their woe
And in the coils of your animal dream
May restive innocence pant until dawn!...
I am awake. Pale and wondrous presence,
Moist with tears I did not shed, I emerge from
An oblivion softly contoured like a mortal woman, lulled
By itself alone... And breaking forth from a tranquil tomb,
I lean on my arms, anxious and yet supreme,
So much do the slightest stirrings of my vision
Between night and the eye turn to my pride.

Yet I quivered at losing such a divine pain!
I kissed this fine bite on my hand,

Et je ne savais plus de mon antique corps
Insensible, qu'un feu qui brûlait sur mes bords :   100

Adieu, pensai-je, MOI, mortelle sœur, mensonge...

Harmonieuse MOI, différente d'un songe,
Femme flexible et ferme aux silences suivis
D'actes purs !... Front limpide, et par ondes ravis,
Si loin que le vent vague et velu les achève,   105
Longs brins légers qu'au large un vol mêle et soulève,
Dites !... J'étais l'égale et l'épouse du jour,
Seul support souriant que je formais d'amour
À la toute-puissante altitude adorée...

Quel éclat sur mes cils aveuglément dorée,   110
Ô paupières qu'opprime une nuit de trésor,
Je priais à tâtons dans vos ténèbres d'or !
Poreuse à l'éternel qui me semblait m'enclore,
Je m'offrais dans mon fruit de velours qu'il dévore ;
Rien ne me murmurait qu'un désir de mourir   115
Dans cette blonde pulpe au soleil pût mûrir :
Mon amère saveur ne m'était point venue.
Je ne sacrifiais que mon épaule nue
À la lumière ; et sur cette gorge de miel,
Dont la tendre naissance accomplissait le ciel,   120
Se venait assoupir la figure du monde.
Puis dans le dieu brillant, captive vagabonde,
Je m'ébranlais brûlante et foulais le sol plein,
Liant et déliant mes ombres sous le lin.
Heureuse ! À la hauteur de tant de gerbes belles,   125
Qui laissais à ma robe obéir les ombelles,
Dans les abaissements de leur frêle fierté ;
Et si, contre le fil de cette liberté,
Si la robe s'arrache à la rebelle ronce,
L'arc de mon brusque corps s'accuse et me prononce,   130
Nu sous le voile enflé de vivantes couleurs
Que dispute ma race aux longs liens de fleurs !

Je regrette à demi cette vaine puissance...
Une avec le désir, je fus l'obéissance
Imminente, attachée à ces genoux polis ;   135

And I knew no more of the unfeeling body
I left behind than a blazing fire along my edges:

Farewell, I thought, ME, mortal sister, untruth...

Harmonious ME, unlike a dream,
Yielding and firm woman whose silences beget
Pure acts!... Limpid brow, swept away by the waves,
So far as to be hushed by the faint and feathery wind,
Long, wispy strands twirling and gliding upon the open sea,
Say!... I was the equal and the spouse of day,
The sole smiling support which I fashioned from love
For the adored, all-powerful heights...

What radiance upon my eyelashes so dazzlingly gilded,
O eyelids laden with such a bounteous night,
I prayed, groping my way in your shadows of gold!
Suffused with eternity which seemed to envelop me,
I offered the velvety fruit it so lovingly devours,
Nothing whispered in my ear that a desire to die
Might ripen in this fair flesh beneath the sun's warm kiss:
I had yet to discover my bitter taste.
I sacrificed only my bare shoulder
To the light; and upon this honeyed breast,
Whose tender birth did heaven delight,
The curve of the world came to slumber.
Then in god's brilliance, I, the wandering captive,
Sallied forth, burning with desire, and trod the firm earth,
My shadows softly folding and unfolding beneath the linen.
How joyful I was! Immersed in a sea of beauteous sheaves,
Letting the flower clusters bow with meek pride
As they yield to the brush of my dress;
And if, against the gentle flow of this abandon,
The dress snags on a stubborn briar,
My body's curve is suddenly outlined, revealing me
Naked beneath this billowing veil of vivid colours
For which my race vies with the long trailing flowers!

I half regret this vain power...
At one with desire, I was imminent
Obedience bound to these smooth knees;

De mouvements si prompts mes vœux étaient remplis
Que je sentais ma cause à peine plus agile !
Vers mes sens lumineux nageait ma blonde argile,
Et dans l'ardente paix des songes naturels,
Tous ces pas infinis me semblaient éternels.   140
Si ce n'est, ô Splendeur, qu'à mes pieds l'Ennemie,
Mon ombre ! la mobile et la souple momie,
De mon absence peinte effleurait sans effort
La terre où je fuyais cette légère mort.
Entre la rose et moi, je la vois qui s'abrite ;   145
Sur la poudre qui danse, elle glisse et n'irrite
Nul feuillage, mais passe, et se brise partout...
Glisse ! Barque funèbre...

                    Et moi vive, debout,
Dure, et de mon néant secrètement armée,
Mais, comme par l'amour une joue enflammée,   150
Et la narine jointe au vent de l'oranger,
Je ne rends plus au jour qu'un regard étranger...
Oh ! combien peut grandir dans ma nuit curieuse
De mon cœur séparé la part mystérieuse,
Et de sombres essais s'approfondir mon art !...   155
Loin des purs environs, je suis captive, et par
L'évanouissement d'arômes abattue,
Je sens sous les rayons frissonner ma statue,
Des caprices de l'or, son marbre parcouru.
Mais je sais ce que voit mon regard disparu ;   160
Mon œil noir est le seuil d'infernales demeures !
Je pense, abandonnant à la brise les heures
Et l'âme sans retour des arbustes amers,
Je pense, sur le bord doré de l'univers,
À ce goût de périr qui prend la Pythonisse   165
En qui mugit l'espoir que le monde finisse.
Je renouvelle en moi mes énigmes, mes dieux,
Mes pas interrompus de paroles aux cieux,
Mes pauses, sur le pied portant la rêverie,
Qui suit au miroir d'aile un oiseau qui varie,   170
Cent fois sur le soleil joue avec le néant,
Et brûle, au sombre but de mon marbre béant.

My wishes were fulfilled by movements so swift
That I felt my purpose scarcely more agile!
Towards my lucid senses my blond clay swam,
And in the fiery calm of natural dreams,
I believed my boundless steps were everlasting,
If only, O Splendour, it were not for the Enemy at my feet,
My shadow! this deftly moving mummy,
Painted from my absence, brushing ever gently
The earth where I was fleeing this airy death.
Between the rose and me, I see it lurking;
It glides over the twirling dust, never disturbing
A leaf, but passes, and shatters all about...
Glide by! Funeral barque...

                    And I alive, upright,
Strong, and secretly armed with my inner void,
Yet, like a cheek flushed with love and
My nostril drawn to the fragrant orange tree,
I give day no more than a passing glance...
Oh! how much, in my night-long quest,
The mysterious part of my riven heart may swell,
And my art from gloomy endeavours be enriched!...
Far from resplendent surroundings, I am captive,
And wearied by waning scents,
In the sun's rays, I feel my statue quiver,
Its marble rippling with capricious gold.
Yet I know what my vanished gaze can see;
My dark eye is the door to fiery abodes!
I ponder, casting to the wind the hours
And the soul of the bitter shrubs forever departed,
Poised on the gilded edge of the universe, I ponder
The longing to die that takes hold of the Pythia whose
Hope-filled heart howls for the world to end.
Within myself, I renew my enigmas, my gods,
My steps interrupted by prayers to heaven,
My pauses, on a foot bearing a dream that
Follows in a winged mirror a bird's varying flight,
Plays freely with the sunlit void,
And burns at my gaping marble's dark purpose.

Ô dangereusement de son regard la proie !

Car l'œil spirituel sur ses plages de soie
Avait déjà vu luire et pâlir trop de jours   175
Dont je m'étais prédit les couleurs et le cours.
L'ennui, le clair ennui de mirer leur nuance,
Me donnait sur ma vie une funeste avance :
L'aube me dévoilait tout le jour ennemi.
J'étais à demi-morte ; et peut-être, à demi   180
Immortelle, rêvant que le futur lui-même
Ne fût qu'un diamant fermant le diadème
Où s'échange le froid des malheurs qui naîtront
Parmi tant d'autres feux absolus de mon front.

Osera-t-il, le Temps, de mes diverses tombes,   185
Ressusciter un soir favori des colombes,
Un soir qui traîne au fil d'un lambeau voyageur
De ma docile enfance un reflet de rougeur,
Et trempe à l'émeraude un long rose de honte ?

Souvenir, ô bûcher, dont le vent d'or m'affronte,   190
Souffle au masque la pourpre imprégnant le refus
D'être moi-même en flamme une autre que je fus...
Viens, mon sang, viens rougir la pâle circonstance
Qu'ennoblissait l'azur de la sainte distance,
Et l'insensible iris du temps que j'adorai !   195
Viens consumer sur moi ce don décoloré ;
Viens ! que je reconnaisse et que je les haïsse,
Cette ombrageuse enfant, ce silence complice,
Ce trouble transparent qui baigne dans les bois...
Et de mon sein glacé rejaillisse la voix   200
Que j'ignorais si rauque et d'amour si voilée...
Le col charmant cherchant la chasseresse ailée.

Mon cœur fut-il si près d'un cœur qui va faiblir ?
Fut-ce bien moi, grands cils, qui crus m'ensevelir
Dans l'arrière douceur riant à vos menaces...   205
Ô pampres ! sur ma joue errant en fils tenaces,
Ou toi... de cils tissue et de fluides fûts,
Tendre lueur d'un soir brisé de bras confus ?

O perilously the prey of one's own gaze!

For upon its silken shores, the mind's eye
Had already seen countless days glow and wane,
And whose course and colours I could foresee.
The tedium of gazing at their subtle hues
Gave me a sinister start on life:
Dawn unveiled day in all its hostility.
I was half dead; and perhaps half
Immortal, dreaming that the future itself
Was a mere diamond completing the diadem
Where cold swirling sorrows will well up
Amid the sovereign fires glowing upon my brow.

From my many tombs, will Time dare
Resurrect an evening so cherished by doves,
An evening that draws by a wispy thread
A rosy gleam of my quiescent childhood,
And dips in emerald a long flush of shame?

Memory, o pyre whose golden wind assails me,
Breathe on my mask the purple imbuing the refusal
To be another than I once was, myself aflame within...
Come, my blood, come redden the pale circumstance
Ennobled by the saintly blue expanse,
And the imperceptible iris of time I once adored!
Come and consume on me this faded gift;
Come! let me recognize and despise them,
This touchy child, this conniving silence,
This transparent disquiet bathing in the woods...
And let spring forth from my icy breast the voice
I did not know was so hoarse and so veiled in love...
The charming neck seeking the winged huntress.

Was my heart so near a heart that will soon languish?
Was it truly I, great eyelashes, who thought to bury myself
In the lingering sweetness that mocks your threats...
O vine branches! rambling in tenacious tendrils upon my cheek,
Or you... woven of eyelashes and of flowing columns,
An evening's mellow glow disrupted by arms intertwining?

'Que, dans le ciel placés, mes yeux tracent mon temple !
Et que sur moi repose un autel sans exemple !'   210

Criaient de tout mon corps la pierre et la pâleur...
La terre ne m'est plus qu'un bandeau de couleur
Qui coule et se refuse au front blanc de vertige...
Tout l'univers chancelle et tremble sur ma tige,
La pensive couronne échappe à mes esprits,   215
La mort veut respirer cette rose sans prix
Dont la douleur importe à sa fin ténébreuse !

Que si ma tendre odeur grise ta tête creuse,
Ô mort, respire enfin cette esclave de roi :
Appelle-moi, délie !... Et désespère-moi,   220
De moi-même si lasse, image condamnée !
Écoute... N'attends plus... La renaissante année
À tout mon sang prédit de secrets mouvements :
Le gel cède à regret ses derniers diamants...
Demain, sur un soupir des Bontés constellées,   225
Le printemps vient briser les fontaines scellées :
L'étonnant printemps rit, viole... On ne sait d'où
Venu ? Mais la candeur ruisselle à mots si doux
Qu'une tendresse prend la terre à ses entrailles...
Les arbres regonflés et recouverts d'écailles   230
Chargés de tant de bras et de trop d'horizons,
Meuvent sur le soleil leurs tonnantes toisons,
Montent dans l'air amer avec toutes leurs ailes
De feuilles par milliers qu'ils se sentent nouvelles...
N'entends-tu pas frémir ces noms aériens,   235
Ô Sourde !... Et dans l'espace accablé de liens,
Vibrant de bois vivace infléchi par la cime,
Pour et contre les dieux ramer l'arbre unanime,
La flottante forêt de qui les rudes troncs
Portent pieusement à leurs fantasques fronts,   240
Aux déchirants départs des archipels superbes,
Un fleuve tendre, ô mort, et caché sous les herbes ?

Quelle résisterait, mortelle, à ces remous ?
Quelle mortelle ?
                    Moi si pure, mes genoux

'MAY MY EYES FIXED ON THE HEAVENS TRACE MY TEMPLE!
AND MAY AN ALTAR LIKE NO OTHER REPOSE ON ME!'

Thus my body in all its stony pallor cried out...
The earth is no more than a flowing headband of colours
Spurning my vertiginous white brow...
The whole universe totters and trembles upon my stem,
The crown of thought eludes my senses,
Death longs to inhale this priceless rose
Whose sweetness matters to its dark designs!

Should my subtle scent intoxicate your hollow head,
O death, breathe in at last this royal slave;
Summon me, release!... And make me despair,
So weary of myself, this image condemned!
Listen... Wait no more... The year renewed
Foretells secret stirrings to the blood in my veins:
The frost reluctantly yields its last diamonds...
Tomorrow, on a sigh from heaven's Bounties,
Spring will arrive to break the sealed fountains:
Astonishing spring, scorning and violating... Whence will it
Come? Yet its freshness purls with words so sweet
The earth's womb is seized by tenderness...
Trees again swollen and swathed in scales
Laden with plenteous limbs and boundless horizons,
Bear their thunderous fleeces towards the sun,
Soar in the bitter air on myriad
Leafy wings that seem so resplendent and new...
Do you not hear these airy names quiver
O Deaf one!... And in the sky's teeming web,
Resonant with supple wood bowed by its crown,
The tree rowing as one, with and against the gods,
The floating forest whose coarse trunks
Draw reverently to their capricious brows,
To the heart-rending departures of splendid archipelagos,*
A tender stream, O Death, concealed beneath the grass?

Who among mortals could resist turmoil such as this?
What mortal woman?
                    Pure as I may be, my knees

Pressentent les terreurs de genoux sans défense...   245
L'air me brise. L'oiseau perce de cris d'enfance
Inouïs... l'ombre même où se serre mon cœur,
Et roses ! mon soupir vous soulève, vainqueur
Hélas ! des bras si doux qui ferment la corbeille...
Oh ! parmi mes cheveux pèse d'un poids d'abeille,   250
Plongeant toujours plus ivre au baiser plus aigu,
Le point délicieux de mon jour ambigu...
Lumière !... Ou toi, la mort ! Mais le plus prompt me prenne !...
Mon cœur bat ! mon cœur bat ! Mon sein brûle et
    m'entraîne !
Ah ! qu'il s'enfle, se gonfle et se tende, ce dur,   255
Très doux témoin captif de mes réseaux d'azur...

Dur en moi... mais si doux à la bouche infinie !...

Chers fantômes naissants dont la soif m'est unie,
Désirs ! Visages clairs !... Et vous, beaux fruits d'amour,
Les dieux m'ont-ils formé ce maternel contour   260
Et ces bords sinueux, ces plis et ces calices,
Pour que la vie embrasse un autel de délices,
Où mêlant l'âme étrange aux éternels retours,
La semence, le lait, le sang coulent toujours ?
Non ! L'horreur m'illumine, exécrable harmonie !   265
Chaque baiser présage une neuve agonie...
Je vois, je vois flotter, fuyant l'honneur des chairs
Des mânes impuissants les millions amers...
Non, souffles ! Non, regards, tendresses... mes convives,
Peuple altéré de moi suppliant que tu vives,   270
Non, vous ne tiendrez pas de moi la vie !... Allez,
Spectres, soupirs la nuit vainement exhalés,
Allez joindre des morts les impalpables nombres !
Je n'accorderai pas la lumière à des ombres,
Je garde loin de vous l'esprit sinistre et clair...   275
Non ! Vous ne tiendrez pas de mes lèvres l'éclair !...
Et puis... mon cœur aussi vous refuse sa foudre.
J'ai pitié de nous tous, ô tourbillons de poudre !

Grands Dieux ! Je perds en vous mes pas déconcertés !

Je n'implorerai plus que tes faibles clartés,   280
Longtemps sur mon visage envieuse de fondre.

Can sense the terror of defenceless knees...
The air crushes me. With ineffable childhood cries,
The bird pierces... the very shadow of my anguished heart,
And roses! my sigh lifts you, vanquisher
Alas, of the arms so tenderly enfolding the basket...
Oh! there among my tresses, and no more ponderous than a bee,
Whose dizzying flight plummets even more to the sharper kiss,
The delectable moment of my uncertain day gently weighs...
Light!... Or you, death! Let the more prompt take me!
My heart is beating! beating! My breast is burning and drawing
    me away!...
Ah! let it swell, enlarge, and stretch, this hard yet
All too soft witness ensnared in my web of blue sky...

Hard within me... yet so soft to infinity's mouth!...

Dear stirring phantoms, whose thirst is also mine,
Desires! Bright faces!... And you, love's beauteous fruits,
Has heaven fashioned this maternal form,
These sinuous contours and these folds and calices,
So that life might embrace an altar of delights
Where, blending the strange soul with eternal cycles,
Seed, milk, and blood forever flow?
No! Horror illuminates me, abominable harmony!
Each kiss portends a fresh death-throe...
I see gliding, fleeing the flesh's honour,
The embittered multitude of impotent Manes*...
No, breaths! No, glances, tenderness... my guests,
People thirsting for me, imploring that you may live,
No, you shall not get life from me!... Begone,
Spectres, sighs which night exhaled in vain,
Go join the ghostly myriads of the departed!
I shall not yield up light to shadows,
Far from you I keep a clear and ominous mind...
No! You shall not steal lightning from my lips!...
And then... my heart too refuses you its thunderbolt.
I pity us all, O swirls of dust!

Great Gods! In you I lose my anxious way!

I shall beseech no more than your faint gleam,
Yearning for so long to melt upon my face,

Très imminente larme, et seule à me répondre,
Larme qui fais trembler à mes regards humains
Une variété de funèbres chemins ;
Tu procèdes de l'âme, orgueil du labyrinthe,   285
Tu me portes du cœur cette goutte contrainte,
Cette distraction de mon suc précieux
Qui vient sacrifier mes ombres sur mes yeux,
Tendre libation de l'arrière-pensée !
D'une grotte de crainte au fond de moi creusée   290
Le sel mystérieux suinte muette l'eau.
D'où nais-tu ? Quel travail toujours triste et nouveau
Te tire avec retard, larme, de l'ombre amère ?
Tu gravis mes degrés de mortelle et de mère,
Et déchirant ta route, opiniâtre faix,   295
Dans le temps que je vis, les lenteurs que tu fais
M'étouffent... Je me tais, buvant ta marche sûre...
—Qui t'appelle au secours de ma jeune blessure ?

Mais blessure, sanglots, sombres essais, pourquoi ?
Pour qui, joyaux cruels, marquez-vous ce corps froid, 300
Aveugle aux doigts ouverts évitant l'espérance !
Où va-t-il, sans répondre à sa propre ignorance,
Ce corps dans la nuit noire étonné de sa foi ?
Terre trouble... et mêlée à l'algue, porte-moi,
Porte doucement moi... Ma faiblesse de neige   305
Marchera-t-elle tant qu'elle trouve son piège ?
Où traîne-t-il, mon cygne, où cherche-t-il son vol ?

...Dureté précieuse... Ô sentiment du sol,
Mon pas fondait sur toi l'assurance sacrée !
Mais sous le pied vivant qui tâte et qui la crée   310
Et touche avec horreur à son pacte natal,
Cette terre si ferme atteint mon piédestal.
Non loin, parmi ces pas, rêve mon précipice...
L'insensible rocher, glissant d'algues, propice
À fuir (comme en soi-même ineffablement seul).   315
Commence... Et le vent semble au travers d'un linceul
Ourdir de bruits marins une confuse trame,
Mélange de la lame en ruine, et de rame...
Tant de hoquets longtemps, et de râles heurtés,

Tear so imminent, lone response to me,
Tear that sets quivering in this human gaze
Plenteous paths winding to my mournful end;
You well up from the soul, pride of the labyrinth.
You bring me this repressed drop from my heart,
Extracted from my precious essence and
Rising to sacrifice the shadows on my eyes,
Mellow libation of my thought's hidden trove!
From a cavern of fear hollowed out deep within me
Water silently seeps from the mysterious salt.
From what spring do you rise? What toil ever sorrowful and new
Warily draws you, tear, from the bitter depths?
You climb my mortal and maternal rungs,
And, obstinate burden, cleaving a path
Through the time I am living, your slow pace
Stifles me... I fall silent, drinking in your steady advance...
—Who summons you to tend my young wound?

But why this wound, these sobs and gloomy endeavours?
For whom, heartless jewels, do you mark this cold body,
Blind to the outspread fingers avoiding hope!
Silent to its own ignorance, whither bound this body
Alone in the dark night and astounded by its own faith?
Gently bear me, troubled and seaweed-mingled earth
Gently bear me*... Can my pallid weakness
Tread its weary way until it finds its snare?
Where does my wandering swan hope to take flight?

...Precious firmness... O the feel of the earth,
My step founded upon you its sacred reassurance!
But beneath the living foot that feels and creates it,
And horrified to touch the pact of its birth,
This earth so firm reaches my pedestal.
Nearby, amidst these steps, my precipice dreams...
The unfeeling rock, slippery with seaweed, so suited
To vanishing (as if into one's own inexpressible solitude),
Begins... And through a shroud the wind seems
To weave tangled threads of sound wafting from the sea,
A blend of waves crashing in ruins and oars...
Myriad long gasps and rattles colliding, shattering,

Brisés, repris au large... et tous les sorts jetés   320
Éperdument divers roulant l'oubli vorace...

Hélas ! De mes pieds nus qui trouvera la trace
Cessera-t-il longtemps de ne songer qu'à soi ?

Terre trouble, et mêlée à l'algue, porte-moi !

Mystérieuse MOI, pourtant, tu vis encore !   325
Tu vas te reconnaître au lever de l'aurore
Amèrement la même...

                Un miroir de la mer
Se lève... Et sur la lèvre, un sourire d'hier
Qu'annonce avec ennui l'effacement des signes,
Glace dans l'orient déjà les pâles lignes   330
De lumière et de pierre, et la pleine prison
Où flottera l'anneau de l'unique horizon...
Regarde : un bras très pur est vu, qui se dénude.
Je te revois, mon bras... Tu portes l'aube...

                          Ô rude
Réveil d'une victime inachevée... et seuil   335
Si doux... si clair, que flatte, affleurement d'écueil,
L'onde basse, et que lave une houle amortie !...
L'ombre qui m'abandonne, impérissable hostie,
Me découvre vermeille à de nouveaux désirs,
Sur le terrible autel de tous mes souvenirs.   340

Là, l'écume s'efforce à se faire visible ;
Et là, titubera sur la barque sensible
À chaque épaule d'onde, un pêcheur éternel.
Tout va donc accomplir son acte solennel
De toujours reparaître incomparable et chaste,   345
Et de restituer la tombe enthousiaste
Au gracieux état du rire universel.

Salut ! Divinités par la rose et le sel,
Et les premiers jouets de la jeune lumière,
Îles !... Ruches bientôt, quand la flamme première   350
Fera que votre roche, îles que je prédis,
Ressente en rougissant de puissants paradis ;
Cimes qu'un feu féconde à peine intimidées,

Then echoing on the open sea... and the spells there cast,
So wildly different, all rolling voracious oblivion...

Alas! Will he who finds the trail of my bare feet
Cease thinking only of himself for long?

Bear me, troubled and seaweed-strewn earth!

Mysterious ME, you are still alive!
At daybreak, you will recognize yourself
Bitterly the same...

              A mirror is rising from the
Sea... And upon its lip, a smile from yesterday,
Wearily foretold as signs slowly ebbed,
Already freezes in the east the faint lines
Of light and stone, and the teeming prison
Where the horizon's unbroken curve will float...
Behold, a bare arm, so graceful and pale, has appeared.
I see you once again, my arm... Now bearing the dawn...

                                     O rude

Awakening of a victim still present... threshold
So soft... glistening reefy outcrop caressed by
The lapping ebb, and cleansed by the deadened swell!...
The shadow retreating from me, undying sacrifice,
Reveals me flushed with new desires,
Upon the terrible altar of all my memories.

There, the foam strives to be seen;
And there, upon the barque rolling with
Each buffeting wave, an eternal fisherman will teeter.
All things will now perform the solemn act of
Forever returning flawless and supreme,
And of restoring the avid tomb
To the gracious state of universal laughter.

Greetings! Divinities by the rose and salt,
And first playthings of daybreak,
Isles!... Hives soon to be, when the first flame
Will make your rock, isles I foretell,
Feel the blush of the mighty heavens;
Crests no sooner startled than made fruitful by a fire,

Bois qui bourdonnerez de bêtes et d'idées,
D'hymnes d'hommes comblés des dons du juste éther,   355
Îles ! dans la rumeur des ceintures de mer,
Mères vierges toujours, même portant ces marques,
Vous m'êtes à genoux de merveilleuses Parques :
Rien n'égale dans l'air les fleurs que vous placez,
Mais dans la profondeur, que vos pieds sont glacés !   360

De l'âme les apprêts sous la tempe calmée,
Ma mort, enfant secrète et déjà si formée,
Et vous, divins dégoûts qui me donniez l'essor,
Chastes éloignements des lustres de mon sort,
Ne fûtes-vous, ferveur, qu'une noble durée ?   365
Nulle jamais des dieux plus près aventurée
N'osa peindre à son front leur souffle ravisseur,
Et de la nuit parfaite implorant l'épaisseur,
Prétendre par la lèvre au suprême murmure.

Je soutenais l'éclat de la mort toute pure   370
Telle j'avais jadis le soleil soutenu...
Mon corps désespéré tendait le torse nu
Où l'âme, ivre de soi, de silence et de gloire,
Prête à s'évanouir de sa propre mémoire,
Écoute, avec espoir, frapper au mur pieux   375
Ce cœur,—qui se ruine à coups mystérieux
Jusqu'à ne plus tenir que de sa complaisance
Un frémissement fin de feuille, ma présence...

Attente vaine, et vaine... Elle ne peut mourir
Qui devant son miroir pleure pour s'attendrir.   380

Ô n'aurait-il fallu, folle, que j'accomplisse
Ma merveilleuse fin de choisir pour supplice
Ce lucide dédain des nuances du sort ?
Trouveras-tu jamais plus transparente mort
Ni de pente plus pure où je rampe à ma perte   385
Que sur ce long regard de victime entr'ouverte,
Pâle, qui se résigne et saigne sans regret ?
Que lui fait tout le sang qui n'est plus son secret ?
Dans quelle blanche paix cette pourpre la laisse,
À l'extrême de l'être, et belle de faiblesse !   390

Wood set to hum with creatures and fancies,
With hymns of men burdened with heaven's just bounty,
Isles! in the murmuring of the encircling sea,
Mothers virgin still, even bearing these marks,
To me you are wondrous, kneeling Fates:
Nothing matches the flowers you sprinkle in the air,
But in the depths, how icy-cold your feet!

Beneath the hushed temples, the soul's preparations,
My death, stealthy child already fully formed,
And you, divine loathing which gave my soul wings,
Chaste distancing from the lustra* of my fate,
Were you, burning passion, but a noble interlude?
No one who ever ventured so near to the gods
Dared paint upon her brow their abductor's breath
Or, imploring night's pure and fathomless depths,
Aspire through her lips to the supreme murmur.

I withstood death's all-powerful allure
Just as I had once withstood the sun...
My despairing body bared its breast
Where the soul, drunk on itself, silence and glory,
Ready to fade away from its own memory,
Listens in hope to this heart, worn down by
Mysterious blows, knocking on the pious wall
Until all it can endure of its own kindness is
A leaf's faint quiver, my presence...

Vain, so vain this expectation... She who weeps
From self-pity before the looking-glass cannot die.

O, madwoman that I am, should I not have fulfilled
My wonderful desire to choose as my torment
This lucid disdain for fate's varying hues?
Will you ever find a more transparent demise
Or a purer slope where I can crawl to my ruin
Than the fixed gaze of this victim cut open,
Pallid, resigned and bleeding without regret?
Does this blood matter when no longer her secret?
In such lily-white calm this purple leaves her bathed,
At the extremity of being, and beauteously frail!

Elle calme le temps qui la vient abolir,
Le moment souverain ne la peut plus pâlir,
Tant la chair vide baise une sombre fontaine !...
Elle se fait toujours plus seule et plus lointaine...
Et moi, d'un tel destin, le cœur toujours plus près,   395
Mon cortège, en esprit, se berçait de cyprès...
Vers un aromatique avenir de fumée,
Je me sentais conduite, offerte et consumée,
Toute, toute promise aux nuages heureux !
Même, je m'apparus cet arbre vaporeux,   400
De qui la majesté légèrement perdue
S'abandonne à l'amour de toute l'étendue.
L'être immense me gagne, et de mon cœur divin
L'encens qui brûle expire une forme sans fin...
Tous les corps radieux tremblent dans mon essence !...   405

Non, non !... N'irrite plus cette réminiscence !
Sombre lys ! Ténébreuse allusion des cieux,
Ta vigueur n'a pu rompre un vaisseau précieux...
Parmi tous les instants tu touchais au suprême...
—Mais qui l'emporterait sur la puissance même,   410
Avide par tes yeux de contempler le jour
Qui s'est choisi ton front pour lumineuse tour ?

Cherche, du moins, dis-toi, par quelle sourde suite
La nuit, d'entre les morts, au jour t'a reconduite ?
Souviens-toi de toi-même, et retire à l'instinct   415
Ce fil (ton doigt doré le dispute au matin),
Ce fil, dont la finesse aveuglément suivie
Jusque sur cette rive a ramené ta vie...
Sois subtile... cruelle... ou plus subtile !... Mens !...
Mais sache !... Enseigne-moi par quels enchantements,   420
Lâche que n'a su fuir sa tiède fumée,
Ni le souci d'un sein d'argile parfumée,
Par quel retour sur toi, reptile, as-tu repris
Tes parfums de caverne et tes tristes esprits ?

Hier la chair profonde, hier, la chair maîtresse   425
M'a trahie... Oh ! sans rêve, et sans une caresse !...
Nul démon, nul parfum ne m'offrit le péril

She calms time which comes to lay its deathly hands on her,
The moment of reckoning shall not make her paler,
The ashen flesh so kisses a dark fountain!...
She grows ever more alone and more distant...
And my own heart draws ever closer to such a destiny,
I dreamed my cortège was swaying with cypresses...
Towards days redolent of sweet-scented smoke,
I felt I was being led, offered, and consumed,
Promised whole to joyful clouds!
I had a vision of myself as this haze-shrouded tree,
Whose lightly faded splendour
Lovingly yields to the vast expanse.
The immense being takes hold of me, and my
Divine heart's burning incense exhales a boundless form...
All glowing bodies quiver in my essence!...

No, no!... Stir up no more these memories!
Dark lily! Mysterious hint of the heavens,
Your vigour could not break a precious vessel...
Amid all moments you touched on the supreme...
—Yet who could triumph over power itself,
Eager through your eyes to contemplate the day
Which chose your brow as its tower of light?

Seek, at least, ask by what mysterious path
Night brought you back to day from the realm of the dead?
Remember yourself, and reclaim from instinct
This thread (your gilded finger vies for it with dawn),
This silken thread you blindly followed
Has led your life once again to this shore...
Be subtle... cruel... or more subtle still!... Lie!...
Yet know!... Enlighten me, by what wiles,
Coward whom her own tepid breath or the torment of a
Breast of sweet-scented clay could not escape,
By what soul-searching, reptile, did you regain
Your dank lair and your gloomy spirits?

Yesterday the mysterious flesh, the flesh supreme
Betrayed me... Oh! not by a dream, or a caress!...
No demon, no scent lured me with the danger

D'imaginaires bras mourant au col viril ;
Ni, par le Cygne-Dieu, de plumes offensée
Sa brûlante blancheur n'effleura ma pensée...   430

Il eût connu pourtant le plus tendre des nids !
Car toute à la faveur de mes membres unis,
Vierge, je fus dans l'ombre une adorable offrande...
Mais le sommeil s'éprit d'une douceur si grande,
Et nouée à moi-même au creux de mes cheveux,   435
J'ai mollement perdu mon empire nerveux.
Au milieu de mes bras, je me suis faite une autre...
Qui s'aliène ?... Qui s'envole ?... Qui se vautre ?...
À quel détour caché, mon cœur s'est-il fondu ?
Quelle conque a redit le nom que j'ai perdu ?   440
Le sais-je, quel reflux traître m'a retirée
De mon extrémité pure et prématurée,
Et m'a repris le sens de mon vaste soupir ?
Comme l'oiseau se pose, il fallut m'assoupir.

Ce fut l'heure, peut-être, où la devineresse   445
Intérieure s'use et se désintéresse :
Elle n'est plus la même... Une profonde enfant
Des degrés inconnus vainement se défend,
Et redemande au loin ses mains abandonnées.
Il faut céder aux vœux des mortes couronnées   450
Et prendre pour visage un souffle...
                       Doucement,
Me voici : mon front touche à ce consentement...
Ce corps, je lui pardonne, et je goûte à la cendre.
Je me remets entière au bonheur de descendre,
Ouverte aux noirs témoins, les bras suppliciés,   455
Entre des mots sans fin, sans moi, balbutiés.
Dors, ma sagesse, dors. Forme-toi cette absence ;
Retourne dans le germe et la sombre innocence,
Abandonne-toi vive aux serpents, aux trésors.
Dors toujours ! Descends, dors toujours ! Descends, dors, dors !   460

(La porte basse c'est une bague... où la gaze
Passe... Tout meurt, tout rit dans la gorge qui jase...
L'oiseau boit sur ta bouche et tu ne peux le voir...
Viens plus bas, parle bas... Le noir n'est pas si noir...)

Of imaginary arms languishing upon such a potent neck;
Nor did the Swan-God,* whose resplendent whiteness is
Blemished by feathers, lightly brush my thought...

Yet, he would have known the tenderest nest!
For, so happily enfolded in the warmth of my limbs,
I, this virgin lying in the shadows, was a delightful offering...
But sleep was smitten with such softness,
And huddled in my mantle of tresses,
I meekly yielded my nervous dominion.
Embraced in my own arms, I became another...
Who is estranged?... Who vanishes?... Who wallows?
At what hidden turn did my heart melt?
What seashell echoed the name I have lost?
What treacherous ebb drew me back
From my pure and premature edge, and
Stole from me the meaning of my deep sigh?
Just as the bird comes to land, so I had to slumber.

It was, perhaps, the hour when the inner
Soothsayer grows weary and indifferent:
No longer is she the same... A child deep within
Protects herself in vain from realms of the unknown,
Pleading from afar for her hands long forsaken.
The wishes of glorified dead women must be granted
And this face taken as a breath...
                                        Gently,
I am here: my brow is in harmony with this consent...
I forgive this body and taste the ashes.
I abandon myself entirely to the joyous descent,
Bared to the dark's watchful eyes, with tortured arms,
Amid endless muttered words that were not mine.
Now sleep, my wisdom, sleep. Shape this absence;
Return to the seed and to gloomy innocence.
Give yourself up alive to the serpents, to the treasures,
Sleep on! Down, sleep on! Down still, sleep, sleep!

(The low door is a ring... where gauze
Passes... All is dying, laughing in the chattering throat...
The bird sips from your mouth and you cannot see it...
Come, lower still, speak softly... The dark is not so dark...)

Délicieux linceuls, mon désordre tiède,   465
Couche où je me répands, m'interroge et me cède,
Où j'allai de mon cœur noyer les battements,
Presque tombeau vivant dans mes appartements,
Qui respire, et sur qui l'éternité s'écoute,
Place pleine de moi qui m'avez prise toute,   470
Ô forme de ma forme et la creuse chaleur
Que mes retours sur moi reconnaissaient la leur,
Voici que tant d'orgueil qui dans vos plis se plonge
À la fin se mélange aux bassesses du songe !
Dans vos nappes, où lisse elle imitait sa mort   475
L'idole malgré soi se dispose et s'endort,
Lasse femme absolue, et les yeux dans ses larmes,
Quand, de ses secrets nus les antres et les charmes,
Et ce reste d'amour que se gardait le corps
Corrompirent sa perte et ses mortels accords.   480
Arche toute secrète, et pourtant si prochaine,
Mes transports, cette nuit, pensaient briser ta chaîne ;
Je n'ai fait que bercer de lamentations
Tes flancs chargés de jour et de créations !
Quoi ! mes yeux froidement que tant d'azur égare   485
Regardent là périr l'étoile fine et rare,
Et ce jeune soleil de mes étonnements
Me paraît d'une aïeule éclairer les tourments,
Tant sa flamme aux remords ravit leur existence,
Et compose d'aurore une chère substance   490
Qui se formait déjà substance d'un tombeau !...
Ô, sur toute la mer, sur mes pieds, qu'il est beau !
Tu viens !... Je suis toujours celle que tu respires,
Mon voile évaporé me fuit vers tes empires...

...Alors, n'ai-je formé, vains adieux si je vis,   495
Que songes ?... Si je viens, en vêtements ravis,
Sur ce bord, sans horreur, humer la haute écume,
Boire des yeux l'immense et riante amertume,
L'être contre le vent, dans le plus vif de l'air,
Recevant au visage un appel de la mer ;   500
Si l'âme intense souffle, et renfle furibonde
L'onde abrupte sur l'onde abattue, et si l'onde

Delightful shrouds, my warm disarray,
Bed where I spread, question, and surrender myself,
Where I set forth to drown my beating heart,
Like a living tomb within my chambers,
Breathing, and where eternity's pulse resonates,
Realm imbued with me which it took whole,
O form of my form and the hollow warmth
Which my returning senses recognized as their own,
Now this bounteous pride immersed in your folds
Blends in the end with the vileness of dream!
In your sheets where she calmly acted out her death
The reluctant idol lays herself down and drifts off to sleep,
Weary woman, truly supreme, her eyes sunken in tears,
When the recesses and charms of her bare secrets,
And love's afterglow that her body cherished
Thwarted her ruin and her pact with death.
Arch, so mysterious and yet so intimate,
This night's ecstasies longed to throw off your shackles;
Yet all I did was lull with my laments
Your sides teeming with day and myriad creations!
What! my eyes coldly spellbound by such bounteous blue
Watch the faint lone star waning there,
And this young sun of my wonder seems
To illuminate the torments of an ancestress,
So fiercely is remorse burned away by its flames,
And to fashion from dawn a treasured substance
Already taking the shape of a tomb!...
How fine the sun, over the vast sea, over my feet!
Here you come!... I am still the one you breathe in,
My airy veil takes flight, bound for your realms...

...So then, vain farewells if I live, was it all
But a dream?... If in windblown clothes I come
To this edge undaunted, breathing in the swirling spray,
My gaze drinking in this boundless, mocking brine.
My entire being facing into the wind, in the keenest air,
Bearing the sea's full brunt on my face;
If the roused soul gusts and thrusts in all its fury
Curling wave upon shattered wave, and if the billow

Au cap tonne, immolant un monstre de candeur,
Et vient des hautes mers vomir la profondeur
Sur ce roc, d'où jaillit jusque vers mes pensées   505
Un éblouissement d'étincelles glacées,
Et sur toute ma peau que morde l'âpre éveil,
Alors, malgré moi-même, il le faut, ô Soleil,
Que j'adore mon cœur où tu te viens connaître,
Doux et puissant retour du délice de naître,   510
Feu vers qui se soulève une vierge de sang
Sous les espèces d'or d'un sein reconnaissant !

Thunders on the headland, sacrificing a foamy monster,
And surges from the high seas to spew the depths
Upon this rock, casting a dazzling spray
Of icy sparkles towards flowing thoughts,
And upon my skin stung by the bitter awakening,
Then I must, despite myself, O Sun, adore
This heart where you come to know yourself,
The delight of birth gently and potently rekindled,
Fire to which a virgin of blood ascends
Beneath the gold coins of a grateful breast!

ALBUM DE VERS ANCIENS

La fileuse

Lilia... neque nent

Assise, la fileuse au bleu de la croisée
Où le jardin mélodieux se dodeline ;
Le rouet ancien qui ronfle l'a grisée.

Lasse, ayant bu l'azur, de filer la câline
Chevelure, à ses doigts si faibles évasive,   5
Elle songe, et sa tête petite s'incline.

Un arbuste et l'air pur font une source vive
Qui, suspendue au jour, délicieuse arrose
De ses pertes de fleurs le jardin de l'oisive.

Une tige, où le vent vagabond se repose,   10
Courbe le salut vain de sa grâce étoilée,
Dédiant magnifique, au vieux rouet, sa rose.

Mais la dormeuse file une laine isolée ;
Mystérieusement l'ombre frêle se tresse
Au fil de ses doigts longs et qui dorment, filée.   15

Le songe se dévide avec une paresse
Angélique, et sans cesse, au doux fuseau crédule,
La chevelure ondule au gré de la caresse...

Derrière tant de fleurs, l'azur se dissimule,
Fileuse de feuillage et de lumière ceinte :   20
Tout le ciel vert se meurt. Le dernier arbre brûle.

Ta sœur, la grande rose où sourit une sainte,
Parfume ton front vague au vent de son haleine
Innocente, et tu crois languir... Tu es éteinte

Au bleu de la croisée où tu filais la laine.   25

ALBUM OF EARLY VERSE

The Spinner

*Lilies... neither do they spin**

Seated in the blue of the window
Where the melodious garden gently sways, the spinner
Drowses to the hum of the ancient spinning wheel.

Sated with the blue realm and weary of threading
The gentle hair eluding her fingers grown so frail,
She is dreaming, her small head bowed.

A shrub and the pure air form a living spring,
Suspended in light, as she delights in sprinkling
Fallen blossoms upon the garden where she slumbers.

A stem, where wind's capricious breath comes to rest,
Bows with the vain greeting of its starry grace,
Bestowing its splendid rose upon the old spinning wheel.

But the slumbering woman weaves her solitary yarn;
The flimsy shadow is mysteriously braided,
Threaded down along her slender sleepy fingers.

The dream unwinds with heavenly languor,
And ceaselessly, upon the soft and trusting spindle,
The hair undulates at the whim of her caress...

Behind so many flowers, the blue sky is wreathed,
A spinner bounded by leaves and light:
The green sky ebbs away. The last tree is ablaze.

Your sister, the glorious rose wherein smiles a saint,
Scents your dim brow with her innocent breath,
You feel yourself languishing... You have faded

In the blue of the window where you sat spinning wool.

Hélène

Azur ! c'est moi... Je viens des grottes de la mort
Entendre l'onde se rompre aux degrés sonores,
Et je revois les galères dans les aurores
Ressusciter de l'ombre au fil des rames d'or.

Mes solitaires mains appellent les monarques   5
Dont la barbe de sel amusait mes doigts purs ;
Je pleurais. Ils chantaient leurs triomphes obscurs
Et les golfes enfuis aux poupes de leurs barques.

J'entends les conques profondes et les clairons
Militaires rythmer le vol des avirons ;   10
Le chant clair des rameurs enchaîne le tumulte,

Et les Dieux, à la proue héroïque exaltés
Dans leur sourire antique et que l'écume insulte,
Tendent vers moi leurs bras indulgents et sculptés.

Orphée

...Je compose en esprit, sous les myrtes, Orphée
L'Admirable !... Le feu, des cirques purs descend ;
Il change le mont chauve en auguste trophée
D'où s'exhale d'un dieu l'acte retentissant.

Si le dieu chante, il rompt le site tout-puissant ;   5
Le soleil voit l'horreur du mouvement des pierres ;
Une plainte inouïe appelle éblouissants
Les hauts murs d'or harmonieux d'un sanctuaire.

Il chante, assis au bord du ciel splendide, Orphée !
Le roc marche, et trébuche ; et chaque pierre fée   10
Se sent un poids nouveau qui vers l'azur délire !

D'un Temple à demi nu le soir baigne l'essor,
Et soi-même il s'assemble et s'ordonne dans l'or
À l'âme immense du grand hymne sur la lyre !

Helen

Blue realm! it is I... come from death's caverns
To listen to the waves break in sonorous steps,
And again I glimpse the galleys at daybreak
Resurrected from the shadow, swept along by golden oars.

My solitary hands call out to the monarchs
Whose salty beards used to delight my soft fingers;
There I would weep. They would sing of their ancient exploits
And of gulfs fled astern their boats.

I hear the deep conches and the martial clarions
Rhyme in cadence with the sweep of the oars;
The rowers' clear shanty melts into the tumult,

And the Gods, upon the heroic helm exalted
With their ancient smiles scorned by the spume,
Extend to me their carved, indulgent arms.

Orpheus

...In my mind, beneath the myrtles, I compose Orpheus
The Admirable One!... Fire falls from heaven's extravaganza;
It changes the bare mount into a majestic trophy
From which a god's resonant act is exhaled.

Should the god chant, he shatters the all–powerful site;
The sun beholds the horror of moving stones;
An astounding wail calls out to a sanctuary's high
Walls, brilliantly radiating their harmonious gold.

Seated on the edge of the splendid sky, Orpheus sings!
The rock treads, and stumbles; and every nimble stone
Feels a new and deep yearning for blue realms beyond!

Evening bathes a half-naked Temple as it soars,
And gathers itself in the gold attuned to
The boundless soul and majestic hymnals rising from the lyre!

86
Féerie

Naissance de Vénus

De sa profonde mère, encor froide et fumante,
Voici qu'au seuil battu de tempêtes, la chair
Amèrement vomie au soleil par la mer,
Se délivre des diamants de la tourmente.

Son sourire se forme, et suit sur ses bras blancs   5
Qu'éplore l'orient d'une épaule meurtrie,
De l'humide Thétis la pure pierrerie,
Et sa tresse se fraye un frisson sur ses flancs.

Le frais gravier, qu'arrose et fuit sa course agile,
Croule, creuse rumeur de soif, et le facile   10
Sable a bu les baisers de ses bonds puérils ;

Mais de mille regards ou perfides ou vagues,
Son œil mobile mêle aux éclairs de périls
L'eau riante, et la danse infidèle des vagues.

Féerie

La lune mince verse une lueur sacrée,
Toute une jupe d'un tissu d'argent léger,
Sur les bases de marbre où vient l'Ombre songer
Que suit d'un char de perle une gaze nacrée.

Pour les cygnes soyeux qui frôlent les roseaux   5
De carènes de plume à demi lumineuse,
Elle effeuille infinie une rose neigeuse
Dont les pétales font des cercles sur les eaux...

Est-ce vivre ?... Ô désert de volupté pâmée
Où meurt le battement faible de l'eau lamée,   10
Usant le seuil secret des échos de cristal...

La chair confuse des molles roses commence
À frémir, si d'un cri le diamant fatal
Fêle d'un fil de jour toute la fable immense.

Birth of Venus

From her mother's depths, still steaming and cold,
Here on the storm-battered threshold, the flesh,
Bitterly spewed out by the sea and cast to the sun,
Frees itself from the tempest of diamonds.

Her smile appears, and along her pallid arms,
Bathed in pearled tears trickling from a shoulder's wound,
Trails the pure gemstones of watery Thetis,* as
Her tress sends a quiver down her side.

The cool pebbles which her airy steps sprinkle and flee,
Yield beneath her, sounding a hollow thirst, and the soft
Sand has imbibed the kisses of her childlike gambols;

But with myriad treacherous or absent glances,
Her darting eye blends perilous lightning,
Laughing water, and the frolicking waves.

Faery

The slender moon spills a sacred gleam,
A billowing skirt of fine silvery fabric,
Upon marble where the Shadow comes to dream
Trailed by the lustrous veil of a chariot of pearl.

For the silken swans brushing against the reeds
With their half-radiant feathery hulls,
She plucks the leaves from an everlasting snowy rose
Whose fallen petals send forth ripples upon the water...

Is this living?... O desert of swooning sensual delight
Where the faint lapping of silvery water expires,
Wearing away the secret threshold of resounding crystal...

The blended flesh of velvety roses begins
To quiver, should a cry's fatal diamond
Utterly shatter the boundless fable with a wisp of daylight.

Même féerie

La lune mince verse une lueur sacrée,
Comme une jupe d'un tissu d'argent léger,
Sur les masses de marbre où marche et croit songer
Quelque vierge de perle et de gaze nacrée.

Pour les cygnes soyeux qui frôlent les roseaux   5
De carènes de plume à demi lumineuse,
Sa main cueille et dispense une rose neigeuse
Dont les pétales font des cercles sur les eaux.

Délicieux désert, solitude pâmée,
Quand le remous de l'eau par la lune lamée   10
Compte éternellement ses échos de cristal,

Quel cœur pourrait souffrir l'inexorable charme
De la nuit éclatante au firmament fatal,
Sans tirer de soi-même un cri pur comme une arme ?

Baignée

Un fruit de chair se baigne en quelque jeune vasque,
(Azur dans les jardins tremblants) mais hors de l'eau,
Isolant la torsade aux puissances de casque,
Luit le chef d'or que tranche à la nuque un tombeau.

Éclose la beauté par la rose et l'épingle !   5
Du miroir même issue où trempent ses bijoux,
Bizarres feux brisés dont le bouquet dur cingle
L'oreille abandonnée aux mots nus des flots doux.

Un bras vague inondé dans le néant limpide
Pour une ombre de fleur à cueillir vainement   10
S'effile, ondule, dort par le délice vide,

Si l'autre, courbé pur sous le beau firmament,
Parmi la chevelure immense qu'il humecte,
Capture dans l'or simple un vol ivre d'insecte.

Same Faery

The slender moon spills a sacred gleam,
Like a billowing skirt of fine silvery fabric,
Upon blocks of marble where treads, as if dreaming,
Some virgin fashioned from pearl and lustrous gauze.

For the silken swans brushing against the reeds
With their half-radiant feathery hulls,
Her hand plucks and discards a snowy rose
Whose fallen petals send forth ripples upon the water.

Delectable reward, swooning solitude,
When the purling water silvered by the brilliant moon
Counts forevermore its crystal echoes,

What heart could bear the relentless allure
Of dazzling night in the heaven's mortal vault,
Without releasing a cry as piercing as a blade?

Bathed

A fruit of flesh is bathing in some young pool
(Blue sky in the quivering gardens) but out of the water,
Twisting a lock of iron-like hair, gleams
The gilded head severed at the nape by a tomb.

Beauty blossoming forth by the rose and the pin!*
From the very mirror where she dips her jewels,
Strange flickering fires whose sharp scent stings
The ear abandoned to the waves' mellow lapping.

A fair arm immersed in the limpid oblivion
To pluck in vain the shadow of a flower
Frays, ripples, and slumbers in the empty delight,

While the other so pure, folded beneath beauteous heaven,
Amid the bountiful tresses it moistens,
Seizes an insect's heady flight in the rich gold.

Au bois dormant

La princesse, dans un palais de rose pure,
Sous les murmures, sous la mobile ombre dort,
Et de corail ébauche une parole obscure
Quand les oiseaux perdus mordent ses bagues d'or.

Elle n'écoute ni les gouttes, dans leurs chutes,   5
Tinter d'un siècle vide au lointain le trésor,
Ni, sur la forêt vague, un vent fondu de flûtes
Déchirer la rumeur d'une phrase de cor.

Laisse, longue, l'écho rendormir la diane,
Ô toujours plus égale à la molle liane   10
Qui se balance et bat tes yeux ensevelis.

Si proche de ta joue et si lente la rose
Ne va pas dissiper ce délice de plis
Secrètement sensible au rayon qui s'y pose.

César

César, calme César, le pied sur toute chose,
Les poings durs dans la barbe, et l'œil sombre peuplé
D'aigles et des combats du couchant contemplé,
Ton cœur s'enfle, et se sent toute-puissante Cause.

Le lac en vain palpite et lèche son lit rose ;   5
En vain d'or précieux brille le jeune blé ;
Tu durcis dans les nœuds de ton corps rassemblé
L'ordre, qui doit enfin fendre ta bouche close.

L'ample monde, au delà de l'immense horizon,
L'Empire attend l'éclair, le décret, le tison   10
Qui changeront le soir en furieuse aurore.

Heureux là-bas sur l'onde, et bercé du hasard,
Un pêcheur indolent qui flotte et chante, ignore
Quelle foudre s'amasse au centre de César.

In the Sleeping Wood

In a palace of vibrant rose, the princess slumbers
Beneath the whispers, beneath the dappled shadows;
And murmurs in words of coral
When the stray birds peck at her gold rings.

She pays no heed to the drops softly falling,
Chiming over yonder of treasure from times past,
Or to the dulcet flutes wafting above the shadowed forest,
Shredding the whispered phrase of the hunting horn.

Let the echo lull the long reveille,
O you who resembles evermore the climbing liana
Swaying and brushing your sunken eyes.

So close to your cheek, the lingering rose
Will not smooth out these delectable folds
Faintly stirred by the sunbeam's caress.

Caesar

Caesar, calm Caesar, treading all underfoot,
Hard fists in your beard, your gloomy eye brimming with
Eagles and the battles you behold in the sunset,
Your heart swells, believing itself all-powerful Cause.

In vain the lake quivers and laps its rosy bed;
In vain the young wheat gleams of precious gold;
In your body's taut knots you harden
The order which must finally cleave your sealed lips.

The wide world, beyond the boundless horizon,
The Empire awaits the lightning, the decree, the ember
Which will change evening to furious dawn.

Happily rocked by chance out there on the wave,
A fisherman languidly drifts and chants, oblivious to
The thunderbolt swelling within Caesar's heart.

Le bois amical

Nous avons pensé des choses pures
Côte à côte, le long des chemins,
Nous nous sommes tenus par les mains
Sans dire... parmi les fleurs obscures ;

Nous marchions comme des fiancés   5
Seuls, dans la nuit verte des prairies ;
Nous partagions ce fruit de féeries
La lune amicale aux insensés.

Et puis, nous sommes morts sur la mousse,
Très loin, tout seuls parmi l'ombre douce   10
De ce bois intime et murmurant ;

Et là-haut, dans la lumière immense,
Nous nous sommes trouvés en pleurant
Ô mon cher compagnon de silence !

Les vaines danseuses

Celles qui sont des fleurs légères sont venues,
Figurines d'or, et beautés toutes menues
Où s'irise une faible lune... Les voici
Mélodieuses fuir dans le bois éclairci.
De mauves et d'iris et de nocturnes roses   5
Sont les grâces de nuit sous leurs danses écloses.
Que de parfums voilés dispensent leurs doigts d'or !
Mais l'azur doux s'effeuille en ce bocage mort,
Et de l'eau mince luit à peine, reposée
Comme un pâle trésor d'une antique rosée   10
D'où le silence en fleur monte... Encor les voici
Mélodieuses fuir dans le bois éclairci.
Aux calices aimés leurs mains sont gracieuses ;
Un peu de lune dort sur leurs lèvres pieuses
Et leurs bras merveilleux aux gestes endormis   15
Aiment à dénouer sous les myrtes amis
Leurs liens fauves et leurs caresses... Mais certaines,

The Friendly Wood

We thought of pure things
Side by side, along the trails,
We held each other's hand,
Silent... amid the dappled flowers;

We strolled like ones betrothed
Alone, in the meadows' verdant night;
We shared this fruit of faeries
The moon, kind to those who have no sense of it.

And then, we died upon the moss,
Far away, all alone in the gentle shade
Of this loving, whispering wood;

And there, in the boundless light aloft,
We found each other weeping
O my dear companion of silence!

The Vain Dancers

They who are delicate flowers appeared,
Gilded figurines and slender beauties
Tinged with moon's silvery sheen... Behold them
Melodiously gliding off to the illumined wood.
Mallows and irises and nocturnal roses
Pose like graces of night beneath their blossom dance.
What subtle fragrance wafts from their gilded fingers!
But the leafy blue sky gently ebbs in this lifeless grove
And shallow waters scarcely gleam, spread
Like a faint treasure of some ancient dew
Whence silence rises like a flower... Behold them once more
Melodiously gliding off to the illumined wood.
Their hands graciously brush the beloved chalices.
A thread of moonlight lingers upon their virtuous lips
And their delightful arms, languorous with sleep,
Lovingly unfurl beneath the myrtles' merry limbs
Their wild embrace and caresses... Yet some

Moins captives du rythme et des harpes lointaines,
S'en vont d'un pas subtil au lac enseveli
Boire des lys l'eau frêle où dort le pur oubli.   20

Un feu distinct...

Un feu distinct m'habite, et je vois froidement
La violente vie illuminée entière...
Je ne puis plus aimer seulement qu'en dormant
Ses actes gracieux mélangés de lumière.

Mes jours viennent la nuit me rendre des regards,   5
Après le premier temps de sommeil malheureux ;
Quand le malheur lui-même est dans le noir épars
Ils reviennent me vivre et me donner des yeux.

Que si leur joie éclate, un écho qui m'éveille
N'a rejeté qu'un mort sur ma rive de chair,   10
Et mon rire étranger suspend à mon oreille,

Comme à la vide conque un murmure de mer,
Le doute,—sur le bord d'une extrême merveille,
Si je suis, si je fus, si je dors ou je veille ?

Narcisse parle

Narcissæ placandis manibus

Ô frères ! tristes lys, je languis de beauté
Pour m'être désiré dans votre nudité,
Et vers vous, Nymphe, nymphe, ô nymphe des fontaines,
Je viens au pur silence offrir mes larmes vaines.

Un grand calme m'écoute, où j'écoute l'espoir.   5
La voix des sources change et me parle du soir ;
J'entends l'herbe d'argent grandir dans l'ombre sainte,
Et la lune perfide élève son miroir
Jusque dans les secrets de la fontaine éteinte.

Et moi ! de tout mon corps dans ces roseaux jeté,   10
Je languis, ô saphir, par ma triste beauté !

Less bound to the melodic sway and the distant harps,
Steal away on tiptoe to the hidden lake
To drink the lilies' frail water where pure oblivion slumbers.

A Distinct Fire...

A distinct fire burns within me, and coldly I see
Violent life wholly illuminated...
I can no longer love only when sleeping
Its gracious acts suffused with light.

My days come at night to return their glances;
Following on from restless slumber,
When sorrow seeps into darkness itself
They come back to dwell in me and make me see.

Should their joy burst, an echo stirring within
Washes up a mere dead soul on my shore of flesh,
And my unfamiliar laughter lingers at my ear,

Like the sea's murmur in an empty conch,
A doubt—on the edge of an extreme marvel,
If I am, if I was, if I am asleep or awake?

Narcissus Speaks

*To appease the manes of Narcissus**

O brothers! sorrowful lilies, I languish in beauty
For having desired myself in your nudity,
And it is to you, Nymph, nymph, O nymph of the fountains,
I come offering my vain tears to pure silence.

A boundless calm listens to me, where I listen to hope.
The voice of the springs changes and speaks to me of evening;
I hear the silvery grass grow in the saintly shade,
And the treacherous moon holds up its mirror
To the secrets of the extinguished fountain.

And I! Cast flesh and blood into these reeds,
I languish, O sapphire, in my sorrowful beauty!

Je ne sais plus aimer que l'eau magicienne
Où j'oubliai le rire et la rose ancienne.

Que je déplore ton éclat fatal et pur,
Si mollement de moi fontaine environnée,   15
Où puisèrent mes yeux dans un mortel azur
Mon image de fleurs humides couronnée !

Hélas ! L'image est vaine et les pleurs éternels !
À travers les bois bleus et les bras fraternels,
Une tendre lueur d'heure ambigüe existe,   20
Et d'un reste du jour me forme un fiancé
Nu, sur la place pâle où m'attire l'eau triste...
Délicieux démon, désirable et glacé !

Voici dans l'eau ma chair de lune et de rosée,
Ô forme obéissante à mes yeux opposée !   25
Voici mes bras d'argent dont les gestes sont purs !...
Mes lentes mains dans l'or adorable se lassent
D'appeler ce captif que les feuilles enlacent,
Et je crie aux échos les noms des dieux obscurs !...

Adieu, reflet perdu sur l'onde calme et close,   30
Narcisse... ce nom même est un tendre parfum
Au cœur suave. Effeuille aux mânes du défunt
Sur ce vide tombeau la funérale rose.

Sois, ma lèvre, la rose effeuillant le baiser
Qui fasse un spectre cher lentement s'apaiser,   35
Car la nuit parle à demi-voix, proche et lointaine,
Aux calices pleins d'ombre et de sommeils légers.
Mais la lune s'amuse aux myrtes allongés.

Je t'adore, sous ces myrtes, ô l'incertaine,
Chair pour la solitude éclose tristement   40
Qui se mire dans le miroir au bois dormant.
Je me délie en vain de ta présence douce,
L'heure menteuse est molle aux membres sur la mousse
Et d'un sombre délice enfle le vent profond.

Adieu, Narcisse... meurs ! Voici le crépuscule.   45
Au soupir de mon cœur mon apparence ondule,

Now I can love only the enchanted water
Where I forgot laughter and the ancient rose.

    How I lament your pure and fatal brilliance,
Fountain that I so softly encircled,
Where my gaze drew from a mortal yonder
My own image wreathed in moist flowers!

Alas! The image is vain and the tears eternal!
Through the loving arms of the blue-tinged woods,
A gentle gleam of the twilight hour filters,
Fashioning a betrothed from the day's embers
Naked upon the pale spot where I am drawn by the sad water...
Enchanting demon, desirable and frozen!

Here in the water lies my flesh of moon and dew,
O dutiful form opposed to my eyes!
Here are my silvery arms whose gestures are pure!...
My languid hands bathed in delightful gold grow weary
Of calling this captive entwined in leaves, and
I cry out to the echoes the names of gods unknown!...

Farewell, lost reflection upon the calm encircled water,
Narcissus... the mere name summons a tender fragrance
So sweet to the heart. To the manes of the departed,
Scatter over this empty tomb the petals of the funereal rose.

Be, my lip, the rose plucking off the petals of a kiss
To soothe gently a beloved spectre,
Since the night communes in whispers, far and near,
With the chalices brimming with shadows and light slumber.
Yet the moon gambols amid the stretching myrtles.

I idolize you, beneath these myrtles, O wary
Flesh, sorrowfully opening on to solitude,
Beholding yourself in the mirror of the slumbering wood.
I release myself in vain from your tender presence,
The deceitful hour is kind to my limbs upon the moss
And swells the mysterious wind with solemn delight.

    Farewell, Narcissus... die! The gloaming has come.
My image quivers at my heart's deep sigh,

La flûte, par l'azur enseveli module
Des regrets de troupeaux sonores qui s'en vont.
Mais sur le froid mortel où l'étoile s'allume,
Avant qu'un lent tombeau ne se forme de brume,   50
Tiens ce baiser qui brise un calme d'eau fatal !
L'espoir seul peut suffire à rompre ce cristal.
La ride me ravisse au souffle qui m'exile
Et que mon souffle anime une flûte gracile
Dont le joueur léger me serait indulgent !...   55

    Évanouissez-vous, divinité troublée !
Et toi, verse à la lune, flûte isolée,
Une diversité de nos larmes d'argent.

Épisode

Un soir favorisé de colombes sublimes,
La pucelle doucement se peigne au soleil.
Aux nénuphars de l'onde elle donne un orteil
Ultime, et pour tiédir ses froides mains errantes
Parfois trempe au couchant leurs roses transparentes.   5
Tantôt, si d'une ondée innocente, sa peau
Frissonne, c'est le dire absurde d'un pipeau,
Flûte dont le coupable aux dents de pierrerie
Tire un futile vent d'ombre et de rêverie
Par l'occulte baiser qu'il risque sous les fleurs.   10
Mais presque indifférente aux feintes de ces pleurs,
Ni se divinisant par aucune parole
De rose, elle démêle une lourde auréole,
Et tirant de sa nuque un plaisir qui la tord,
Ses poings délicieux pressent la touffe d'or   15
Dont la lumière coule entre ses doigts limpides !
...Une feuille meurt sur ses épaules humides,
Une goutte tombe de la flûte sur l'eau,
Et le pied pur s'épeure comme un bel oiseau
Ivre d'ombre...   20

Across the entombed blue sky, the flute's lilting air
Echoes the regrets of herds departing.
But upon the chill where a star lights up,
Before a tomb of mist slowly enshrouds me,
Accept this kiss stirring the water's mortal calm!
Hope alone is enough to shatter this crystal.
May the ripple snatch me from its banishing breath
And may my breath bring to life a slender flute
Whose evanescent player is kind to me!...

 Vanish now, dimming divinity!
And you, meek and solitary flute, shed before the moon
 Our bounteous silvery tears.

Episode

One evening graced with splendid doves,
The maiden gently combs her hair in the sun's rich glow.
Her toe brushes the water lilies in a final caress, and
To warm her cold and restless hands, bathes
From time to time their rosy clarity in the setting sun.
Should her skin ever quiver at some innocent ripple,
It is no more than the senseless utterance of a reed pipe,
A flute whose guilty player with teeth of gemstones
Draws a futile breath woven of shadow and dream
By the furtive kiss he dares steal beneath the flowers.
But unmoved almost by this pretence of tears,
And not wanting to be made a god by any word of rose
She untangles her ponderous halo of tresses,
And drawing from her nape a pleasure there entwined,
Her comely fists clasp the golden locks
Whose brightness spills between her limpid fingers!
...A leaf is dying upon her glistening shoulders,
A drop falls to the water from the flute
And her pure foot takes fright like a beauteous bird
Intoxicated by the shadows...

Vue

Si la plage planche, si
L'ombre sur l'œil s'use et pleure
Si l'azur est larme, ainsi
Au sel des dents pure affleure

La vierge fumée ou l'air   5
Que berce en soi puis expire
Vers l'eau debout d'une mer
Assoupie en son empire

Celle qui sans les ouïr
Si la lèvre au vent remue   10
Se joue à évanouir
Mille mots vains où se mue

Sous l'humide éclair de dents
Le très doux feu du dedans.

Valvins

Si tu veux dénouer la forêt qui t'aère
Heureuse, tu te fonds aux feuilles, si tu es
Dans la fluide yole à jamais littéraire,
Traînant quelques soleils ardemment situés

Aux blancheurs de son flanc que la Seine caresse   5
Émue, ou pressentant l'après-midi chanté,
Selon que le grand bois trempe une longue tresse,
Et mélange ta voile au meilleur de l'été.

Mais toujours près de toi que le silence livre
Aux cris multipliés de tout le brut azur,   10
L'ombre de quelque page éparse d'aucun livre

Tremble, reflet de voile vagabonde sur
La poudreuse peau de la rivière verte
Parmi le long regard de la Seine entr'ouverte.

View

If the beach slants, if
The shadow on the eye ebbs and weeps,
If the blue heaven turns into a tear, then
Over the salt-glazed teeth wafts

The virgin breath or the air
Lulled and breathed out
To the sheer wall of a sea*
Languorous in its kingdom

She who without hearing them
Whenever the lip stirs in the wind
Plays at scattering
A myriad vain words where

Beneath the moist flash of teeth
The gentle flame flickers within.

Valvins

If you wish to untangle the forest that cools you,
Happily you melt into the leaves, if you glide by
In the smooth and ever literary yawl,
Trailing a few suns that shimmer on

Its dazzling white sides caressed by
The purling Seine, or foretelling the song-filled afternoon,
As the great wood dips a flowing tress and
Blends your sail with summer's glory.

Yet ever close to you, whom the silence yields
To cries resounding in the stark blue sky,
The shadow of a scattered page from some book

Flickers, a glimmer of a sail drifting along
The green river's powdery skin bounded by
The languid gaze of the gently opening Seine.

Été

À Francis Viélé-Griffin

Été, roche d'air pur, et toi, ardente ruche,
Ô mer ! Éparpillée en mille mouches sur
Les touffes d'une chair fraîche comme une cruche,
Et jusque dans la bouche où bourdonne l'azur,

Et toi, maison brûlante, Espace, cher Espace   5
Tranquille, où l'arbre fume et perd quelques oiseaux,
Où crève infiniment la rumeur de la masse
De la mer, de la marche et des troupes des eaux,

Tonnes d'odeurs, grands ronds par les races heureuses
Sur le golfe qui mange et qui monte au soleil,   10
Nids purs, écluses d'herbe, ombres des vagues creuses,
Bercez l'enfant ravie en un poreux sommeil,

Aux cieux vainement tonne un éclat de matière,
Embrasse-t-il les mers, consume-t-il les monts,
Verse-t-il à la vie un torrent de lumière   15
Et fait-il dans les cœurs hennir tous les démons,

Toi, sur le sable tendre où s'abandonne l'onde,
Où sa puissance en pleurs perd tous ses diamants,
Toi qu'assoupit l'ennui des merveilles du monde,
Vierge sourde aux clameurs d'éternels éléments,   20

Tu te fermes sur toi, serrant ta jeune gorge,
Âme toute à l'amour de sa petite nuit,
Car ces tumultes purs, cet astre fou qui forge
L'or brut d'événements bêtes comme le bruit,

Te font baiser les seins de ton être éphémère,   25
Chérir ce peu de chair comme un jeune animal
Et victime et dédain de la splendeur amère
Choyer le doux orgueil de s'aimer comme un mal.

Fille exposée aux dieux que l'Océan constelle
D'écume qu'il arrache aux miroirs du soleil,   30
Aux jeux universels tu préfères mortelle,
Toute d'ombre et d'amour, ton île de sommeil,

Summer

For Francis Viélé-Griffin

Summer, rock of pure air, and you, blazing hive,
O sea! Teeming with shimmering specks upon
The clumps of flesh cool like a pitcher,
And into the mouth where the blue sky hums,

And you, flaming house, Space, dear Tranquil Space,
Where the tree smoulders and sheds a few birds,
Where the sea's purling mass, advancing in
Legions of waves, tirelessly crashes,

Fragrant casks, great ripples by the joyous races
Above the gulf devouring and soaring to the sun,
Pure nests, sluices of grass, shadows of resonant waves,
Lull the enchanted girl into a porous slumber.

In the heavens a burst of matter thunders in vain,
Sets the sea ablaze, consumes the mountains,
Spills a torrent of light upon life below
And within its heart of hearts makes the demons bray,

You, languishing upon the soft sand where the sea ebbs,
Where its plenteous tears shed their sparkle,
You who are soothed by tedium of the world's wonders,
Virgin oblivious to the clamour of the eternal elements,

You curl up, clasping your young neck,
Soul enrapt by the love of its short night,
For this pure tumult, this frenzied star forging
The raw gold of events, foolish like sound,

Makes you kiss the breasts of your fleeting being,
To cherish this bit of flesh like a young animal
And, scornful victim of the bitter splendour,
To pamper self-love's gentle pride like an evil.

Girl exposed to the gods that the Ocean speckles
With foam snatched from the shimmering sun,
You prefer, mortal woman all shadow and love,
Your island of languor to universal games.

Cependant du haut ciel foudroyant l'heure humaine,
Monstre altéré de temps, immolant le futur,
Le Sacrificateur Soleil roule et ramène   35
Le jour après le jour sur les autels d'azur...

Mais les jambes, (dont l'une est fraîche et se dénoue
De la plus rose), les épaules, le sein dur,
Le bras qui se mélange à l'écumeuse joue
Brillent abandonnés autour du vase obscur   40

Où filtrent les grands bruits pleins de bêtes puisées
Dans les cages de feuille et les mailles de mer
Par les moulins marins et les huttes rosées
Du jour... Toute la peau dore les treilles d'air.

Profusion du soir

POÈME ABANDONNÉ...

À Paul Claudel

Du Soleil soutenant la puissante paresse
Qui plane et s'abandonne à l'œil contemplateur,
Regard !... Je bois le vin céleste, et je caresse
Le grain mystérieux de l'extrême hauteur.

Je porte au sein brûlant ma lucide tendresse,   5
Je joue avec les feux de l'antique inventeur ;
Mais le dieu par degrés qui se désintéresse
Dans la pourpre de l'air s'altère avec lenteur.

Laissant dans le champ pur battre toute l'idée,
Les travaux du couchant dans la sphère vidée   10
Connaissent sans oiseaux leur ancienne grandeur.

L'Ange frais de l'œil nu pressent dans sa pudeur,
Haute nativité d'étoile élucidée,
Un diamant agir qui perce la splendeur...

*

Ô Soir, tu viens épandre un délice tranquille,   15
Horizon des sommeils, stupeur des cœurs pieux,

Yet from high heaven shattering the human hour,
Monster thirsting for time, sacrificing the future,
Sun the High Priest rolls on, leading
A procession of days to heaven's altars...

Yet her legs (one cool and freeing itself from
The rosier one), her shoulders, her firm breast,
Her arm blending with the foamy cheek
Linger in brilliant abandon around the gloomy vase

Where rumbling echoes seep in, teeming of creatures
Drawn from leafy cages and the meshed sea
By marine mills and the dewy huts
Of light... Her entire skin gilds the trellises of air.

Profusion of Evening

ABANDONED POEM...

For Paul Claudel

Enduring the Sun's mighty languor
Soaring and yielding to the contemplative eye,
Gaze!... I drink the heavenly wine, and caress
The mysterious grain of the loftiest heights.

Bearing my lucid tenderness in the burning breast,
I gambol with the fires of the ancient inventor;
But the god, grown ever more distant,
Slowly declines in the crimson-flushed air.

Leaving the entire thought wrangle in the pure realm,
The toil of sunset in the emptied expanse
Rejoices in all its birdless grandeur.

The fresh Angel of the naked eye senses in its modesty,
Nativity on high of a brilliant star,
The action of a diamond piercing the splendour...

*

O Evening, you come pouring forth a calm delight,
Horizon of slumber, languor of devout hearts,

Persuasive approche, insidieux reptile,
Et rose que respire un mortel immobile
Dont l'œil doré s'engage aux promesses des cieux !

*

Sur tes ardents autels son regard favorable   20
Brûle, l'âme distraite, un passé précieux.
Il adore dans l'or qui se rend adorable
Bâtir d'une vapeur un temple mémorable,
Suspendre au sombre éther son risque et son récif,
Et vole, ivre des feux d'un triomphe passif,   25
Sur l'abîme aux ponts d'or rejoindre la Fortune ;
—Tandis qu'aux bords lointains du Théâtre pensif,
Sous un masque léger glisse la mince lune...

*

...Ce vin bu, l'homme bâille, et brise le flacon.
Aux merveilles du vide il garde une rancune ;   30
Mais le charme du soir fume sur le balcon
Une confusion de femme et de flocon...

*

—Ô Conseil !... Station solennelle !... Balance
D'un doigt doré pesant les motifs du silence !
Ô sagesse sensible entre les dieux ardents !   35
—De l'espace trop beau, préserve-moi, balustre !
Là, m'appelle la mer !... Là, se penche l'illustre
Vénus Vertigineuse avec ses bras fondants !

*

Mon œil, quoiqu'il s'attache au sort souple des ondes,
Et boive comme en songe à l'éternel verseau,   40
Garde une chambre fixe et capable des mondes ;
Et ma cupidité des surprises profondes
Voit à peine au travers du transparent berceau
Cette femme d'écume et d'algue et d'or que roule
Sur le sable et le sel la meule de la houle.   45

*

Persuasive arrival, insidious reptile,
Rose inhaled by a motionless mortal
Whose gilded eye pledges to heaven's promises!

*

Upon your flaming altars its kind gaze
Dreamily consumes a treasured past.
In the ever-wondrous gold, it delights in
Fashioning a memorable temple from vapours,
In suspending its risk and reef in the gloomy firmament,
And, heady with the fires of passive triumph, flies
Above the golden-bridged abyss to meet with Fortune;
—While on the remote edges of thought's Theatre,
The slender moon slips beneath a thin mask...

*

...This wine drunk, the man yawns and breaks the flagon,
Bearing a grudge against the wonders of the void;
But evening's enchantment brings its mingled fragrance
Of woman and smoke wreathing up to the balcony...

*

—O Counsel!... Solemn station!... Scales weighing
The motifs of silence with a gilded finger!
O perceptible wisdom between the fiery gods!
—Save me, baluster, from the sublime beauty of this expanse!
Over yonder, the sea lures me!... There in all her splendour leans
Venus the Vertiginous with her melting arms!

*

My eye, though bound to the waves' smooth fate, and
Drinking from the eternal water-carrier as if in a dream,
Keeps an unchanging realm where other worlds may thrive;
And my craving for deep wonders
Can scarcely see through the transparent cradle
This woman of gold, foam and seaweed churned by
The grinding swell upon the salt and the sand.

*

Pourtant je place aux cieux les ébats d'un esprit ;
Je vois dans leurs vapeurs des terres inconnues,
Des déesses de fleurs feindre d'être des nues,
Des puissances d'orage d'errer à demi nues,
Et sur les roches d'air du soir qui s'assombrit,   50
Telle divinité s'accoude. Un ange nage.
Il restaure l'espace à chaque tour de rein.
Moi, qui jette ici-bas l'ombre d'un personnage,
Toutefois délié dans le plein souverain,
Je me sens qui me trempe, et pur qui me dédaigne !   55
Vivant au sein futur le souvenir marin,
Tout le corps de mon choix dans mes regards se baigne !

*

Une crête écumeuse, énorme et colorée,
Barre, puissamment pure, et plisse le parvis.
Roule jusqu'à mon cœur la distance dorée,   60
Vague !... Croulants soleils aux horizons ravis,
Tu n'iras pas plus loin que la ligne ignorée
Qui divise les dieux des ombres où je vis.

*

Une volute lente et longue d'une lieue
Semant les charmes lourds de sa blanche torpeur   65
Où se joue une joie, une soif d'être bleue,
Tire le noir navire épuisé de vapeur...

*

Mais pesants et neigeux les monts du crépuscule,
Les nuages trop pleins et leurs seins copieux,
Toute la majesté de l'Olympe recule,   70
Car voici le signal, voici l'or des adieux,
Et l'espace a humé la barque minuscule...

*

Lourds frontons du sommeil toujours inachevés,
Rideaux bizarrement d'un rubis relevés
Pour le mauvais regard d'une sombre planète,   75
Les temps sont accomplis, les désirs se sont tus,

Yet I place the frolics of a mind in the heavens;
I glimpse unknown lands in its mists,
Goddesses of flowers parading as clouds,
The mighty storm wandering half naked,
And upon the rock where the evening's light ebbs,
Some divinity is leaning. An angel swims,
Restoring space at every stroke.
Casting a person's shadow here below,
Though released into the supreme plenitude,
I feel steeped in pure self-loathing!
Reliving the sea's memory in the heart of the future,
My entire chosen body bathes in my gaze!

*

A foamy crest, colossal and coloured,
Envelops and creases the concourse in a potent sweep.
Roll across the golden distance to my heart,
Wave!... Waning suns snatched from the horizons,
You shall not venture beyond the mysterious line
Separating the gods from the shadows where I dwell.

*

A languid whorl, a league in length
Scattering the ponderous charms of its white torpor
Where a joy gambols, yearning to be blue,
Tugs the black ship sapped of steam...

*

But the snow-clad mountains of dusk,
The brimming clouds' ample bosom,
All of Olympus' majesty recedes,
For here is the signal, here is the gold of farewells,
And space has engulfed the tiny barque...

*

Ponderous pediments of slumber, ever incomplete,
Curtains strangely fastened by a ruby
For the scowling gaze of a downcast planet,
Time has run its course, and desire has fallen silent,

Et dans la bouche d'or, bâillements combattus,
S'écartèlent les mots que charmait le poète...
    Les temps sont accomplis, les désirs se sont tus.

                              *

    Adieu, Adieu !... Vers vous, ô mes belles images,   80
Mes bras tendent toujours insatiable port !
Venez, effarouchés, hérissant vos plumages,
Voiliers aventureux que talonne la mort !
Hâtez-vous, hâtez-vous !... La nuit presse !... Tantale
Va périr ! Et la joie éphémère des cieux !   85
Une rose naguère aux ténèbres fatale,
Une toute dernière rose occidentale
Pâlit affreusement sur le soir spacieux...
    Je ne vois plus frémir au mât du belvédère
Ivre de brise un sylphe aux couleurs de drapeau,   90
Et ce grand port n'est plus qu'un noir débarcadère
Couru du vent glacé que sent venir ma peau !

    Fermez-vous ! Fermez-vous ! Fenêtres offensées !
Grands yeux qui redoutez la véritable nuit !
    Et toi, de ces hauteurs d'astres ensemencées,   95
Accepte, fécondé de mystère et d'ennui,
Une maternité muette de pensées...

Anne

À André Lebey

Anne qui se mélange au drap pâle et délaisse
Des cheveux endormis sur ses yeux mal ouverts
Mire ses bras lointains tournés avec mollesse
Sur la peau sans couleur du ventre découvert.

Elle vide, elle enfle d'ombre sa gorge lente,   5
Et comme un souvenir pressant ses propres chairs,
Une bouche brisée et pleine d'eau brûlante
Roule le goût immense et le reflet des mers.

Enfin désemparée et libre d'être fraîche,
La dormeuse déserte aux touffes de couleur   10

And in the golden mouth struggling not to yawn,
The words the poet enchanted are torn asunder...
   Time has run its course, and desire has fallen silent.

*

   Farewell, farewell!... My open arms still offer
You, O wondrous images, their insatiable haven!
Your ruffled feathers bristling in fright, come
Adventurous sailboats with death hard on your heels!
Hurry, hurry!... Night is closing in!... Tantalus
Shall perish! And the sky's fleeting delight!
A rose once fatal to the shadows,
One last rose from the west
Grows ghastly pale in the boundless twilight...
   I no longer see quivering on the belvedere's mast
A flag-coloured sylph, heady with the breeze,
And this great port is now a mere black landing stage
Swept by an icy wind which my skin can feel draw near!

   Close now! Offended windows! Close!
Huge eyes dreading true night!
   And you, pregnant with mystery and tedium,
Accept from these star-seeded heights
A motherhood of silent thoughts...

Anne

For André Lebey

Anne, who blends with the pale sheet and abandons
Her slumbering tresses draped over her half-opened eyes,
Gazes at her remote arms languidly lying
Upon the colourless skin of her uncovered waist.

Her breast gently sinks and swells with shadow
And like a memory pressing its own skin,
A shattered mouth brimming with scalding water
Swirls the boundless savour and sparkle of the seas.

At last cast adrift and bound for coolness,
The languid sleeper dappled in colour

Flotte sur son lit blême, et d'une lèvre sèche,
Tette dans la ténèbre un souffle amer de fleur.

Et sur le linge où l'aube insensible se plisse,
Tombe, d'un bras de glace effleuré de carmin,
Toute une main défaite et perdant le délice   15
À travers ses doigts nus dénoués de l'humain.

Au hasard ! À jamais, dans le sommeil sans hommes
Pur des tristes éclairs de leurs embrassements,
Elle laisse rouler les grappes et les pommes
Puissantes, qui pendaient aux treilles d'ossements,   20

Qui riaient, dans leur ambre appelant les vendanges,
Et dont le nombre d'or de riches mouvements
Invoquait la vigueur et les gestes étranges
Que pour tuer l'amour inventent les amants...

                              *

Sur toi, quand le regard de leurs âmes s'égare,   25
Leur cœur bouleversé change comme leurs voix,
Car les tendres apprêts de leur festin barbare
Hâtent les chiens ardents qui tremblent dans ces rois...

À peine effleurent-ils de doigts errants ta vie,
Tout leur sang les accable aussi lourd que la mer,   30
Et quelque violence aux abîmes ravie
Jette ces blancs nageurs sur tes roches de chair...

Récifs délicieux, Île toute prochaine,
Terre tendre, promise aux démons apaisés,
L'amour t'aborde, armé des regards de la haine,   35
Pour combattre dans l'ombre une hydre de baisers !

                              *

Ah, plus nue et qu'imprègne une prochaine aurore,
Si l'or triste interroge un tiède contour,
Rentre au plus pur de l'ombre où le Même s'ignore,
Et te fais un vain marbre ébauché par le jour !   40

Laisse au pâle rayon ta lèvre violée
Mordre dans un sourire un long germe de pleur,

Floating on her pale bed, and with a parched lip,
Sucks at a blossom's bitter breath in the dark.

And upon the linen where dawn furtively creases,
An icy arm brushed with carmine lets slip
A hand, limp and losing its grip on delight
Through its bare fingers freed from their human bond.

By chance! Forever, in a sleep devoid of men,
Away from the gloomy thunderbolt of their loving embraces,
She lets roll the great clusters of grapes and apples
Dangling on the trellises of bones,

Pleading amid amber-hued laughter for the grape harvest
And whose golden ratio* in its plenteous movements
Summoned the strength and the strange gestures
Invented by lovers to kill off love...

*

When the gaze of their souls goes astray on you,
Their distraught hearts change like their voices,
For the tender preparations of their barbarous feast
Stir the fiery dogs quivering within these kings...

No sooner do their errant fingers lightly brush your life,
Than all their blood engulfs them like a heavy sea
And a violent tempest torn from the depths
Tosses these pale swimmers on to your fleshy rocks.

Delectable reefs, Island so near,
Gentle land promised to the placated demons,
Love lands on your shores, bristling with spiteful looks,
To battle a hydra of kisses in the shadows!

*

Ah, ever more naked and suffused with an imminent dawn,
Should the mournful gold timidly test a tepid contour,
Withdraw into the darkest shadow where the Same is unknown,
And make of yourself a worthless marble object wrought by day!

In the pale sunbeam, may your violated lip
Bite with a smile a long welling tear,

Masque d'âme au sommeil à jamais immolée
Sur qui la paix soudaine a surpris la douleur !

Plus jamais redorant tes ombres satinées,   45
La vieille aux doigts de feu qui fendent les volets
Ne viendra t'arracher aux grasses matinées
Et rendre au doux soleil tes joyeux bracelets...

Mais suave, de l'arbre extérieur, la palme
Vaporeuse remue au delà du remords,   50
Et dans le feu, parmi trois feuilles, l'oiseau calme
Commence le chant seul qui réprime les morts.

Air de Sémiramis

À *Camille Mauclair*

Dès l'aube, chers rayons, mon front songe à vous ceindre !
À peine il se redresse, il voit d'un œil qui dort
Sur le marbre absolu, le temps pâle se peindre,
L'heure sur moi descendre et croître jusqu'à l'or...

*

...*Existe* !... *Sois enfin toi-même* ! dit l'Aurore,   5
Ô grande âme, il est temps que tu formes un corps !
Hâte-toi de choisir un jour digne d'éclore,
Parmi tant d'autres feux, les immortels trésors !

Déjà, contre la nuit lutte l'âpre trompette !
Une lèvre vivante attaque l'air glacé ;   10
L'or pur, de tout en tour, éclate et se répète,
Rappelant tout l'espace aux splendeurs du passé !

Remonte aux vrais regards ! Tire-toi de tes ombres,
Et comme du nageur, dans le plein de la mer,
Le talon tout-puissant l'expulse des eaux sombres,   15
Toi, frappe au fond de l'être ! Interpelle ta chair,

Traverse sans retard ses invisibles trames,
Épuise l'infini de l'effort impuissant,

Soul's mask forever surrendered to sleep
Where a sudden peace has taken pain by surprise!

Never again regilding your satiny shadows
Shall the old woman whose fiery fingers cleave the shutters,
Come to wrench you from a lingering slumber
And return your joyous bracelets to the gentle sun...

But the hazy palm on the yonder tree
Lightly stirs beyond remorse,
And in the fire, nestled between three leaves, the tranquil bird
Begins the one song that quells the dead.

Semiramis' Air

For Camille Mauclair

Since dawn, beloved rays, my brow has dreamed of encircling you!
No sooner raised than it sees with an eye yet asleep
Pale time caressing the lustrous marble,
Light descending on me and turning gold...

*

...Exist! At last be yourself! Dawn murmurs,
O great soul, it is time for you to take corporeal form!
Hasten to choose a day worthy of opening up
Your everlasting treasures amongst so many other fires!

Already, the rasping trumpet struggles with night!
A living lip assails the icy air;
From tower to tower, pure gold bursts and echoes,
Recalling all space to the glories of the past!

Rise to the real gaze! Haul yourself from your shadows,
And like the swimmer out on the sea, whose all-powerful heel
Thrusts him out of the dark waters,
Touch the depths of your being! Summon your flesh,

Cross undeterred its indomitable webs,
Exhaust the infinity of its helpless endeavour,

Et débarrasse-toi d'un désordre de drames
Qu'engendrent sur ton lit les monstres de ton sang !   20

J'accours de l'Orient suffire à ton caprice !
Et je te viens offrir mes plus purs aliments ;
Que d'espace et de vent ta flamme se nourrisse !
Viens te joindre à l'éclat de mes pressentiments !

*

—Je réponds !... Je surgis de ma profonde absence !   25
Mon cœur m'arrache aux morts que frôlait mon sommeil,
Et vers mon but, grand aigle éclatant de puissance,
Il m'emporte !... Je vole au-devant du soleil !

Je ne prends qu'une rose et fuis... La belle flèche
Au flanc !... Ma tête enfante une foule de pas...   30
Ils courent vers ma tour favorite, où la fraîche
Altitude m'appelle, et je lui tends les bras !

Monte, ô Sémiramis, maîtresse d'une spire
Qui d'un cœur sans amour s'élance au seul honneur !
Ton œil impérial a soif du grand empire   35
À qui ton spectre dur fait sentir le bonheur...

Ose l'abîme ! Passe un dernier pont de roses !
Je t'approche, péril ! Orgueil plus irrité !
Ces fourmis sont à moi ! Ces villes sont mes choses,
Ces chemins sont les traits de mon autorité !   40

C'est une vaste peau de fauve que mon royaume !
J'ai tué le lion qui portait cette peau ;
Mais encor le fumet du féroce fantôme
Flotte chargé de mort, et garde mon troupeau !

Enfin, j'offre au soleil le secret de mes charmes !   45
Jamais il n'a doré de seuil si gracieux !
De ma fragilité je goûte les alarmes
Entre le double appel de la terre et des cieux.

Repas de ma puissance, intelligible orgie,
Quel parvis vaporeux de toits et de forêts   50
Place aux pieds de la pure et divine vigie,
Ce calme éloignement d'événements secrets !

And escape from the tangled knot of passions
Which the monsters of your blood beget on your bed!

I rush from the East to satisfy your whims!
And I come to you bearing my purest fare;
Let wind and space nourish your flames!
Come join the brilliance of my intuitions!

*

—I reply!... I surge from the depths of my absence!
My heart wrenches me from the dead encountered fleetingly in my sleep
And, like a great eagle brimming with strength, bears me
Towards my goal!... I fly faster than the sun!

I pluck just one rose and flee... That splendid arrow
By my flank!... My head begets a horde of steps...
They rush towards my chosen tower, where the cool
Heights draw me, and I stretch out my arms to it!

Arise, O Semiramis, mistress of a spire
Soaring with a loveless heart to its true glory!
Your imperial eye thirsts for the great empire
Upon which your harsh sceptre thrusts happiness...

Dare the abyss!... Cross the one last bridge of roses!
I approach you, peril! My pride ever more incensed!
These ants are all mine! These cities are my chattels,
These paths are the mark of my authority!

My kingdom is the boundless skin of a wolf!
I slayed the lion that wore this skin;
Yet the death–imbued smell of the ferocious phantom
Still lingers and guards my flock!

At last, I offer the sun the secret of my charms,
Never has it gilded a threshold so gracious!
I relish the dangers of my fragility
Between the double call of heaven and earth.

Feast of my potency, intelligible orgy,
What a hazy concourse of rooftops and forests
This tranquil expanse of hidden events
Lays at the feet of the pure and divine sentinel!

L'âme enfin sur ce faîte a trouvé ses demeures !
Ô de quelle grandeur, elle tient sa grandeur
Quand mon cœur soulevé d'ailes intérieures   55
Ouvre au ciel en moi-même une autre profondeur !

Anxieuse d'azur, de gloire consumée,
Poitrine, gouffre d'ombre aux narines de chair,
Aspire cet encens d'âmes et de fumée
Qui monte d'une ville analogue à la mer !   60

Soleil, soleil, regarde en toi rire mes ruches !
L'intense et sans repos Babylone bruit,
Toute rumeurs de chars, clairons, chaînes de cruches
Et plaintes de la pierre au mortel qui construit.

Qu'ils flattent mon désir de temples implacables,   65
Les sons aigus de scie et les cris des ciseaux,
Et ces gémissements de marbres et de câbles
Qui peuplent l'air vivant de structure et d'oiseaux !

Je vois mon temple neuf naître parmi les mondes,
Et mon vœu prendre place au séjour des destins ;   70
Il semble de soi-même au ciel monter par ondes
Sous le bouillonnement des actes indistincts.

Peuple stupide, à qui ma puissance m'enchaîne,
Hélas ! mon orgueil même a besoin de tes bras !
Et que ferait mon cœur s'il n'aimait cette haine   75
Dont l'innombrable tête est si douce à mes pas ?

Plate, elle me murmure une musique telle
Que le calme de l'onde en fait de sa fureur,
Quand elle se rapaise aux pieds d'une mortelle
Mais qu'elle se réserve un retour de terreur.   80

En vain j'entends monter contre ma face auguste
Ce murmure de crainte et de férocité :
À l'image des dieux la grande âme est injuste
Tant elle s'appareille à la nécessité !

Des douceurs de l'amour quoique parfois touchée,   85
Pourtant nulle tendresse et nuls renoncements

The soul has finally found its abode upon this height!
O from what grandeur it draws its grandeur
When my heart uplifted by inner wings
Opens to the heavens another depth within me!

Breast, yearning for the blue yonder and consumed by glory,
Chasm of shadow with nostrils of flesh,
Inhale this incense of souls and of smoke
Wreathing up from a city resembling the sea!

Sun, sun, behold my hives rejoicing in you!
Bustling and restless Babylon murmurs,
All astir with chariots, clarions, chains of pitchers
And the stone's lament to the mortal who builds.

May they flatter my desire with implacable temples,
The shrill screech of saws, the rasp of chisels,
And these grinding moans of marble and cables
Filling the air with architecture and birds!

I see my new temple begotten amongst the worlds,
And my vow find its true abode among destinies;
It seems to soar aloft from itself in waves
Beneath the bustling blur of activity.

Foolish people, to whom my power shackles me,
Alas! my very pride longs for your strong hands!
And what would my poor heart do without loving
This hatred's immeasurable head so gentle to my steps?

Flatly, it murmurs to me such a music as the
Calm into which the sea turns its stormy rage,
When it abates at the feet of a mortal while
Still holding in reserve a new reign of terror.

In vain I hear this murmur of fear and ferocity
Rising against my noble and worthy stature;
Like the gods, the great soul is unjust
Such does it match necessity!

Though love's pleasures may have sometimes moved me,
No tenderness or renunciation can

Ne me laissent captive et victime couchée
Dans les puissants liens du sommeil des amants !

Baisers, baves d'amour, basses béatitudes,
Ô mouvements marins des amants confondus,   90
Mon cœur m'a conseillé de telles solitudes,
Et j'ai placé si haut mes jardins suspendus

Que mes suprêmes fleurs n'attendent que la foudre
Et qu'en dépit des pleurs des amants les plus beaux,
À mes roses, la main qui touche tombe en poudre :   95
Mes plus doux souvenirs bâtissent des tombeaux !

Qu'ils sont doux à mon cœur les temples qu'il enfante
Quand tiré lentement du songe de mes seins,
Je vois un monument de masse triomphante
Joindre dans mes regards l'ombre de mes desseins !   100

Battez, cymbales d'or, mamelles cadencées,
Et roses palpitant sur ma pure paroi !
Que je m'évanouisse en mes vastes pensées,
Sage Sémiramis, enchanteresse et roi !

L'amateur de poèmes

Si je regarde tout à coup ma véritable pensée, je ne me console
pas de devoir subir cette parole intérieure sans personne et sans
origine ; ces figures éphémères ; et cette infinité d'entreprises
interrompues par leur propre facilité, qui se transforment l'une
dans l'autre, sans que rien ne change avec elles. Incohérente sans   5
le paraître, nulle instantanément comme elle est spontanée, la
pensée, par sa nature, manque de style.

MAIS je n'ai pas tous les jours la puissance de proposer à mon
attention quelques êtres nécessaires, ni de feindre les obstacles
spirituels qui formeraient une apparence de commencement, de   10
plénitude et de fin, au lieu de mon insupportable fuite.

UN poème est une durée, pendant laquelle, lecteur, je respire
une loi qui fut préparée ; je donne mon souffle et les machines de
ma voix ; ou seulement leur pouvoir, qui se concilie avec le silence.

Leave me captive or as victim lying
In the potent clutches of lovers' slumber!

Kisses, love's slaver, vile bliss,
O rolling billows of lovers entwined,
My heart has counselled me to such solitude,
And I placed my hanging gardens* so high above

That my uppermost flowers await only thunderbolts
And despite the weeping of beauteous lovers,
The hand that dares touch my roses turns to ashes:
My gentlest memories are building tombs!

My heart so delights in the temples it begets
When slowly drawn from the dream of my breasts,
I glimpse a monument whose towering mass
Satisfies in my gaze the shadow of my designs!

Clash, O golden cymbals, breasts beating in time,
And roses quivering on the purity of my wall!
May I swoon in my boundless thoughts,
Wise Semiramis, enchantress and king!

The Lover of Poems

If I suddenly look at my true thought, I take no comfort in having to endure this internal language, without source or speaker; these evanescent figures; and these infinite enquiries interrupted by their own fluency, blending one into the next, without anything altering with them. Incoherent without appearing to be so, instantly negated by its spontaneity, thought, by its very nature, lacks style.

But I do not have every day the power to provide my concentration with certain necessary elements, nor to feign the spiritual impediments that would create some semblance of beginning, abundance, and ending, instead of my unbearable flight.

A poem has a lasting duration, in the course of which I, the reader, breathe a time-honoured law; I provide my breathing and the mechanisms of my voice; or merely their potential which can be reconciled with silence.

JE m'abandonne à l'adorable allure : lire, vivre où mènent les   15
mots. Leur apparition est écrite. Leurs sonorités concertées.
Leur ébranlement se compose, d'après une méditation antérieure,
et ils se précipiteront en groupes magnifiques ou purs, dans la
résonance. Même mes étonnements sont assurés : ils sont cachés
d'avance, et font partie du nombre.   20

MÛ par l'écriture fatale, et si le mètre toujours futur enchaîne
sans retour ma mémoire, je ressens chaque parole dans toute sa
force, pour l'avoir indéfiniment attendue. Cette mesure qui me
transporte et que je colore, me garde du vrai et du faux. Ni le
doute ne me divise, ni la raison ne me travaille. Nul hasard, mais   25
une chance extraordinaire se fortifie. Je trouve sans effort le langage de ce bonheur ; et je pense par artifice, une pensée toute
certaine, merveilleusement prévoyante,—aux lacunes calculées,
sans ténèbres involontaires, dont le mouvement me commande et
la quantité me comble : une pensée singulièrement achevée.   30

I give myself over to the delightful rhythm: reading, living wherever words may lead me. They are written down as they appear. Their sonorities are harmonized. Their disrupted flow takes shape along premeditated lines and they rush off to resonate in splendid or pure groups. Even my surprise is guaranteed: it is concealed in advance, and forms part of number.

Stirred by the fatal act of writing, and should the everlasting metre irreversibly enslave my memory, I feel the full force of each word, by virtue of having indefinitely awaited it. This rhythm uplifting my soul and which I imbue with colour shields me from what is true and false. I am neither riven by doubt nor troubled by reason. This is not by chance, but an extraordinary stroke of good luck grows ever stronger. Effortlessly I find the language of this delight; and out of pretence I think—a thought that is utterly certain and wondrously provident—of the calculated gaps, free of unwitting obscurities, whose movement steers me and whose quantity fulfils me: an outstandingly perfected thought.

CHARMES

Aurore

À Paul Poujaud

La confusion morose
Qui me servait de sommeil,
Se dissipe dès la rose
Apparence du soleil.
Dans mon âme je m'avance,   5
Tout ailé de confiance :
C'est la première oraison !
À peine sorti des sables,
Je fais des pas admirables
Dans les pas de ma raison.   10

Salut ! encore endormies
À vos sourires jumeaux,
Similitudes amies
Qui brillez parmi les mots !
Au vacarme des abeilles   15
Je vous aurai par corbeilles,
Et sur l'échelon tremblant
De mon échelle dorée,
Ma prudence évaporée
Déjà pose son pied blanc.   20

Quelle aurore sur ces croupes
Qui commencent de frémir !
Déjà s'étirent par groupes
Telles qui semblaient dormir :
L'une brille, l'autre bâille ;   25
Et sur un peigne d'écaille
Égarant ses vagues doigts,
Du songe encore prochaine,
La paresseuse l'enchaîne
Aux prémisses de sa voix.   30

CHARMS

Dawn

For Paul Poujaud

The gloomy disarray
That served me as sleep
Melts away with
Dawn's rosy gleam.
In my soul I set forth,
Fully fledged with confidence:
This is the day's first orison!
Scarcely risen from the sands,
I take splendid steps
In the steps of my reason.

Greetings! still slumbering ones,
To your paired smiles,
Friendly likenesses
Glowing amid words!
To the din of the bees,
I shall have you in basketfuls,
And upon the trembling rung
Of my golden ladder
My light-headed caution
Already places its white foot.

What a dawn over these crests
Now beginning to quiver!
Those who seemed to be sleeping
Already stretch out in clusters:
One glistens, the other yawns;
And letting her idle fingers stray
Over a tortoiseshell comb,
The languid girl binds
Night's lingering dream
To the first fruits of her voice.

Quoi ! c'est vous, mal déridées !
Que fîtes-vous, cette nuit,
Maîtresses de l'âme, Idées,
Courtisanes par ennui ?
—Toujours sages, disent-elles,   35
Nos présences immortelles
Jamais n'ont trahi ton toit !
Nous étions non éloignées,
Mais secrètes araignées
Dans les ténèbres de toi !   40

Ne seras-tu pas de joie
Ivre ! à voir de l'ombre issus
Cent mille soleils de soie
Sur tes énigmes tissus ?
Regarde ce que nous fîmes :   45
Nous avons sur tes abîmes
Tendu nos fils primitifs,
Et pris la nature nue
Dans une trame ténue
De tremblants préparatifs...   50

Leur toile spirituelle,
Je la brise, et vais cherchant
Dans ma forêt sensuelle
Les oracles de mon chant.
Être ! Universelle oreille !   55
Toute l'âme s'appareille
À l'extrême du désir...
Elle s'écoute qui tremble
Et parfois ma lèvre semble
Son frémissement saisir.   60

Voici mes vignes ombreuses,
Les berceaux de mes hasards !
Les images sont nombreuses
À l'égal de mes regards...
Toute feuille me présente   65
Une source complaisante
Où je bois ce frêle bruit...

What! it is you, scarcely cheerful ones!
What did you do, then, this night,
Mistresses of the soul, Ideas, turned
Courtesans out of boredom?
—Sensible as always, they reply,
Never has our immortal presence
Betrayed your roof!
We were not far away,
But lurked like stealthy spiders
In your gloomy depths!

Will you not be wild with
Delight! to see emerge from the dark
The myriad silken suns
Woven upon your enigmas?
Behold what we have brought forth:
Over your abyss we have
Spun our primitive threads
And ensnared bare nature
In a finely laced weft
Of flurried activity...

I break their spiritual web
And venture forth to search
My sensual forest for
The oracles of my chant.
Being! Universal ear!
The entire soul sets sail for
The far reaches of desire...
It listens to itself quiver within
And my lips at times seem
To seize its faint stirring.

Here are my shady vines,
The cradles of my chance!
The images are boundless
Just like my glances...
Each leaf offers me
An obliging spring
Where I drink this faint sound...

Tout m'est pulpe, tout amande,
Tout calice me demande
Que j'attende pour son fruit.   70

Je ne crains pas les épines !
L'éveil est bon, même dur !
Ces idéales rapines
Ne veulent pas qu'on soit sûr :
Il n'est pour ravir un monde   75
De blessure si profonde
Qui ne soit au ravisseur
Une féconde blessure,
Et son propre sang l'assure
D'être le vrai possesseur.   80

J'approche la transparence
De l'invisible bassin
Où nage mon Espérance
Que l'eau porte par le sein.
Son col coupe le temps vague   85
Et soulève cette vague
Que fait un col sans pareil...
Elle sent sous l'onde unie
La profondeur infinie,
Et frémit depuis l'orteil.   90

Au platane

À André Fontainas

Tu penches, grand Platane, et te proposes nu,
　　Blanc comme un jeune Scythe,
Mais ta candeur est prise, et ton pied retenu
　　Par la force du site.

Ombre retentissante en qui le même azur   5
　　Qui t'emporte, s'apaise,
La noire mère astreint ce pied natal et pur
　　À qui la fange pèse.

All is pith, all is kernel to me.
All leaf-clustered chalices compel me
To await their fruit.

I fear not the thorns!
Though arduous, the waking is delightful!
Such perfect plundering
Would rather deny us the certainty:
In ravishing a world there is
No wound so deep
That is not a fruitful one
To the ravisher,
And his own blood assures him
Of being the true owner.

I approach the limpid sheen
Of the invisible pool
Where bathes my Hope
Which the water draws by the breast.
Her neck cleaves time's gentle flow
And raises this wave which
No other neck could match...
Beneath the shimmering swell
She feels the fathomless depths,
And quivers up from her toe.

To the Plane Tree

For André Fontainas

You lean, great Plane Tree, and offer yourself bare,
    White as a young Scythian,
But your pale being is held fast, and your feet gripped
    By the strength of the site.

Resonant shadow where the same blue sky which
    Sweeps you, comes peacefully to rest,
The dark mother restrains this pure native foot
    Burdened by the mire.

De ton front voyageur les vents ne veulent pas ;
    La terre tendre et sombre,
Ô Platane, jamais ne laissera d'un pas
    S'émerveiller ton ombre !

Ce front n'aura d'accès qu'aux degrés lumineux
    Où la sève l'exalte ;
Tu peux grandir, candeur, mais non rompre les nœuds   15
    De l'éternelle halte !

Pressens autour de toi d'autres vivants liés
    Par l'hydre vénérable ;
Tes pareils sont nombreux, des pins aux peupliers,
    De l'yeuse à l'érable,   20

Qui, par les morts saisis, les pieds échévelés
    Dans la confuse cendre,
Sentent les fuir les fleurs, et leurs spermes ailés
    Le cours léger descendre.

Le tremble pur, le charme, et ce hêtre formé   25
    De quatre jeunes femmes,
Ne cessent point de battre un ciel toujours fermé,
    Vêtus en vain de rames.

Ils vivent séparés, ils pleurent confondus
    Dans une seule absence,   30
Et leurs membres d'argent sont vainement fendus
    À leur douce naissance.

Quand l'âme lentement qu'ils expirent le soir
    Vers l'Aphrodite monte,
La vierge doit dans l'ombre, en silence, s'asseoir,   35
    Toute chaude de honte.

Elle se sent surprendre, et pâle, appartenir
    À ce tendre présage
Qu'une présente chair tourne vers l'avenir
    Par un jeune visage...   40

Mais toi, de bras plus purs que les bras animaux,
    Toi qui dans l'or les plonges,

The winds cast aside your restless top;
    The dark tender earth
Shall never, O Plane Tree, allow your shadow
    Marvel at a step!

This crown may caress only the resplendent heights
    Where the sap exalts it;
You may grow, white being, but not break the knots
    Of the eternal end!

Sense around you other living beings, bound
    By the venerable hydra;
Your equals are many, from the pine to the poplar,
    From the ilex to the maple,

Who, by the dead tightly clutched, their feet dishevelled
    And mingling with the ashes,
Feel the flowers take flight, and their winged seeds
    Twirl down the lightsome way.

The pure aspen, the hornbeam, and this beech tree
    Shaped like four young women,
Never weary of whipping an ever-heedless sky,
    Vainly clad in oars.

Separated they live, together they weep
    Blended in a single absence,
And their silvery limbs are riven in vain
    At their sweet moment of birth.

When the soul they slowly exhale at evening
    Ascends towards Aphrodite
The virgin must sit silently in the shade,
    Flushed warm with shame.

She is taken by surprise and pales, feeling she
    Belongs to this gentle omen
Which the youthful face of the present flesh
    Turns towards the future...

Yet you, with arms more fair than animal arms,
    Who bathe them in gold,

Toi qui formes au jour le fantôme des maux
    Que le sommeil fait songes,

Haute profusion de feuilles, trouble fier   45
    Quand l'âpre tramontane
Sonne, au comble de l'or, l'azur du jeune hiver
    Sur tes harpes, Platane,

Ose gémir !... Il faut, ô souple chair du bois,
    Te tordre, te détordre,   50
Te plaindre sans te rompre, et rendre aux vents la voix
    Qu'ils cherchent en désordre !

Flagelle-toi !... Parais l'impatient martyr
    Qui soi-même s'écorche,
Et dispute à la flamme impuissante à partir   55
    Ses retours vers la torche !

Afin que l'hymne monte aux oiseaux qui naîtront,
    Et que le pur de l'âme
Fasse frémir d'espoir les feuillages d'un tronc
    Qui rêve de la flamme,   60

Je t'ai choisi, puissant personnage d'un parc,
    Ivre de ton tangage,
Puisque le ciel t'exerce, et te presse, ô grand arc,
    De lui rendre un langage !

Ô qu'amoureusement des Dryades rival,   65
    Le seul poète puisse
Flatter ton corps poli comme il fait du Cheval
    L'ambitieuse cuisse !...

—Non, dit l'arbre. Il dit : *Non !* par l'étincellement
    De sa tête superbe,   70
Que la tempête traite universellement
    Comme elle fait une herbe !

You who shape by day ghostly sorrows
   Which sleep turns to dreams,

Lofty profusion of leaves, haughty tumult,
   When the bitter north wind rings
Early winter's blue sky at its golden zenith
   Upon your harps, O Plane Tree,

Dare to groan!... You must, O limber flesh of wood,
   Twist and untwist,
Lament without breaking, and restore to the wind
   The wild voice it seeks!

Flog yourself!... Appear the impatient martyr
   Who flays himself,
And dispute with the flame that can never be free,
   Its return to the torch!

So that the hymn may rise to birds as yet unborn,
   And that the soul's purity
May fill with hope the foliage of a trunk
   Dreaming of the flame,

I have chosen you, towering presence of a park,
   Heady with your own pitching,
For the sky tests and impels you, O great bow,
   To give it language!

O how lovingly, rival of the Dryads,*
   May the poet alone
Caress your lustrous body, as he would
   The Horse's potent thigh!...

—No, says the tree. It says: *No!* by the gleaming sway
   Of its glorious crown,
Which the tempest treats universally
   As it would a blade of grass!

Cantique des colonnes

À Léon-Paul Fargue

Douces colonnes, aux
Chapeaux garnis de jour,
Ornés de vrais oiseaux
Qui marchent sur le tour,

Douces colonnes, ô   5
L'orchestre de fuseaux !
Chacun immole son
Silence à l'unisson.

—Que portez-vous si haut,
Égales radieuses ?   10
—Au désir sans défaut
Nos grâces studieuses !

Nous chantons à la fois
Que nous portons les cieux !
Ô seule et sage voix   15
Qui chantes pour les yeux !

Vois quels hymnes candides !
Quelle sonorité
Nos éléments limpides
Tirent de la clarté !   20

Si froides et dorées
Nous fûmes de nos lits
Par le ciseau tirées,
Pour devenir ces lys !

De nos lits de cristal   25
Nous fûmes éveillées,
Des griffes de métal
Nous ont appareillées.

Pour affronter la lune,
La lune et le soleil,   30

Canticle of the Columns

For Léon–Paul Fargue

Gentle columns, capped
With the day's warm glow,
Adorned with real birds
Ambling about the rim.

Gentle columns, O
Orchestra of spindles!
Each one offering up
Its silence in unison.

—What do you raise aloft,
Radiant Equals?
—To the flawless desire
Our studious graces!

We sing as one of
How we bear the heavens!
O sole and wise voice,
Singing for the eyes!

Behold what pure white hymns!
What resonance
Our limpid elements
Draw from light!

So cold and so gilded
Out of our beds
We were drawn by the chisel,
To become these lilies!

From our beds of crystal
We were roused,
Talons of metal
Fashioned us alike.

To confront the moon,
The moon and the sun,

On nous polit chacune
Comme ongle de l'orteil !

Servantes sans genoux,
Sourires sans figures,
La belle devant nous   35
Se sent les jambes pures.

Pieusement pareilles,
Le nez sous le bandeau
Et nos riches oreilles
Sourdes au blanc fardeau,   40

Un temple sur les yeux
Noirs pour l'éternité,
Nous allons sans les dieux
À la divinité !

Nos antiques jeunesses,   45
Chair mate et belles ombres,
Sont fières des finesses
Qui naissent par les nombres !

Filles des nombres d'or,
Fortes des lois du ciel,   50
Sur nous tombe et s'endort
Un dieu couleur de miel.

Il dort content, le Jour,
Que chaque jour offrons
Sur la table d'amour   55
Étale sur nos fronts.

Incorruptibles sœurs,
Mi-brûlantes, mi-fraîches,
Nous prîmes pour danseurs
Brises et feuilles sèches,   60

Et les siècles par dix,
Et les peuples passés,
C'est un profond jadis,
Jadis jamais assez !

Each one was polished
Like a toenail!

Maids unbending,
Smiles without a face,
Beauty before us
Feels her legs pure.

Piously alike,
Our noses beneath the bandeau,
And our ornate ears
Deaf to the white burden.

A temple upon the eyes,
Dark for all eternity.
We set forth without the gods
To seek divinity!

Our ancient youthfulness,
Dull flesh and delightful shadows,
Take pride in the refinements
Born of numbers!

Daughters of the golden ratio,*
Nurtured on heaven's laws,
Upon us descends and slumbers
A honey-coloured god.

Peacefully sleeps the Day
Which we offer each day
On love's table,
So still upon our brows.

Incorruptible sisters,
Half blazing, half cool,
We took as dancers
Gentle winds and withered leaves,

And centuries in tens,
And peoples departed,
This distant long ago was
Never long ago enough!

Sous nos mêmes amours   65
Plus lourdes que le monde
Nous traversons les jours
Comme une pierre l'onde !

Nous marchons dans le temps
Et nos corps éclatants   70
Ont des pas ineffables
Qui marquent dans les fables...

L'abeille

À Francis de Miomandre

Quelle, et si fine, et si mortelle,
Que soit ta pointe, blonde abeille,
Je n'ai, sur ma tendre corbeille,
Jeté qu'un songe de dentelle.

Pique du sein la gourde belle,   5
Sur qui l'Amour meurt ou sommeille,
Qu'un peu de moi-même vermeille,
Vienne à la chair ronde et rebelle !

J'ai grand besoin d'un prompt tourment :
Un mal vif et bien terminé   10
Vaut mieux qu'un supplice dormant !

Soit donc mon sens illuminé
Par cette infime alerte d'or
Sans qui l'Amour meurt ou s'endort !

Poésie

Par la surprise saisie,
Une bouche qui buvait
Au sein de la Poésie
En sépare son duvet :

Beneath our equal love
More ponderous than the world
We pass through days
As a stone through water!

We tread our way through time
And our gleaming bodies
Take ineffable steps that
Leave their print in fables...

The Bee

For Francis de Miomandre

However fine, and mortal,
Your sting may be, golden bee,
Over my tender basket
I have spread a mere dream of lace.

Prick the beauteous gourd-like breast,
Where Love slumbers or dies,
So that a little of my vermillion being
May rise to the round resistant flesh!

I long for a sudden torment:
A sharp pain promptly ended
Is more desirable than a lingering agony!

May my senses be illumined
By this tiny golden alarm
Without which Love slumbers or dies!

Poetry

Taken by surprise,
A mouth that was drinking
At Poetry's breast
Withdraws its downy lip:

—Ô ma mère Intelligence,   5
De qui la douceur coulait,
Quelle est cette négligence
Qui laisse tarir son lait !

À peine sur ta poitrine,
Accablé de blancs liens,   10
Me berçait l'onde marine
De ton cœur chargé de biens ;

À peine, dans ton ciel sombre,
Abattu sur ta beauté,
Je sentais, à boire l'ombre,   15
M'envahir une clarté !

Dieu perdu dans son essence,
Et délicieusement
Docile à la connaissance
Du suprême apaisement,   20

Je touchais à la nuit pure,
Je ne savais plus mourir,
Car un fleuve sans coupure
Me semblait me parcourir...

Dis, par quelle crainte vaine,   25
Par quelle ombre de dépit,
Cette merveilleuse veine
À mes lèvres se rompit ?

Ô rigueur, tu m'es un signe
Qu'à mon âme je déplus !   30
Le silence au vol de cygne
Entre nous ne règne plus !

Immortelle, ta paupière
Me refuse mes trésors,
Et la chair s'est faite pierre   35
Qui fut tendre sous mon corps !

Des cieux même tu me sèvres,
Par quel injuste retour ?

—O mother Intelligence,
From whom such softness flowed,
What negligence this is
To let its milk run dry!

No sooner resting upon your breast,
Burdened by white bonds, than
I was lulled by the ocean swell
Of your heart's rich bounty;

No sooner had I swooped down
On the beauty in your gloomy sky, than
I felt, as I drank the shadows,
My being suffused with light!

God languishing in his essence,
And so delightfully
Willing to understand
Appeasement's supremacy,

I touched pure night,
I knew not how to die,
For an unbroken river
Seemed to flow through me...

Tell me, what vain fear,
What spite-filled shadow,
Made this wonderful vein
Break off at my lips?

O severity, you are a sign
That I offended my soul!
The silence of a swan's flight
No longer reigns between us!

Immortal one, your eyelid
Denies me my treasures, and
The flesh once soft beneath my body
Has now turned to stone!

You cut me off from heaven itself,
Out of what unfair change of heart?

Que seras-tu sans mes lèvres ?
Que serai-je sans amour ?   40

Mais la Source suspendue
Lui répond sans dureté :
—Si fort vous m'avez mordue
Que mon cœur s'est arrêté !

Les pas

Tes pas, enfants de mon silence,
Saintement, lentement placés,
Vers le lit de ma vigilance
Procèdent muets et glacés.

Personne pure, ombre divine,   5
Qu'ils sont doux, tes pas retenus !
Dieux !... tous les dons que je devine
Viennent à moi sur ces pieds nus !

Si, de tes lèvres avancées,
Tu prépares pour l'apaiser,   10
À l'habitant de mes pensées
La nourriture d'un baiser,

Ne hâte pas cet acte tendre,
Douceur d'être et de n'être pas,
Car j'ai vécu de vous attendre,   15
Et mon cœur n'était que vos pas.

La ceinture

Quand le ciel couleur d'une joue
Laisse enfin les yeux le chérir
Et qu'au point doré de périr
Dans les roses le temps se joue,

Devant le muet de plaisir   5
Qu'enchaîne une telle peinture,
Dans une Ombre à libre ceinture
Que le soir est près de saisir.

What will you be without my lips?
What shall I be without love?

Yet the now silent Font
Replies without bitterness:
—You bit me so hard that
My heart stopped beating!

The Footsteps

Your steps, children of my silence,
Soft and saintly their tread,
Approach the bed of my vigil,
In hushed and frozen procession.

Pure one, shadow so divine,
How light, your cautious steps!
Gods!... all the gifts I can imagine
Come to me on these bare feet!

If, with willing lips,
You are preparing to appease
The dweller of my thoughts
With the nourishment of a kiss,

Do not hasten this tender act,
Gentleness of being and not being,
For I have awaited your coming,
And my heart was but your steps.

The Girdle

When the sky flushed like a cheek
At last lets the eyes savour it,
And as it expires in a golden glow,
Time frolics amid the roses,

Before one hushed with delight,
Enchanted by such a painting,
A Shadow dances in a flowing girdle
Which evening will soon sweep away.

Cette ceinture vagabonde
Fait dans le souffle aérien   10
Frémir le suprême lien
De mon silence avec ce monde...

Absent, présent... Je suis bien seul,
Et sombre, ô suave linceul !

La dormeuse

À Lucien Fabre

Quels secrets dans son cœur brûle ma jeune amie,
Âme par le doux masque aspirant une fleur ?
De quels vains aliments sa naïve chaleur
Fait ce rayonnement d'une femme endormie ?

Souffles, songes, silence, invincible accalmie,   5
Tu triomphes, ô paix plus puissante qu'un pleur,
Quand de ce plein sommeil l'onde grave et l'ampleur
Conspirent sur le sein d'une telle ennemie.

Dormeuse, amas doré d'ombres et d'abandons,
Ton repos redoutable est chargé de tels dons,   10
Ô biche avec langueur longue auprès d'une grappe,

Que malgré l'âme absente, occupée aux enfers,
Ta forme au ventre pur qu'un bras fluide drape,
Veille ; ta forme veille, et mes yeux sont ouverts.

Fragments du Narcisse

Cur aliquid vidi ?

Que tu brilles enfin, terme pur de ma course !

Ce soir, comme d'un cerf, la fuite vers la source
Ne cesse qu'il ne tombe au milieu des roseaux,
Ma soif me vient abattre au bord même des eaux.
Mais, pour désaltérer cette amour curieuse,   5
Je ne troublerai pas l'onde mystérieuse :

This girdle freely trailing
Sets quivering in the air's breath
The supreme thread binding
My silence to this world...

Absent, present... I am truly alone,
O soft shroud, in the deepening gloom.

The Slumbering Woman

For Lucien Fabre

What secrets are burning in my young friend's heart,
Soul inhaling a flower through the gentle mask?
From what scant sustenance does the innocent warmth
Of this slumbering woman so radiantly glow?

Breath, dream, silence, invincible calm,
You triumph, O serenity more potent than a tear,
When sleep's heavy swell and great sweep
Conspire on the breast of such a foe.

Slumbering woman, golden mass of shadow and surrender,
Your daunting repose is laden with such gifts,
O languorous doe stretched out beside a grape cluster,

Which, though the soul may be absent, absorbed in hell,
Your form, with its soft waist draped by a flowing arm,
Keeps vigil; your form is awake, and my eyes are open.

Fragments of Narcissus

*Why did I see something?**

How you shine at last, pure end of my course!

This evening, the flight towards the spring, like a stag's,
Will not cease until it falls amidst the reeds,
My thirst brings me to my knees by the water's edge.
Yet, to slake this inquisitive love,
I shall not trouble the mysterious water:

Nymphes ! si vous m'aimez, il faut toujours dormir !
La moindre âme dans l'air vous fait toutes frémir ;
Même, dans sa faiblesse, aux ombres échappée,
Si la feuille éperdue effleure la napée,   10
Elle suffit à rompre un univers dormant...
Votre sommeil importe à mon enchantement,
Il craint jusqu'au frisson d'une plume qui plonge !
Gardez-moi longuement ce visage pour songe
Qu'une absence divine est seule à concevoir !   15
Sommeil des nymphes, ciel, ne cessez de me voir !

Rêvez, rêvez de moi !... Sans vous, belles fontaines,
Ma beauté, ma douleur, me seraient incertaines.
Je chercherais en vain ce que j'ai de plus cher,
Sa tendresse confuse étonnerait ma chair,   20
Et mes tristes regards, ignorants de mes charmes,
À d'autres que moi-même adresseraient leurs larmes...

Vous attendiez, peut-être, un visage sans pleurs,
Vous calmes, vous toujours de feuilles et de fleurs,
Et de l'incorruptible altitude hantées,   25
Ô Nymphes !... Mais docile aux pentes enchantées
Qui me firent vers vous d'invincibles chemins,
Souffrez ce beau reflet des désordres humains !

Heureux vos corps fondus, Eaux planes et profondes !
Je suis seul !... Si les Dieux, les échos et les ondes   30
Et si tant de soupirs permettent qu'on le soit !
Seul !... mais encor celui qui s'approche de soi
Quand il s'approche aux bords que bénit ce feuillage...
Des cimes, l'air déjà cesse le pur pillage ;
La voix des sources change, et me parle du soir ;   35
Un grand calme m'écoute, où j'écoute l'espoir.
J'entends l'herbe des nuits croître dans l'ombre sainte,
Et la lune perfide élève son miroir
Jusque dans les secrets de la fontaine éteinte...
Jusque dans les secrets que je crains de savoir,   40
Jusque dans le repli de l'amour de soi-même,
Rien ne peut échapper au silence du soir...
La nuit vient sur ma chair lui souffler que je l'aime.

Nymphs! if you love me, you must sleep on!
The slightest stirring in the air makes you all shiver;
Even if, in its weakness broken free from the shadows,
The distraught leaf brushes against the Napaeae,*
It is sufficient to disturb a slumbering universe...
My enchantment cannot live without your sleep,
It fears even the quiver of a dropping feather!
Long may you keep for me this face as a dream
Which a divine absence alone can conceive!
Slumber of the nymphs, sky, never stop seeing me!

Dream, dream of me!... Without you, splendid fountains,
My beauty and my grief would be uncertain.
I would seek in vain what I hold most dear,
Its bewildered tenderness would astound my flesh,
And my sorrowful gaze, blind to my charms,
Would shed tears for others than me...

　　Perhaps you were awaiting a face without tears,
You, calm Nymphs, ever fashioned of foliage and flowers,
And haunted by the incorruptible heights!...
Yet yielding to the enchanted slopes
Whose invincible paths led me to you,
Endure this beautiful reflection of human disarray!

　　Happy your blended bodies, deep and still Waters!
I am alone!... Should the Gods, the echoes and the ripples
And the plenteous sighs allow it so!
Alone!... and yet one who approaches himself
As he nears this leaf-blessed verge...
　　The air already ceases its pure plunder of the heights;
The voice of the springs changes, and speaks to me of evening;
A great calm listens to me, where I listen to hope.
I hear the night grass growing in the sacred shadows,
And the treacherous moon holds aloft its mirror
To the secrets of the lifeless fountain...
To the secrets that I dread knowing,
To the sanctuary of self-love,
Nothing eludes the hush of evening...
Night comes whispering over my flesh I so love.

Sa voix fraîche à mes vœux tremble de consentir ;
À peine, dans la brise, elle semble mentir,   45
Tant le frémissement de son temple tacite
Conspire au spacieux silence d'un tel site.

   Ô douceur de survivre à la force du jour,
Quand elle se retire enfin rose d'amour,
Encore un peu brûlante, et lasse, mais comblée,   50
Et de tant de trésors tendrement accablée
Par de tels souvenirs qu'ils empourprent sa mort,
Et qu'ils la font heureuse agenouiller dans l'or,
Puis s'étendre, se fondre, et perdre sa vendange,
Et s'éteindre en un songe en qui le soir se change.   55
   Quelle perte en soi-même offre un si calme lieu !
L'âme, jusqu'à périr, s'y penche pour un Dieu
Qu'elle demande à l'onde, onde déserte, et digne
Sur son lustre, du lisse effacement d'un cygne...
   À cette onde jamais ne burent les troupeaux !   60
D'autres, ici perdus, trouveraient le repos,
Et dans la sombre terre, un clair tombeau qui s'ouvre...
Mais ce n'est pas le calme, hélas ! que j'y découvre !
Quand l'opaque délice où dort cette clarté,
Cède à mon corps l'horreur du feuillage écarté,   65
Alors, vainqueur de l'ombre, ô mon corps tyrannique,
Repoussant aux forêts leur épaisseur panique,
Tu regrettes bientôt leur éternelle nuit !
Pour l'inquiet Narcisse, il n'est ici qu'ennui !
Tout m'appelle et m'enchaîne à la chair lumineuse   70
Que m'oppose des eaux la paix vertigineuse !

Que je déplore ton éclat fatal et pur,
Si mollement de moi, fontaine environnée,
Où puisèrent mes yeux dans un mortel azur,
Les yeux mêmes et noirs de leur âme étonnée !   75

Profondeur, profondeur, songes qui me voyez,
     Comme ils verraient une autre vie,
Dites, ne suis-je pas celui que vous croyez,
     Votre corps vous fait-il envie ?

Its fresh voice nervously quavers with consent;
In the breeze, it scarcely seems to lie,
So faithfully does the quivering of its tacit temple
Conspire with the boundless silence of this site.

   O how sweet it is to survive day's intensity,
When finally it fades, flushed with love,
Still faintly glowing, weary yet fulfilled,
And with a trove of treasures lovingly overwhelmed
By such memories that melt its demise to crimson
And make it happily kneel in gold,
Then spread, evanesce, and squander its harvest
Before ebbing into a dream that fades to evening.
   What loss within is begotten by so calm an expanse!
To the point of perishing, the soul reaches out
For the Heavenly which it beseeches from the waters,
Forsaken yet worthy of the silken brush of a swan...
   Never did herds drink this water!
Others, lost here, might find repose,
And in the dark earth, a bright tomb opens...
But, alas, it is not calm I find here!
When the shadowy delight where this brightness slumbers
Yields to my body the horror of foliage cast aside,
Then, vanquisher of the shadows, O cruel body of mine,
Thrusting their fearful obscurity to the forests,
Soon you will yearn for their eternal night!
There is nothing here but tedium for troubled Narcissus!
All draws and binds me to the resplendent flesh
Confronting me in the water's immeasurable tranquillity!

How I lament your pure and fatal glare,
Fount which my arms so tenderly enfold,
Where my eyes draw up from the mortal blue,
The same dark eyes of their astonished soul!

Depths, depths, dreams that see me,
     Just as they might glimpse another life,
Tell me, am I not the one you imagine,
     Do you not desire your own body?

Cessez, sombres esprits, cet ouvrage anxieux   80
      Qui se fait dans l'âme qui veille ;
Ne cherchez pas en vous, n'allez surprendre aux cieux
      Le malheur d'être une merveille :
Trouvez dans la fontaine un corps délicieux...

Prenant à vos regards cette parfaite proie,   85
Du monstre de s'aimer faites-vous un captif ;
Dans les errants filets de vos longs cils de soie
Son gracieux éclat vous retienne pensif ;

Mais ne vous flattez pas de le changer d'empire.
      Ce cristal est son vrai séjour ;   90
      Les efforts mêmes de l'amour !
Ne le sauraient de l'onde extraire qu'il n'expire...

PIRE.
     Pire ?...
         Quelqu'un redit *Pire*... Ô moqueur !
Écho lointaine est prompte à rendre son oracle !
De son rire enchanté, le roc brise mon cœur,   95
      Et le silence, par miracle,
Cesse !... parle, renaît, sur la face des eaux...
Pire ?...
      Pire destin !... Vous le dites, roseaux,
Qui reprîtes des vents ma plainte vagabonde !
Antres, qui me rendez mon âme plus profonde,   100
Vous renflez de votre ombre une voix qui se meurt...
Vous me le murmurez, ramures !... Ô rumeur
Déchirante, et docile aux souffles sans figure,
Votre or léger s'agite, et joue avec l'augure...
Tout se mêle de moi, brutes divinités !   105
Mes secrets dans les airs sonnent ébruités,
Le roc rit ; l'arbre pleure ; et par sa voix charmante,
Je ne puis jusqu'aux cieux que je ne me lamente
D'appartenir sans force à d'éternels attraits !
Hélas ! entre les bras qui naissent des forêts,   110
Une tendre lueur d'heure ambiguë existe...
Là, d'un reste du jour, se forme un fiancé,
Nu, sur la place pâle où m'attire l'eau triste,
Délicieux démon désirable et glacé !

Cease, solemn spirits, this anxious toil
      Welling up in the watchful soul;
Seek not within yourselves, nor startle in the heavens
      The misfortune of being a wonder
Find in the fount a delightful body...

Ensnaring this perfect prey in your gaze,
Surrender yourself to the monster of self-love;
In the stray web of your long silky lashes
May its gracious glare mesmerize you;

But do not think you can change its empire.
      This crystal is its true domain;
      Even love's toils could no sooner
Withdraw it from the water than it breathes its last...

LAST.
      Last?...
              A voice calls back *Last*... O mocker!
Distant Echo* is quick to deliver her oracle!
The rock's enchanted laugh breaks my heart,
      And, by some miracle, the silence is
Broken!... speaks, is reborn upon the glassy water...
Last?
      Fate will have the last laugh!... So you say, reeds,
You who caught my lament drifting on the winds!
Lairs restoring my deeper soul,
You swell an ailing voice with your shadow...
You whisper it to me, boughs!... O harrowing
Murmur, yet obedient to the faceless breaths,
Your light gold stirs, and gambols with the augur...
Everything meddles with my restless being, brute divinities!
My secrets revealed now fill the air,
The rock laughs; the tree weeps; and by its charming rustle,
I can but lament to the heavens that
I am helplessly bound to eternal charms!
Alas! between the outstretched limbs of the forests
A tender gleam of doubtful light lingers...
There, from a remnant of ebbing day, a betrothed is formed,
Naked on the palely lit spot where the sad waters draw me,
Delectable demon, desirable and ice-cold!

Te voici, mon doux corps de lune et de rosée,   115
Ô forme obéissante à mes vœux opposée !
Qu'ils sont beaux, de mes bras les dons vastes et vains !
Mes lentes mains, dans l'or adorable se lassent
D'appeler ce captif que les feuilles enlacent ;
Mon cœur jette aux échos l'éclat des noms divins !...   120

   Mais que ta bouche est belle en ce muet blasphème !

   Ô semblable !... Et pourtant plus parfait que moi-même,
Éphémère immortel, si clair devant mes yeux,
Pâles membres de perle, et ces cheveux soyeux,
Faut-il qu'à peine aimés, l'ombre les obscurcisse,   125
Et que la nuit déjà nous divise, ô Narcisse,
Et glisse entre nous deux le fer qui coupe un fruit !
Qu'as-tu ?
          Ma plainte même est funeste ?...
                       Le bruit
Du souffle que j'enseigne à tes lèvres, mon double,
Sur la limpide lame a fait courir un trouble !...   130
Tu trembles !... Mais ces mots que j'expire à genoux
Ne sont pourtant qu'une âme hésitante entre nous,
Entre ce front si pur et ma lourde mémoire...
Je suis si près de toi que je pourrais te boire,
Ô visage !... Ma soif est un esclave nu...   135
   Jusqu'à ce temps charmant je m'étais inconnu,
Et je ne savais pas me chérir et me joindre !
Mais te voir, cher esclave, obéir à la moindre
Des ombres dans mon cœur se fuyant à regret,
Voir sur mon front l'orage et les feux d'un secret,   140
Voir, ô merveille, voir ! ma bouche nuancée
Trahir... peindre sur l'onde une fleur de pensée,
Et quels événements étinceler dans l'œil !
J'y trouve un tel trésor d'impuissance et d'orgueil,
Que nulle vierge enfant échappée au satyre,   145
Nulle ! aux fuites habiles, aux chutes sans émoi,
Nulle des nymphes, nulle amie, ne m'attire
Comme tu fais sur l'onde, inépuisable Moi !...

I see you now, soft body made of moon and dew,
Obedient form contrary to my yearning!
How fine the bountiful and fruitless offerings of my arms!
My slender hands lovingly bathed in gold weary
Of calling to this captive wreathed in leaves;
My heart casts out to the echoes the wonder of names divine!...

But how beauteous your mouth in this silent blasphemy!

O mirror image!... And yet more perfect than myself,
Ephemeral immortal, so clear before my eyes,
Must these fair pearly limbs, and that silken hair,
So scarcely loved, vanish into the gloom,
Must night already divide us, O Narcissus,
And slip between us the blade that slices the fruit!
What ails you?

     Is even my lament baleful?...

            The sigh
Of the breath that I teach your lips, my double,
Stirs a ripple on the limpid blade!...
You are quivering!... Yet these words I whisper here on my knees
Are no more than a hesitant soul between us,
Between this brow so pure and my ponderous memory...
You are so close I could drink you,
O face!... My thirst is a stripped slave...

Until this bewitching hour I was a stranger to myself,
Not knowing how to cherish or commune with my soul!
But to see you, beloved slave, obey the faintest
Shades sorrowfully taking flight within my heart,
To see the fire and the fury of a secret upon my brow,
To see, O marvel, to see! my finely shadowed mouth
Betray... and paint a blossoming thought upon the waters,
And what stirs in the gleaming eye!
I find there such a trove of helplessness and pride
That no young virgin child who eluded the zephyr,
Not one! nimble in her flight, unruffled in her fall,
Not one of the nymphs, no friend, entices me
As you do to the water, boundless I!...

II

Fontaine, ma fontaine, eau froidement présente,
Douce aux purs animaux, aux humains complaisante
Qui d'eux-mêmes tentés suivent au fond la mort,
Tout est songe pour toi, Sœur tranquille du Sort !
À peine en souvenir change-t-il un présage,   5
Que pareille sans cesse à son fuyant visage,
Sitôt de ton sommeil les cieux te sont ravis !
Mais si pure tu sois des êtres que tu vis,
Onde, sur qui les ans passent comme les nues,
Que de choses pourtant doivent t'être connues,   10
Astres, roses, saisons, les corps et leurs amours !
    Claire, mais si profonde, une nymphe toujours
Effleurée, et vivant de tout ce qui l'approche,
Nourrit quelque sagesse à l'abri de sa roche,
À l'ombre de ce jour qu'elle peint sous les bois.   15
Elle sait à jamais les choses d'une fois...
    Ô présence pensive, eau calme qui recueilles
Tout un sombre trésor de fables et de feuilles,
L'oiseau mort, le fruit mûr, lentement descendus,
Et les rares lueurs des clairs anneaux perdus.   20
Tu consommes en toi leur perte solennelle ;
Mais, sur la pureté de ta face éternelle,
L'amour passe et périt...
                    Quand le feuillage épars
Tremble, commence à fuir, pleure de toutes parts,
Tu vois du sombre amour s'y mêler la tourmente,   25
L'amant brûlant et dur ceindre la blanche amante,
Vaincre l'âme... Et tu sais selon quelle douceur
Sa main puissante passe à travers l'épaisseur
Des tresses que répand la nuque précieuse,
S'y repose, et se sent forte et mystérieuse ;   30
Elle parle à l'épaule et règne sur la chair.
    Alors les yeux fermés à l'éternel éther
Ne voient plus que le sang qui dore leurs paupières ;
Sa pourpre redoutable obscurcit les lumières
D'un couple aux pieds confus qui se mêle, et se ment.   35
Ils gémissent... La Terre appelle doucement

II

Fountain, my fountain, water coldly tranquil before me,
Fresh to pure animals, life-giving to humans
Who, lured by themselves, trail death into the depths,
All is dream to you, serene Sister of Fate!
Scarcely does it change an omen to memory,
Than, forever true to its fleeting face,
The heavens are wrested from your slumber!
But however pure you remain of the beings you have seen,
O water, where the years drift by like clouds,
What myriad things you must nonetheless know,
Stars, roses, seasons, bodies and their love!
   Clear, yet so deep, a nymph forever
Lightly touched, and living off what comes her way,
Nurtures some wisdom in the shade of her rock,
In this dappled light she paints beneath the woods.
She knows forevermore things that happened once...
   O thinking presence, still water gathering
An entire gloomy trove of fables and foliage,
The dead bird and the ripe fruit that slowly descended,
And the rare glimmering of long-lost shiny rings.
You consume their solemn loss within you;
Yet, on your timeless face so pure,
Love passes and perishes...
              When the scattered leaves
Quiver, begin to take flight, and stream down all around,
You see there sombre love mingling its torment,
The ardent, hard lover enfolding his love's fair skin,
Vanquishing the spirit... And you know how gently
His powerful fingers slip through the plenteous
Locks tumbling from her precious nape,
Come to rest there and feel their own power and mystery;
They speak to the shoulder and hold sway over the flesh.
   Then the eyes closed to the eternal firmament
Merely see the blood gilding their eyelids;
Its formidable crimson obscures the light
Of a couple, with feet entwined, who blend and whisper their lies.
They moan... The Earth draws tenderly down

Ces grands corps chancelants, qui luttent bouche à bouche,
Et qui, du vierge sable osant battre la couche,
Composeront d'amour un monstre qui se meurt...
Leurs souffles ne font plus qu'une heureuse rumeur,   40
L'âme croit respirer l'âme toute prochaine,
Mais tu sais mieux que moi, vénérable fontaine,
Quels fruits forment toujours ces moments enchantés !

    Car, à peine les cœurs calmes et contentés
D'une ardente alliance expirée en délices,   45
Des amants détachés tu mires les malices,
Tu vois poindre des jours de mensonges tissus,
Et naître mille maux trop tendrement conçus !

    Bientôt, mon onde sage, infidèle et la même,
Le Temps mène ces fous qui crurent que l'on aime   50
Redire à tes roseaux de plus profonds soupirs !
Vers toi, leurs tristes pas suivent leurs souvenirs...

    Sur tes bords, accablés d'ombres et de faiblesse,
Tout éblouis d'un ciel dont la beauté les blesse
Tant il garde l'éclat de leurs jours les plus beaux,   55
Ils vont des biens perdus trouver tous les tombeaux...
'Cette place dans l'ombre était tranquille et nôtre !'
'L'autre aimait ce cyprès,' se dit le cœur de l'autre,
'Et d'ici, nous goûtions le souffle de la mer !'
Hélas ! la rose même est amère dans l'air...   60
Moins amers les parfums des suprêmes fumées
Qu'abandonnent au vent les feuilles consumées !...

    Ils respirent ce vent, marchent sans le savoir,
Foulent aux pieds le temps d'un jour de désespoir...
Ô marche lente, prompte, et pareille aux pensées   65
Qui parlent tour à tour aux têtes insensées !
La caresse et le meurtre hésitent dans leurs mains,
Leur cœur, qui croit se rompre au détour des chemins,
Lutte, et retient à soi son espérance étreinte.
Mais leurs esprits perdus courent ce labyrinthe   70
Où s'égare celui qui maudit le soleil !
Leur folle solitude, à l'égal du sommeil,
Peuple et trompe l'absence ; et leur secrète oreille
Partout place une voix qui n'a point de pareille.
Rien ne peut dissiper leurs songes absolus ;   75

These great teetering bodies, tussling mouth to mouth
And, daring to press the bed of virgin sand,
Will fashion from love a dying monster...
Their breaths now fade to a gratified murmur,
The soul believes it breathes in the other's soul.
But you know better than I, venerable fountain,
What fruits such enchanted moments bring forth!

   For no sooner are their hearts calm and contented
From a burning union that expired in raptures
Than you mirror the malice of the detached lovers,
You see days woven of deceit begin to dawn
And the birth of myriad woes all too tenderly begotten!

   Soon, wise waters, faithless and unchanging,
Time leads these fools who believed in love
To repeat even deeper sighs to your reeds!
Towards you, their sorrowful steps trail their memories...

   Upon your banks, ponderous with weakness and shadow,
Dazzled by a sky whose beauty scars them,
So bright it retains the brilliance of their finest days,
They will find where their lost yearning lies entombed...
'This shaded nook was serene and all ours!'
'The other loved this cypress,' said the same's heart,
'And from here, we could savour the sea's briny breath!'
Alas! even the rose is bitter on the air...
Less bitter is the scent of smoke borne aloft,
Abandoned by the burnt leaves to the winds!...

   They breathe in this wind, tread unaware,
Trample underfoot a time brimming with day's despair...
O slow and prompt their steps, like the thoughts
Which speak in turn in their incensed heads!
Their hands waver between murder and the caress,
Their hearts, expecting to break at every turn in the path,
Struggle and cling tightly to hope.
Yet their bewildered minds roam this labyrinth
Where he who scorns the sun goes astray!
Their raging solitude, just like their slumber,
Deceives and fills the emptiness; and their secret ear
Places all round a voice that has no equal...
Nothing can dissipate their dreams' unreachable realm;

Le soleil ne peut rien contre ce qui n'est plus !
Mais s'ils traînent dans l'or leurs yeux secs et funèbres,
Ils se sentent des pleurs défendre leurs ténèbres
Plus chères à jamais que tous les feux du jour !
Et dans ce corps caché tout marqué de l'amour   80
Que porte amèrement l'âme qui fut heureuse,
Brûle un secret baiser qui la rend furieuse...

Mais moi, Narcisse aimé, je ne suis curieux
            Que de ma seule essence ;
Tout autre n'a pour moi qu'un cœur mystérieux,   85
            Tout autre n'est qu'absence.
Ô mon bien souverain, cher corps, je n'ai que toi !
Le plus beau des mortels ne peut chérir que soi...
        Douce et dorée, est-il une idole plus sainte,
De toute une forêt qui se consume, ceinte,   90
Et sise dans l'azur vivant par tant d'oiseaux ?
Est-il don plus divin de la faveur des eaux,
Et d'un jour qui se meurt plus adorable usage
Que de rendre à mes yeux l'honneur de mon visage ?
Naisse donc entre nous que la lumière unit   95
De grâce et de silence un échange infini !

        Je vous salue, enfant de mon âme et de l'onde,
Cher trésor d'un miroir qui partage le monde !
Ma tendresse y vient boire, et s'enivre de voir
Un désir sur soi-même essayer son pouvoir !   100
        Ô qu'à tous mes souhaits, que vous êtes semblable !
Mais la fragilité vous fait inviolable,
Vous n'êtes que lumière, adorable moitié
D'une amour trop pareille à la faible amitié !

        Hélas ! la nymphe même a séparé nos charmes !   105
Puis-je espérer de toi que de vaines alarmes ?
Qu'ils sont doux les périls que nous pourrions choisir !
Se surprendre soi-même et soi-même saisir,
Nos mains s'entremêler, nos maux s'entre-détruire,
Nos silences longtemps de leurs songes s'instruire,   110
La même nuit en pleurs confondre nos yeux clos,
Et nos bras refermés sur les mêmes sanglots
Étreindre un même cœur, d'amour prêt à se fondre...

The sun is helpless against what is no more!
But if they trail in the gold their dry and mournful eyes,
Tears well up to guard their inner gloom
Infinitely more treasured than all of day's fires!
And in this body's love-scarred recesses,
Still bitterly borne by a once joyous soul,
Smoulders a secret kiss that enrages it...

Yet I, beloved Narcissus, seek to know
       Only my own essence;
The hearts of others are a mystery to me,
       All others are mere absence.
O my sovereign possession, dear body, you are all that I have!
The most beauteous of mortals can cherish only himself*...
   Is there a more saintly or gently gilded idol,
Bounded by a blazing forest and set
Against a blue realm teeming with birds?
Is there a gift more divine than the water's kindness,
A more delightful way to spend the ebbing day than
To grant my eyes the honour of my face?
Let there be between us, whom light brings together,
Unending communion of silence and grace!
   I greet you, child of my soul and the waters,
Beloved treasure of a mirror dividing the world!
My tenderness comes here to drink, wild
To behold desire test its potency on itself!
   O how attuned you are to my every wish!
Yet frailty makes you inviolable,
You are merely light, adorable half
Of a love all too similar to feeble friendship!
   Alas! the very nymph has riven our charms!
Is futile fright all that I can expect from you?
How bitter-sweet the perils were we to choose!
To surprise and seize one's very self,
Our hands entwining, our evils tearing one another asunder,
Our silences long learning of each other's dreams,
The same night bathed in tears uniting our closed eyes,
And our arms enfolding the same sobs
Extinguish the same heart, ready to melt in love...

Quitte enfin le silence, ose enfin me répondre,
Bel et cruel Narcisse, inaccessible enfant,   115
Tout orné de mes biens que la nymphe défend...

III

...Ce corps si pur, sait-il qu'il me puisse séduire ?
De quelle profondeur songes-tu de m'instruire,
Habitant de l'abîme, hôte si spécieux
D'un ciel sombre ici-bas précipité des cieux ?...
    Ô le frais ornement de ma triste tendance   5
Qu'un sourire si proche, et plein de confidence,
Et qui prête à ma lèvre une ombre de danger
Jusqu'à me faire craindre un désir étranger !
Quel souffle vient à l'onde offrir ta froide rose !...
J'aime... J'aime !... Et qui donc peut aimer autre chose   10
Que soi-même ?...
                    Toi seul, ô mon corps, mon cher corps,
Je t'aime, unique objet qui me défends des morts !
....
Formons, toi sur ma lèvre, et moi, dans mon silence,
Une prière aux dieux qu'émus de tant d'amour
Sur sa pente de pourpre ils arrêtent le jour !...   15
Faites, Maîtres heureux, Pères des justes fraudes,
Dites qu'une lueur de rose ou d'émeraudes
Que des songes du soir votre sceptre reprit,
Pure, et toute pareille au plus pur de l'esprit,
Attende, au sein des cieux, que tu vives et veuilles,   20
Près de moi, mon amour, choisir un lit de feuilles,
Sortir tremblant du flanc de la nymphe au cœur froid,
Et sans quitter mes yeux, sans cesser d'être moi,
Tendre ta forme fraîche, et cette claire écorce...
Oh ! te saisir enfin !... Prendre ce calme torse   25
Plus pur que d'une femme et non formé de fruits...
Mais, d'une pierre simple est le temple où je suis,
Où je vis... Car je vis sur tes lèvres avares !...
    Ô mon corps, mon cher corps, temple qui me sépares
De ma divinité, je voudrais apaiser   30
Votre bouche... Et bientôt, je briserais, baiser,

End thus the silence, dare finally to answer me,
Beauteous and cruel Narcissus, unreachable child,
All adorned with my treasures forbidden by the nymph...

III

...Does this body so pure know it can charm me?
From what depths do you think to teach me,
Denizen of the abyss, deceptive host
Of a sombre sky cast down here from the heavens?...
   O cool adornment of my sorrowful spirit,
This smile so close and brimming with secrecy,
Shading my lip with a tinge of risk and
Making me fear even unfamiliar desire!
What breath comes to the water offering your cold rose!...
I love... I love!... And who then could love anyone
Other than himself?...

                         O body of mine, my dear body, I love
You alone, the one object guarding me from the dead!
....
Let us make, you upon my lip and I in my silence,
A prayer so that the gods, touched by such bounteous love,
May stop the day's crimson ebbing!...
Joyful Masters, Fathers of just deceit, you must act,
Declare that a glimmer of rose or of emerald
Drawn from evening's dreams by your sceptre,
Pure in its likeness to a mind's true essence,
Wait in the bosom of heaven until you, my love,
Live and choose a bed of leaves next to me,
Emerge quivering from the side of the cold-hearted nymph,
And without leaving in my gaze, or ceasing to be me,
Offer your cool form, and this fair skin...
Ah, to seize you at last!... Embrace this calm torso
Purer than a woman's and not formed of fruit...
But the temple that I am and where I dwell is fashioned
From a single stone... For I dwell on your miserly lips!...
   O body of mine, beloved body, temple estranging me
From my god, I long to appease
  Your mouth... And soon, I may break, kiss,

Ce peu qui nous défend de l'extrême existence,
Cette tremblante, frêle, et pieuse distance
Entre moi-même et l'onde, et mon âme, et les dieux !...
    Adieu... Sens-tu frémir mille flottants adieux ?   35
Bientôt va frissonner le désordre des ombres !
L'arbre aveugle vers l'arbre étend ses membres sombres,
Et cherche affreusement l'arbre qui disparaît...
Mon âme ainsi se perd dans sa propre forêt,
Où la puissance échappe à ses formes suprêmes...   40
L'âme, l'âme aux yeux noirs, touche aux ténèbres mêmes,
Elle se fait immense et ne rencontre rien...
Entre la mort et soi, quel regard est le sien !

    Dieux ! de l'auguste jour, le pâle et tendre reste
Va des jours consumés joindre le sort funeste ;   45
Il s'abîme aux enfers du profond souvenir !
Hélas ! corps misérable, il est temps de s'unir...
Penche-toi... Baise-toi. Tremble de tout ton être !
L'insaisissable amour que tu me vins promettre
Passe, et dans un frisson, brise Narcisse, et fuit...   50

La pythie

À Pierre Louÿs

Hæc effata silet ; pallor simul occupat ora.
Virgile, Æn, IV

La Pythie, exhalant la flamme
De naseaux durcis par l'encens,
Haletante, ivre, hurle !... l'âme
Affreuse, et les flancs mugissants !
Pâle, profondément mordue,   5
Et la prunelle suspendue
Au point le plus haut de l'horreur,
Le regard qui manque à son masque
S'arrache vivant à la vasque,
À la fumée, à la fureur !   10

What little shields us from the extremity of being,
This shivering, frail, and holy distance
Between me and the water, my soul and the gods!...
    Farewell... Can you hear the myriad wafting farewells?
The disarray of shadows will soon begin to quiver here!
The blind tree stetches out its dark limbs to another,
Frantically groping for the vanishing tree...
My soul goes astray in its own forest,
Where power evades its supreme forms...
The soul, the dark-eyed soul touches darkness itself,
Growing ever larger and encountering nothing...
What a gaze there is between death and self!

    Gods! the pale and tender remnant of splendid day
Sets forth to join the gloomy fate of days expended;
It plunges into memory's fathomless abyss!
Alas! wretched body, it is time to unite...
Lean forward... Kiss. Quiver with all your being!
The elusive love you came promising me
Passes, then shivering, breaks Narcissus and takes flight...

The Pythia

For Pierre Louÿs
To these words, she [Dido] fell silent and her face grew pale.*
Vergil, *Aeneid*, 4

    The Pythia, exhaling her flame
    From incense-flared nostrils,
    Panting, frenzied, screaming!... her soul
    Hideous, her flanks writhing!
    Pallid, deeply wounded,
    And her pupil suspended
    On the pinnacle of horror,
    The gaze absent from her mask
    Is wrenched alive from the fountain,
    From the smoke, from the rage!

Sur le mur, son ombre démente
Où domine un démon majeur,
Parmi l'odorante tourmente
Prodigue un fantôme nageur,
De qui la transe colossale,   15
Rompant les aplombs de la salle,
Si la folle tarde à hennir,
Mime de noirs enthousiasmes,
Hâte les dieux, presse les spasmes
De s'achever dans l'avenir !   20

Cette martyre en sueurs froides,
Ses doigts sur ses doigts se crispant,
Vocifère entre les ruades
D'un trépied qu'étrangle un serpent :
—Ah ! maudite !... Quels maux je souffre !   25
Toute ma nature est un gouffre !
Hélas ! Entr'ouverte aux esprits,
J'ai perdu mon propre mystère !...
Une Intelligence adultère
Exerce un corps qu'elle a compris !   30

Don cruel ! Maître immonde, cesse
Vite, vite, ô divin ferment,
De feindre une vaine grossesse
Dans ce pur ventre sans amant !
Fais finir cette horrible scène !   35
Vois de tout mon corps l'arc obscène
Tendre à se rompre pour darder,
Comme son trait le plus infâme,
Implacablement au ciel l'âme
Que mon sein ne peut plus garder !   40

Qui me parle, à ma place même ?
Quel écho me répond : Tu mens !
Qui m'illumine ?... Qui blasphème ?
Et qui, de ces mots écumants,
Dont les éclats hachent ma langue,   45
La fait brandir une harangue
Brisant la bave et les cheveux

Her frenzied shadow upon the wall
Where a great demon looms,
Amid the sweet-smelling tumult
Casts a ghostly swimmer,
Whose colossal trance,
Shattering the harmony of the hall,
If she so crazed retains her chaff,
Mimics dark obsession,
Hastens the gods and urges the violent surge
To perish in the future!

This martyr bathed in an icy sweat,
Her fingers clutching at her fingers,
Seethes at each kick of
A tripod entwined by a serpent:
—Ah! cursed!... What woes I suffer!
My entire being is an abyss!
Alas! Laid bare to the spirits,
I have lost my own mystery!...
An adulterous Intelligence now
Controls the flesh it embodies!

Cruel gift! Wicked Master, cease
Quickly, quickly, O divine ferment,
Feigning a futile pregnancy
In this womb untouched by a lover!
Put an end to this ghastly scene!
Behold my body's obscene bow
Stretched to breaking point
To shoot, as its most vile arrow
Remorselessly heavenward, the soul
Which my bosom can no longer contain!

Who speaks to me, in place of me?
What echo answers me: You are a liar!
Who illumines me?... Who blasphemes?
And who, with these frothing words burst forth,
Whose barbed outpourings shred my tongue,
Makes it utter a harangue which
Breaks through the slaver and the locks

Que mâche et trame le désordre
D'une bouche qui veut se mordre
Et se reprendre ses aveux ?   50

Dieu ! Je ne me connais de crime
Que d'avoir à peine vécu !...
Mais si tu me prends pour victime
Et sur l'autel d'un corps vaincu
Si tu courbes un monstre, tue   55
Ce monstre, et la bête abattue,
Le col tranché, le chef produit
Par les crins qui tirent les tempes,
Que cette plus pâle des lampes
Saisisse de marbre la nuit !   60

Alors, par cette vagabonde
Morte, errante, et lune à jamais,
Soit l'eau des mers surprise, et l'onde
Astreinte à d'éternels sommets !
Que soient les humains faits statues,   65
Les cœurs figés, les âmes tues,
Et par les glaces de mon œil,
Puisse un peuple de leurs paroles
Durcir en un peuple d'idoles
Muet de sottise et d'orgueil !   70

Eh ! Quoi !... Devenir la vipère
Dont tout le ressort de frissons
Surprend la chair que désespère
Sa multitude de tronçons !...
Reprendre une lutte insensée !...   75
Tourne donc plutôt ta pensée
Vers la joie enfuie, et reviens,
Ô mémoire, à cette magie
Qui ne tirait son énergie
D'autres arcanes que des tiens !   80

Mon cher corps... Forme préférée,
Fraîcheur par qui ne fut jamais
Aphrodite désaltérée,
Intacte nuit, tendres sommets,

Munched and tangled by the tumult
Of a mouth keen to bite itself
And withdraw its own avowals?

God! I am not guilty of any crime
Except that of having scarcely lived!...
But if you choose me as your victim
And upon the altar of a vanquished body
If you subdue a monster, kill
That monster, and the beast slain,
The throat slit, the head held aloft
By the hair wrenching its temples,
May that palest of lamps
Transform night to marble!

So, may this wandering soul,
Lifelessly adrift and remote for all time,
Startle the sea's waters, and thrust
The wave to an eternal summit!
May all men be turned to statues,
Their hearts frozen, their souls silenced,
And may my icy gaze
Harden a people by their words
Into a people of idols struck
Dumb with stupidity and pride!

Hey! What!... Become the viper
Whose entire quivering spring
Surprises the flesh driven to despair
By its bounteous coils!...
Begin again a senseless struggle!...
Cast then your mind back
To vanished joy, and return,
O memory, to this magic which
Drew its energy from
No other mystery than your own!

Beloved body of mine!... Chosen form,
Freshness that never
Slaked Aphrodite's thirst,
Night intact, tender summits,

Et vos partages indicibles   85
D'une argile en îles sensibles,
Douce matière de mon sort,
Quelle alliance nous vécûmes,
Avant que le don des écumes
Ait fait de toi ce corps de mort !   90

Toi, mon épaule, où l'or se joue
D'une fontaine de noirceur,
J'aimais de te joindre ma joue
Fondue à sa même douceur !...
Ou, soulevée à mes narines,   95
Ouverte aux distances marines,
Les mains pleines de seins vivants,
Entre mes bras aux belles anses
Mon abîme a bu les immenses
Profondeurs qu'apportent les vents !   100

Hélas ! ô roses, toute lyre
Contient la modulation !
Un soir, de mon triste délire
Parut la constellation !
Le temple se change dans l'antre,   105
Et l'ouragan des songes entre
Au même ciel qui fut si beau !
Il faut gémir, il faut atteindre
Je ne sais quelle extase, et ceindre
Ma chevelure d'un lambeau !   110

Ils m'ont connue aux bleus stigmates
Apparus sur ma pauvre peau ;
Ils m'assoupirent d'aromates
Laineux et doux comme un troupeau ;
Ils ont, pour vivant amulette,   115
Touché ma gorge qui halète
Sous les ornements vipérins ;
Étourdie, ivre d'empyreumes,
Ils m'ont, au murmure des neumes,
Rendu des honneurs souterrains.   120

And visible islands you
Fashioned silently from clay,
Soft substance of my fate,
How we delighted in our union
Before the foam's bounty
Turned you into this deathly body!

You, my shoulder, where the playful gold
Scoffs at a fountain of darkness,
I loved to feel my cheek upon you
Melting into its own softness!...
Or, raised to my nose,
Opened wide to the sea's expanse,
My hands brimming with living breasts,
Within my arms' tender coves
My abyss drew in the fathomless
Depths borne by the winds!

Alas, O roses, every lyre
Is rich in cadence!
One evening, out of my sad delirium
The constellation appeared!
The temple changes to a den
And the tempest of dreams sweeps across
The same sky that was once so splendid!
Now I must moan, and go seek
Who knows what ecstasy, and
Truss my flowing locks!

They knew me by the blue stigmata
Which appeared on my wretched skin;
They dulled me with herbs
Woolly and soft as a flock of sheep;
As a living amulet, they
Touched my heaving breast
Beneath the serpentine ornaments;
Dazed and dizzied by empyreuma,*
Beneath the earth they paid respect to me
To the murmur of neumes.*

Qu'ai-je donc fait qui me condamne
Pure, à ces rites odieux ?
Une sombre carcasse d'âne
Eût bien servi de ruche aux dieux !
Mais une vierge consacrée,　　　　　　　　　125
Une conque neuve et nacrée
Ne doit à la divinité
Que sacrifice et que silence,
Et cette intime violence
Que se fait la virginité !　　　　　　　　　130

Pourquoi, Puissance Créatrice,
Auteur du mystère animal,
Dans cette vierge pour matrice,
Semer les merveilles du mal ?
Sont-ce les dons que tu m'accordes ?　　　　135
Crois-tu, quand se brisent les cordes,
Que le son jaillisse plus beau ?
Ton plectre a frappé sur mon torse,
Mais tu ne lui laisses la force
Que de sonner comme un tombeau !　　　　140

Sois clémente, sois sans oracles !
Et de tes merveilleuses mains,
Change en caresses les miracles,
Retiens les présents surhumains !
C'est en vain que tu communiques　　　　　145
À nos faibles tiges, d'uniques
Commotions de ta splendeur !
L'eau tranquille est plus transparente
Que toute tempête parente
D'une confuse profondeur !　　　　　　　　150

Va, la lumière la divine
N'est pas l'épouvantable éclair
Qui nous devance et nous devine
Comme un songe cruel et clair !
Il éclate !... Il va nous instruire !...　　　155
Non !... La solitude vient luire
Dans la plaie immense des airs

What have I so pure done to be
Condemned to these hideous rites?
A gloomy carcass of a donkey
Might have served as a hive to the gods!
Yet a consecrated virgin,
A new and nacreous conch
Owes the divinity
Only sacrifice and silence,
And this inner harm which
Virginity inflicts upon itself!

Why, Creative Power,
Maker of animal mystery,
Sow the wonders of evil in
This virgin you take as a womb?
Are these the talents you grant me?
Do you believe that when the strings snap
A more beauteous sound flows forth?
Your plectrum has struck my chest,
Yet you leave it with just the strength
To resound like a tomb!

Be merciful, without oracles!
And with your wondrous hands,
Change miracles to caresses,
Clasp the superhuman offerings!
In vain do you convey your
Splendour's unique quivering
To our frail stems!
Still water is clearer
Than any tempest that begets
These murky depths!

Away with you, the light divine
Is not the frightful flash of lightning
Which outsmarts and sees through us
Like a cruel and lucid dream!
It explodes!... It will then enlighten us!...
No!... Solitude comes to gleam
In the air's bounteous wound

Où nulle pâle architecture,
Mais la déchirante rupture
Nous imprime de purs déserts !   160

N'allez donc, mains universelles,
Tirer de mon front orageux
Quelques suprêmes étincelles !
Les hasards font les mêmes jeux !
Le passé, l'avenir sont frères   165
Et par leurs visages contraires
Une seule tête pâlit
De ne voir où qu'elle regarde
Qu'une même absence hagarde
D'îles plus belles que l'oubli.   170

Noirs témoins de tant de lumières
Ne cherchez plus... Pleurez, mes yeux !
Ô pleurs dont les sources premières
Sont trop profondes dans les cieux !...
Jamais plus amère demande !...   175
Mais la prunelle la plus grande
De ténèbres se doit nourrir !...
Tenant notre race atterrée,
La distance désespérée
Nous laisse le temps de mourir !   180

Entends, mon âme, entends ces fleuves !
Quelles cavernes sont ici ?
Est-ce mon sang ?... Sont-ce les neuves
Rumeurs des ondes sans merci ?
Mes secrets sonnent leurs aurores !   185
Tristes airains, tempes sonores,
Que dites-vous de l'avenir !
Frappez, frappez, dans une roche,
Abattez l'heure la plus proche...
Mes deux natures vont s'unir !   190

Ô formidablement gravie,
Et sur d'effrayants échelons,
Je sens dans l'arbre de ma vie
La mort monter de mes talons !

Where, not pale architecture,
But the rending split
Imprints pure deserts upon us!

So do not, universal hands,
Draw from my stormy brow
A few supreme sparks!
Chance plays the same games!
The past and the future are brothers
And by their opposing faces
A single head turns pale
From seeing wherever it may gaze
Only the same wild absence of
Islands more beautiful than oblivion.

Black witnesses of so many gleaming stars
Search no more... Weep then, eyes of mine!...
O tears welling up from fathomless
Springs aloft in the heavens!...
Never was there a more bitter plea!...
Yet the largest pupil
Must nourish itself on darkness!...
Holding our race earthbound,
The despairing distance
Allows us the time to die!

Listen, my soul, listen to these rivers!
What caverns are these?
Is it my blood?... Are these the fresh
Murmurings of the merciless waves?
My secrets summon their dawn!
Lamentable bits of bronze, resounding temples,
May you foresee what is yet to come!
Strike, strike at a rock,
Strike down the nearest hour...
My double nature shall soon be one!

O perilously scaled,
And upon terrifying rungs,
I feel within the tree of my being
Death rising from my heels!

Le long de ma ligne frileuse   195
Le doigt mouillé de la fileuse
Trace une atroce volonté !
Et par sanglots grimpe la crise
Jusque dans ma nuque où se brise
Une cime de volupté !   200

Ah ! brise les portes vivantes !
Fais craquer les vains scellements,
Épais troupeau des épouvantes,
Hérissé d'étincellements !
Surgis des étables funèbres   205
Où te nourrissaient mes ténèbres
De leur fabuleuse foison !
Bondis, de rêves trop repue,
Ô horde épineuse et crépue,
Et viens fumer dans l'or, Toison !   210

*

Telle, toujours plus tourmentée,
Déraisonne, râle et rugit
La prophétesse fomentée
Par les souffles de l'or rougi.
Mais enfin le ciel se déclare !   215
L'oreille du pontife hilare
S'aventure dans le futur :
Une attente sainte la penche,
Car une voix nouvelle et blanche
Échappe de ce corps impur.   220

*

Honneur des Hommes, Saint LANGAGE,
Discours prophétique et paré,
Belles chaînes en qui s'engage
Le dieu dans la chair égaré,
Illumination, largesse !   225
Voici parler une Sagesse
Et sonner cette auguste Voix
Qui se connaît quand elle sonne

Along my quivering figure
The spinner's moistened finger
Traces a dreadful intent!
And the panic ascends in sobs
To my nape where it surges forth
Into a peak of sensual delight!

Ah! Let the living doors burst open!
Crack open the vain seals,
Thronging herd of terrors
Bristling with sparks!
Burst forth from funeral byres
Where my darkness nourished you
With its wondrous profusion!
Too gorged with dreams, leap up
You prickly and rough-wrought drove,
Come steaming, Fleece, in gold!

*

Thus, even more tormented,
The prophetess raves, rattles,
And bellows, fomented by
The breath of reddened gold.
But at last heaven intervenes!
The laughter-wracked high priest
Turns his ear towards the future:
She is bowed down by saintly expectation,
For a new and innocent voice
Slips out of this impure body.

*

Honour of Man, Holy LANGUAGE,
Ornate and provident speech,
Splendid chains entwining
The god lost in the flesh,
Illumination, generosity!
Now a Wisdom speaks,
Ringing out in that revered Voice
Which knows full well it is

N'être plus la voix de personne
Tant que des ondes et des bois !   230

Le sylphe

Ni vu ni connu
Je suis le parfum
Vivant et défunt
Dans le vent venu !

Ni vu ni connu   5
Hasard ou génie ?
À peine venu
La tâche est finie !

Ni lu ni compris ?
Aux meilleurs esprits   10
Que d'erreurs promises !

Ni vu ni connu,
Le temps d'un sein nu
Entre deux chemises !

L'insinuant

Ô Courbes, méandre,
Secrets du menteur,
Est-il art plus tendre
Que cette lenteur ?

Je sais où je vais,   5
Je t'y veux conduire,
Mon dessein mauvais
N'est pas de te nuire...

(Quoique souriante
En pleine fierté,   10
Tant de liberté
La désoriente !)

No longer anyone's voice
But rather that of the seas and forests!

The Sylph

Neither seen nor known
I am the perfume
Living and dead
On the wind borne!

Neither seen nor known
Genius or chance?
No sooner come
The task is done!

Neither read nor understood?
To the sharpest minds
What errors are promised!

Neither seen nor known,
The glimpse of a bare breast
Between two garments!

The Beguiler

O Twists and turns,
The deceiver's wiles,
Is there an art more tender
Than this languor?

I know where I go,
To where I long to take you,
My dark intention
Means you no harm...

(Though she smiles
Brimming with pride,
So much freedom
Bewilders her!)

Ô Courbes, méandres,
Secrets du menteur,
Je veux faire attendre   15
Le mot le plus tendre.

La fausse morte

Humblement, tendrement, sur le tombeau charmant,
     Sur l'insensible monument,
Que d'ombres, d'abandons, et d'amour prodiguée,
     Forme ta grâce fatiguée,
Je meurs, je meurs sur toi, je tombe et je m'abats,   5

Mais à peine abattu sur le sépulcre bas,
Dont la close étendue aux cendres me convie,
Cette morte apparente, en qui revient la vie,
Frémit, rouvre les yeux, m'illumine et me mord,
Et m'arrache toujours une nouvelle mort   10
     Plus précieuse que la vie.

Ébauche d'un serpent

À Henri Ghéon

Parmi l'arbre, la brise berce
La vipère que je vêtis ;
Un sourire, que la dent perce
Et qu'elle éclaire d'appétits,
Sur le Jardin se risque et rôde,   5
Et mon triangle d'émeraude
Tire sa langue à double fil...
Bête je suis, mais bête aiguë,
De qui le venin quoique vil
Laisse loin la sage ciguë !   10

Suave est ce temps de plaisance !
Tremblez, mortels ! Je suis bien fort
Quand jamais à ma suffisance,
Je bâille à briser le ressort !

O Twists and turns,
The deceiver's wiles,
I want to hold back longer
The word most tender.

Death Brushes Her Lightly

Humbly, gently, upon the delightful tomb,
    Upon the unfeeling monument,
Which your weary grace fashions
    From shadows, yieldings, and bounteous love,
I am dying, dying on you, I sink and languish.

Yet, no sooner do I slump on the low sepulchre,
Whose bounded plot summons me to ashes,
Than she, I thought dead and now come back to life,
Quivers, opens her eyes, illumes and bites me,
Wrenching from me an ever-new death
    More precious than life.

Sketch of a Serpent

For Henri Ghéon

Whispering through the leaves, the breeze
Sways the viper I wear;
A smile, pierced by a fang
Glistening with relish,
Roams and lurks above the Garden.
And my emerald triangle
Darts out its double-edged tongue...
Beast that I am, yet a sharp one,
Whose venom though vile
Can outsmart the wise hemlock!

How sweet these languid days!
Tremble, mortals! I am strong
When, never wide enough,
My yawn stretches as if to snap the spring!

La splendeur de l'azur aiguise   15
Cette guivre qui me déguise
D'animale simplicité ;
Venez à moi, race étourdie !
Je suis debout et dégourdie,
Pareille à la nécessité !   20

Soleil, soleil !... Faute éclatante !
Toi qui masques la mort, Soleil,
Sous l'azur et l'or d'une tente
Où les fleurs tiennent leur conseil ;
Par d'impénétrables délices,   25
Toi, le plus fier de mes complices,
Et de mes pièges le plus haut,
Tu gardes les cœurs de connaître
Que l'univers n'est qu'un défaut
Dans la pureté du Non-être !   30

Grand Soleil, qui sonnes l'éveil
À l'être, et de feux l'accompagnes,
Toi qui l'enfermes d'un sommeil
Trompeusement peint de campagnes,
Fauteur des fantômes joyeux   35
Qui rendent sujette des yeux
La présence obscure de l'âme,
Toujours le mensonge m'a plu
Que tu répands sur l'absolu,
Ô roi des ombres fait de flamme !   40

Verse-moi ta brute chaleur,
Où vient ma paresse glacée
Rêvasser de quelque malheur
Selon ma nature enlacée...
Ce lieu charmant qui vit la chair   45
Choir et se joindre m'est très cher !
Ma fureur, ici, se fait mûre ;
Je la conseille et la recuis,
Je m'écoute, et dans mes circuits,
Ma méditation murmure...   50

The blue splendour whets
This wyvern cloaking me
In animal simplicity;
Come unto me, bewildered race!
I am upright and alert,
A match for necessity!

Sun, O sun!... Dazzling fault!
You who shroud death, Sun,
Beneath the blue and gold vault
Where flowers hold counsel;
By unfathomable delights,
You, the proudest of my accomplices,
And the loftiest of my snares,
You shield all hearts from knowing
That the universe is but a blemish
In the purity of Non-being!

Great Sun, who sound the call
To being, and intensify by fire,
You who enfold it in a slumber
Cunningly painted with landscapes,
Fabricator of joyful fantasies
Blurring the vision of
The soul's obscure presence,
I have always loved the lie
You spread across the universe,
O king of shadows fashioned from flame!

Pour me your blistering heat,
Where my icy languor may
Muse on some misfortune which
Matches my entwined nature...
How dear to me this delightful place
Where flesh fell and blended!
Here my fury ripens;
I counsel and ponder it,
I am attuned to myself, and
My meditation murmurs through my coils...

Ô Vanité ! Cause Première !
Celui qui règne dans les Cieux,
D'une voix qui fut la lumière
Ouvrit l'univers spacieux.
Comme las de son pur spectacle,   55
Dieu lui-même a rompu l'obstacle
De sa parfaite éternité ;
Il se fit Celui qui dissipe
En conséquences, son Principe,
En étoiles, son Unité.   60

Cieux, son erreur ! Temps, sa ruine !
Et l'abîme animal, béant !...
Quelle chute dans l'origine
Étincelle au lieu de néant !...
Mais, le premier mot de son Verbe,   65
MOI !... Des astres le plus superbe
Qu'ait parlés le fou créateur,
Je suis !... Je serai !... J'illumine
La diminution divine
De tous les feux du Séducteur !   70

Objet radieux de ma haine,
Vous que j'aimais éperdument,
Vous qui dûtes de la géhenne
Donner l'empire à cet amant,
Regardez-Vous dans ma ténèbre !   75
Devant Votre image funèbre,
Orgueil de mon sombre miroir,
Si profond fut Votre malaise
Que Votre souffle sur la glaise
Fut un soupir de désespoir !   80

En vain, Vous avez, dans la fange,
Pétri de faciles enfants,
Qui de Vos actes triomphants
Tout le jour Vous fissent louange !
Sitôt pétris, sitôt soufflés,   85
Maître Serpent les a sifflés,
Les beaux enfants que Vous créâtes !

O Vanity! First Cause!
He who reigns in Heaven,*
With a voice created from light itself
Opened the boundless universe.
As if weary of his own spectacle,
God shattered the obstacle
Of his perfect eternity;
He became the One who fragments
His Principle into consequences,
His Unity into stars.

Heaven, his error! Time, his downfall!
And the gaping animal abyss!...
What a fall in the beginning
A spark instead of oblivion!...
Yet, the first word of his Language was
ME!... The most splendid star
Uttered by the mad creator,
I am!... I shall be... I illumine
The heavenly decline
Of all the Seducer's fires!

Radiant object of my loathing,
You whom I passionately loved.
You who had to give dominion
Over Gehenna* to this lover,
Behold Yourself in my gloom!
Before Your mournful image,
Pride and joy of my sombre glass,
So profound was Your disquiet
That Your breath upon the clay
Was a sigh of despair!

In vain, You modelled out of
The mire docile children who
Might have given day-long praise
To Your triumphal deeds!
No sooner moulded, no sooner blown,
Than Master Serpent whistled up
The beautiful children You created!

Holà ! dit-il, nouveaux venus !
Vous êtes des hommes tout nus,
Ô bêtes blanches et béates !   90

À la ressemblance exécrée,
Vous fûtes faits, et je vous hais !
Comme je hais le Nom qui crée
Tant de prodiges imparfaits !
Je suis Celui qui modifie,   95
Je retouche au cœur qui s'y fie,
D'un doigt sûr et mystérieux !...
Nous changerons ces molles œuvres,
Et ces évasives couleuvres
En des reptiles furieux !   100

Mon Innombrable Intelligence
Touche dans l'âme des humains
Un instrument de ma vengeance
Qui fut assemblé de tes mains !
Et ta Paternité voilée,   105
Quoique, dans sa chambre étoilée,
Elle n'accueille que l'encens,
Toutefois l'excès de mes charmes
Pourra de lointaines alarmes
Troubler ses desseins tout-puissants !   110

Je vais, je viens, je glisse, plonge,
Je disparais dans un cœur pur !
Fut-il jamais de sein si dur
Qu'on n'y puisse loger un songe ?
Qui que tu sois, ne suis-je point   115
Cette complaisance qui poind
Dans ton âme lorsqu'elle s'aime ?
Je suis au fond de sa faveur
Cette inimitable saveur
Que tu ne trouves qu'à toi-même !   120

Ève, jadis, je la surpris,
Parmi ses premières pensées,
La lèvre entr'ouverte aux esprits
Qui naissaient des roses bercées.

Hello, he exclaims, you newcomers!
You men are stark naked,
O self-righteous pale beasts!

In abhorrent likeness
Were you begotten, and I loathe you
As I loathe the Name that creates
So many defective prodigies!
I am He who alters, He who
Retouches the heart that trusts it,
With a sure and mysterious finger!...
We shall change these feeble works,
And these slippery grass snakes
Into furious reptiles!

My Boundless Intelligence
Touches within man's soul
An instrument of my vengeance
Assembled by your hands!
And though your veiled Paternity
In its star-studded vault may
Welcome only sweet-smelling incense,
Yet my plenteous charms
Can trouble with distant alarms
Its all-powerful designs!

I come, I go, I slide, I dive,
I vanish into a pure heart!
Was there ever a bosom so hard
As to stop a dream settling there?
Whoever you may be, am I not
This self-satisfaction welling up
Within your soul, when enamoured of itself?
In the depths of its favour, I am
That flavour beyond compare
Found only in yourself!

Long ago I surprised Eve,
Absorbed in her first thoughts,
Her lips half opened to spirits
Rising up from the swaying roses.

Cette parfaite m'apparut,　　　　　　　125
Son flanc vaste et d'or parcouru
Ne craignant le soleil ni l'homme ;
Tout offerte aux regards de l'air
L'âme encore stupide, et comme
Interdite au seuil de la chair.　　　　　130

Ô masse de béatitude,
Tu es si belle, juste prix
De la toute sollicitude
Des bons et des meilleurs esprits !
Pour qu'à tes lèvres ils soient pris　　135
Il leur suffit que tu soupires !
Les plus purs s'y penchent les pires,
Les plus durs sont les plus meurtris...
Jusques à moi, tu m'attendris,
De qui relèvent les vampires !　　　　140

Oui ! De mon poste de feuillage
Reptile aux extases d'oiseau,
Cependant que mon babillage
Tissait de ruses le réseau,
Je te buvais, ô belle sourde !　　　　145
Calme, claire, de charmes lourde,
Je dominais furtivement,
L'œil dans l'or ardent de ta laine,
Ta nuque énigmatique et pleine
Des secrets de ton mouvement !　　　150

J'étais présent comme une odeur,
Comme l'arôme d'une idée
Dont ne puisse être élucidée
L'insidieuse profondeur !
Et je t'inquiétais, candeur,　　　　　155
Ô chair mollement décidée,
Sans que je t'eusse intimidée,
À chanceler dans la splendeur !
Bientôt, je t'aurai, je parie,
Déjà ta nuance varie !　　　　　　　160

This perfection appeared to me,
Her ample flank rippling with gold
Fearing neither sun nor man;
All bared to the air's gaze,
The soul still senseless, as though
Forbidden on the threshold of the flesh.

O mass of bliss,
How beauteous you are, a just reward
For the immeasurable kindness
To the fine, indeed the finest minds!
To draw them to your lips
You need merely sigh!
The purest are smitten the worst,
The hardest are the most deeply wounded...
You touch even my heart
From which vampires spring!

Yes! From my leafy lair,
Reptile rapturous like a bird,
While my babble wove
A web of artful wiles,
I drank you in, unwitting beauty!
Clear and calm in my ponderous charms,
I was craftily commanding
The eye in your lustrous gold fleece,
Your enigmatic nape brimming
With the secrets of your movement!

I lingered like a scent,
Like the aroma of an idea
Whose sinister depths
Cannot be illuminated!
And I troubled your pale being,
O slackly wrought flesh,
Without having daunted you,
To waver in the splendour!
Soon, I wager, you will be mine,
Your subtle hues are already changing!

(La superbe simplicité
Demande d'immenses égards !
Sa transparence de regards,
Sottise, orgueil, félicité,
Gardent bien la belle cité !   165
Sachons lui créer des hasards,
Et par ce plus rare des arts,
Soit le cœur pur sollicité ;
C'est là mon fort, c'est là mon fin,
À moi les moyens de ma fin !)   170

Or, d'une éblouissante bave,
Filons les systèmes légers
Où l'oisive et l'Ève suave
S'engage en de vagues dangers !
Que sous une charge de soie   175
Tremble la peau de cette proie
Accoutumée au seul azur !...
Mais de gaze point de subtile,
Ni de fil invisible et sûr,
Plus qu'une trame de mon style !   180

Dore, langue ! dore-lui les
Plus doux des dits que tu connaisses !
Allusions, fables, finesses,
Mille silences ciselés,
Use de tout ce qui lui nuise :   185
Rien qui ne flatte et ne l'induise
À se perdre dans mes desseins,
Docile à ces pentes qui rendent
Aux profondeurs des bleus bassins
Les ruisseaux qui des cieux descendent !   190

Ô quelle prose non pareille,
Que d'esprit n'ai-je pas jeté
Dans le dédale duveté
De cette merveilleuse oreille !
Là, pensais-je, rien de perdu ;   195
Tout profite au cœur suspendu !
Sûr triomphe ! si ma parole,

(Superb simplicity
Demands the greatest care!
Its transparent gaze,
Stupidity, pride, and bliss so ably
Guard the walls of the grand citadel!
Let us contrive some risks for it,
And by the rarest artistry,
Tempt the purest heart;
That is my talent, that is my acute flair,
I alone chose the means of my end!)

So, from a dazzling slaver,
Let us weave delicate webs
Where soft and languid Eve
Is drawn into unforeseen danger!
May the skin of this prey that has grown
Accustomed to only the blue expanse
Quiver beneath the plenteous silk!...
Yet there is no finer gauze,
No gossamer thread to match
The stylish weft I spin!

Gild them, tongue, gild for her the
Sweetest words you know!
Allusions, fables, niceties,
A myriad crafted silences,
Use any means that may do her harm:
All that may flatter and lead her
Astray in my designs,
Yielding to these slopes where
Streams from the heavens flow back
To the lakes' blue depths!

O what peerless prose,
What dazzling wit did I not cast
Into the downy maze
Of this wondrous ear!
Nothing, I thought, is lost there;
All benefits the suspended heart!
Triumph is assured! if my words

De l'âme obsédant le trésor,
Comme une abeille une corolle
Ne quitte plus l'oreille d'or !   200

'Rien, lui soufflais-je, n'est moins sûr
Que la parole divine, Ève !
Une science vive crève
L'énormité de ce fruit mûr !
N'écoute l'Être vieil et pur   205
Qui maudit la morsure brève !
Que si ta bouche fait un rêve,
Cette soif qui songe à la sève,
Ce délice à demi futur,
C'est l'éternité fondante, Ève !'   210

Elle buvait mes petits mots
Qui bâtissaient une œuvre étrange ;
Son œil, parfois, perdait un ange
Pour revenir à mes rameaux.
Le plus rusé des animaux   215
Qui te raille d'être si dure,
Ô perfide et grosse de maux,
N'est qu'une voix dans la verdure !
—Mais sérieuse l'Ève était
Qui sous la branche l'écoutait !   220

'Âme,' disais-je, 'doux séjour
De toute extase prohibée,
Sens-tu la sinueuse amour
Que j'ai du Père dérobée ?
Je l'ai, cette essence du Ciel,   225
À des fins plus douces que miel
Délicatement ordonnée...
Prends de ce fruit... Dresse ton bras !
Pour cueillir ce que tu voudras
Ta belle main te fut donnée !'   230

Quel silence battu d'un cil !
Mais quel souffle sous le sein sombre
Que mordait l'Arbre de son ombre !
L'autre brillait, comme un pistil !

Laying siege to the soul's treasure
Like a bee in a flower's whorl,
Never leave the golden ear!

'Nothing,' I whispered, 'Eve, is less certain
Than the divine word!
Living knowledge bursts
The enormity of this ripe fruit!
Heed not the ancient and pure Being
Who cursed the swift bite!
For should your mouth dream,
This thirst longing for sap,
This near-imminent delight, Eve,
Is eternity slowly melting!'

She drank in my trifling words,
All building a mysterious work;
At times her gaze drifted from an angel's trail
To return to my bough.
The most cunning of animals
Scorning you for being so hard,
O treacherous one, bloated with wickedness,
Is but a voice among the leaves!
—But solemn Eve was
Listening intently beneath the bough!

'Soul,' said I, 'sweet sanctuary
Of all forbidden delights,
Can you feel the sinuous love
I stole from the Father?
For purposes sweeter than honey,
I have delicately designed
This essence from Heaven...
Taste this fruit... Raise your arm!
You were given that lovely hand
To pluck what you will!'

What silence a closing eyelash begets!
Yet what a breath from the dark breast
Which the tree's shadow has bitten!
The other gleamed like a pistil!

—*Siffle, siffle* ! me chantait-il !   235
Et je sentais frémir le nombre,
Tout le long de mon fouet subtil,
De ces replis dont je m'encombre :
Ils roulaient depuis le béryl
De ma crête, jusqu'au péril !   240

Génie ! Ô longue impatience !
À la fin, les temps sont venus,
Qu'un pas vers la neuve Science
Va donc jaillir de ces pieds nus !
Le marbre aspire, l'or se cambre !   245
Ces blondes bases d'ombre et d'ambre
Tremblent au bord du mouvement !...
Elle chancelle, la grande urne,
D'où va fuir le consentement
De l'apparente taciturne !   250

Du plaisir que tu te proposes
Cède, cher corps, cède aux appâts !
Que ta soif de métamorphoses
Autour de l'Arbre du Trépas
Engendre une chaîne de poses !   255
Viens sans venir ! forme des pas
Vaguement comme lourds de roses...
Danse, cher corps... Ne pense pas !
Ici les délices sont causes
Suffisantes au cours des choses !...   260

Ô follement que je m'offrais
Cette infertile jouissance :
Voir le long pur d'un dos si frais
Frémir la désobéissance !...
Déjà délivrant son essence   265
De sagesse et d'illusions,
Tout l'Arbre de la Connaissance
Échevelé de visions,
Agitait son grand corps qui plonge
Au soleil, et suce le songe !   270

—*Hiss, hiss!* it hummed to me!
And along my smooth curving whip,
I felt a quiver flow down
Through my ponderous coils,
Rippling from my beryl* crest
To my tapered tip of peril!

Genius! O tedious impatience!
Now the time has finally come
When a step towards new Science
Will spring forth from these bare feet!
The marble inhales, the gold stretches!
These light-coloured foundations of amber and shade
Quiver on the verge of movement!...
The great urn totters and from it
Will seep the consent of
She who seemed so reserved!

Yield, dear body, yield to the
Enticing pleasure you dream of!
May your longing for transformation
Beget a ring of poses
Around the Tree of Death!
Come, without appearing to! Tread
Lightly, as though burdened with roses...
Dance, dear body... Push aside your thoughts!
Here delights are causes
Sufficient to the course of things!...

O how wildly I indulged in
This barren rapture:
To behold a back's graceful curve
Shudder in defiance!...
Yielding so soon its essence
Of wisdom and illusion,
The entire Tree of Knowledge
Dishevelled by visions,
Tossed its towering form, thrusting itself
To the sun and sucking at dreams!

Arbre, grand Arbre, Ombre des Cieux,
Irrésistible Arbre des arbres,
Qui dans les faiblesses des marbres,
Poursuis des sucs délicieux,
Toi qui pousses tels labyrinthes   275
Par qui les ténèbres étreintes
S'iront perdre dans le saphir
De l'éternelle matinée,
Douce perte, arôme ou zéphir,
Ou colombe prédestinée,   280

Ô Chanteur, ô secret buveur
Des plus profondes pierreries,
Berceau du reptile rêveur
Qui jeta l'Ève en rêveries,
Grand Être agité de savoir,   285
Qui toujours, comme pour mieux voir,
Grandis à l'appel de ta cime,
Toi qui dans l'or très pur promeus
Tes bras durs, tes rameaux fumeux,
D'autre part, creusant vers l'abîme,   290

Tu peux repousser l'infini
Qui n'est fait que de ta croissance,
Et de la tombe jusqu'au nid
Te sentir toute Connaissance !
Mais ce vieil amateur d'échecs,   295
Dans l'or oisif des soleils secs,
Sur ton branchage vient se tordre ;
Ses yeux font frémir ton trésor.
Il en cherra des fruits de mort,
De désespoir et de désordre !   300

Beau serpent, bercé dans le bleu,
Je siffle, avec délicatesse,
Offrant à la gloire de Dieu
Le triomphe de ma tristesse...
Il me suffit que dans les airs,   305
L'immense espoir de fruits amers
Affole les fils de la fange...

Tree, mighty Tree, Shadow of Heaven,
Irresistible Tree of trees,
Seeking the delicious sap
In the marble's imperfections,
You who spread such a tangled maze to
Where the tightly clutched darkness is drawn
To vanish in the sapphire expanse
Of everlasting morning.
Sweet loss, scent, zephyr
Or predestined dove,

O Singer, O secret drinker
Of deep-buried gemstones,
Cradle of the languorous reptile
That lulled Eve into dreamy slumber,
Great Being astir with knowledge,
And, all the better to see,
Growing at your crown's command,
You who display in lustrous gold
Your hard boughs, your hazy limbs,
While sending forth roots into the abyss,

You may push back infinity
Which is but the measure of your growth,
And from the tomb to the nest aloft
Feel you are all Knowledge!
Yet this old lover of chess,
Bathed in the glow of expiring suns,
Comes coiling on your boughs;
His gaze makes your bounty quiver.
From it will fall fruits of death,
Disarray, and despair!

Splendid serpent, swayed in the blue,
Delicately I hiss,
Offering to the glory of God
The triumph of my sorrow...
It suffices me if, in the air,
The boundless hope of bitter fruit
Should drive the children of the mire mad...

—Cette soif qui te fit géant,
Jusqu'à l'Être exalte l'étrange
Toute-Puissance du Néant !   310

Les grenades

Dures grenades entr'ouvertes
Cédant à l'excès de vos grains,
Je crois voir des fronts souverains
Éclatés de leurs découvertes !

Si les soleils par vous subis,   5
Ô grenades entre-bâillées
Vous ont fait d'orgueil travaillées
Craquer les cloisons de rubis,

Et que si l'or sec de l'écorce
À la demande d'une force   10
Crève en gemmes rouges de jus,

Cette lumineuse rupture
Fait rêver une âme que j'eus
De sa secrète architecture.

Le vin perdu

J'ai, quelque jour, dans l'Océan,
(Mais je ne sais plus sous quels cieux),
Jeté, comme offrande au néant,
Tout un peu de vin précieux...

Qui voulut ta perte, ô liqueur ?   5
J'obéis peut-être au devin ?
Peut-être au souci de mon cœur,
Songeant au sang, versant le vin ?

Sa transparence accoutumée
Après une rose fumée   10
Reprit aussi pure la mer...

—This thirst that made you grow so immense
Exalts, to the point of Being, the mysterious
Power of almighty Nothingness!

Pomegranates

Hard sundered pomegranates
Yielding to the surfeit of seeds,
I think of you as sovereign brows
Burst open by their discoveries!

If the suns you have weathered,
O pomegranates with rind agape,
Leave you so swollen with pride
As to crack open the partitioned rubies,

And if the peel's wizened gold
Obeying some force within,
Burst in red juicy gems,

This glistening rupture
Leads a soul I once had to dream
Of its secret architecture.

Lost Wine

One day, into the Ocean
(Yet beneath what skies I no longer recall),
I cast, as though an offering to oblivion,
More than a little precious wine...

Who, O liquor, willed your demise?
Did I perhaps bow to some oracle?
Or perhaps some anxiety of my soul,
Dreaming of blood and pouring the wine?

After a rosy spume,
The sea became limpid once more,
As pure as it was before...

Perdu ce vin, ivres les ondes !...
J'ai vu bondir dans l'air amer
Les figures les plus profondes...

Intérieur

Une esclave aux longs yeux chargés de molles chaînes
Change l'eau de mes fleurs, plonge aux glaces
   prochaines,
Au lit mystérieux prodigue ses doigts purs ;
Elle met une femme au milieu de ces murs
Qui, dans ma rêverie errant avec décence,   5
Passe entre mes regards sans briser leur absence,
Comme passe le verre au travers du soleil,
Et de la raison pure épargne l'appareil.

Le Cimetière marin

Μή, φίλα ψυχά, βίον ἀθάνατον
σπεῦδε, τὰν δ' ἔμπρακτον ἄντλει μαχανάν.
Pindare, *Pythiques*, III

Ce toit tranquille, où marchent des colombes,
Entre les pins palpite, entre les tombes ;
Midi le juste y compose de feux
La mer, la mer, toujours recommencée !
Ô récompense après une pensée   5
Qu'un long regard sur le calme des dieux !

Quel pur travail de fins éclairs consume
Maint diamant d'imperceptible écume,
Et quelle paix semble se concevoir !
Quand sur l'abîme un soleil se repose,   10
Ouvrages purs d'une éternelle cause,
Le Temps scintille et le Songe est savoir.

Stable trésor, temple simple à Minerve,
Masse de calme, et visible réserve,
Eau sourcilleuse, Œil qui gardes en toi   15

Lost was the wine, drunken the waves!...
I saw fathomless shapes
Leaping in the briny air...

Interior

A slave girl, her long eyes burdened with soft chains,
Changes the water of my flowers, immerses herself
    in the nearby mirrors,
Lavishes her delicate fingers at the mysterious bed;
She places a woman within these walls
Who, wandering light-footed in my daydreams,
Slips between my glances without disturbing their absence,
As a glass passes across the sun's ray,
Sparing the workings of pure reason.

The Graveyard by the Sea

> Do not aspire, dear soul, to immortal
> life, but exhaust the realm of the possible.*
> Pindar, Pythian [Odes], 3

This tranquil roof, where doves amble,
Quivers between the pines, between the tombs;
Noon the just composes with flames
The sea, the sea, eternally renewed!
O what rich reward after a thought
A languid gaze upon the calm of the gods!

What finely wrought lightning consumes
Many a diamond of evanescent foam,
And what peace seems to descend!
When a sun lingers over the abyss,
Supreme workings of an eternal cause,
Time gleams and Dream is knowledge.

Serene trove, simple temple to Minerva,
Boundless expanse, and visible reserve,
Haughty waters, Eye concealing within

Tant de sommeil sous un voile de flamme,
Ô mon silence !... Édifice dans l'âme,
Mais comble d'or aux mille tuiles, Toit !

Temple du Temps, qu'un seul soupir résume,
À ce point pur je monte et m'accoutume,   20
Tout entouré de mon regard marin ;
Et comme aux dieux mon offrande suprême,
La scintillation sereine sème
Sur l'altitude un dédain souverain.

Comme le fruit se fond en jouissance,   25
Comme en délice il change son absence
Dans une bouche où sa forme se meurt,
Je hume ici ma future fumée,
Et le ciel chante à l'âme consumée
Le changement des rives en rumeur.   30

Beau ciel, vrai ciel, regarde-moi qui change !
Après tant d'orgueil, après tant d'étrange
Oisiveté, mais pleine de pouvoir,
Je m'abandonne à ce brillant espace,
Sur les maisons des morts mon ombre passe   35
Qui m'apprivoise à son frêle mouvoir.

L'âme exposée aux torches du solstice,
Je te soutiens, admirable justice
De la lumière aux armes sans pitié !
Je te tends pure à ta place première :   40
Regarde-toi !... Mais rendre la lumière
Suppose d'ombre une morne moitié.

Ô pour moi seul, à moi seul, en moi-même,
Auprès d'un cœur, aux sources du poème,
Entre le vide et l'événement pur,   45
J'attends l'écho de ma grandeur interne,
Amère, sombre et sonore citerne,
Sonnant dans l'âme un creux toujours futur !

Sais-tu, fausse captive des feuillages,
Golfe mangeur de ces maigres grillages,   50
Sur mes yeux clos, secrets éblouissants,

So much slumber beneath a flaming veil,
O my silence!... Edifice in the soul,
Yet gilded loft, Roof of a myriad tiles!

Temple of Time, distilled in a single sigh,
I climb and become attuned to the upper reaches,
Bounded by the gaze I cast upon the sea;
And as my ultimate offering to the gods,
The gleaming and still expanse sprinkles
A sovereign distain on high.

As a fruit melts into pleasure,
Changing its absence to pure delight
In a mouth where its shape dissolves,
Here I breathe in smoke I shall become,
And the sky sings to the consumed soul
Of shores fading to a gentle murmur.

Beauteous sky, true sky, it is I you see change!
After so much pride, after so much strange
Languor, yet brimming with vigour,
I surrender myself to this dazzling space,
My shadow slips over the houses of the dead
Subduing me to its frail movement.

With my soul bared to the torches of the solstice,
I can withstand you, admirable justice
Of light, armed with your merciless weapons!
I return you pure to your primal place:
Look at yourself!... Yet to reflect light
Supposes a half in deep shadow.

O for me alone, to me alone, within myself,
Close to a heart, at the poem's source,
Between the void and the pure event,
I await the echo of my grandeur within,
Bitter, sombre, and resonant cistern,
An ever-future hollow resounding in the soul!

Do you know, false captive of the leaves,
Gulf devouring these flimsy trellises,
Dazzling secrets upon my closed eyes,

Quel corps me traîne à sa fin paresseuse,
Quel front l'attire à cette terre osseuse ?
Une étincelle y pense à mes absents.

Fermé, sacré, plein d'un feu sans matière,   55
Fragment terrestre offert à la lumière,
Ce lieu me plaît, dominé de flambeaux,
Composé d'or, de pierre et d'arbres sombres,
Où tant de marbre est tremblant sur tant d'ombres ;
La mer fidèle y dort sur mes tombeaux !   60

Chienne splendide, écarte l'idolâtre !
Quand solitaire au sourire de pâtre,
Je pais longtemps, moutons mystérieux,
Le blanc troupeau de mes tranquilles tombes,
Éloignes-en les prudentes colombes,   65
Les songes vains, les anges curieux !

Ici venu, l'avenir est paresse.
L'insecte net gratte la sécheresse ;
Tout est brûlé, défait, reçu dans l'air
À je ne sais quelle sévère essence...   70
La vie est vaste, étant ivre d'absence,
Et l'amertume est douce, et l'esprit clair.

Les morts cachés sont bien dans cette terre
Qui les réchauffe et sèche leur mystère.
Midi là-haut, Midi sans mouvement   75
En soi se pense et convient à soi-même...
Tête complète et parfait diadème,
Je suis en toi le secret changement.

Tu n'as que moi pour contenir tes craintes !
Mes repentirs, mes doutes, mes contraintes   80
Sont le défaut de ton grand diamant...
Mais dans leur nuit toute lourde de marbres,
Un peuple vague aux racines des arbres
A pris déjà ton parti lentement.

Ils ont fondu dans une absence épaisse,   85
L'argile rouge a bu la blanche espèce,
Le don de vivre a passé dans les fleurs !

What body drags me to its languid end,
What mind lures it to the bone-rich soil?
A spark therein ponders my absent ones.

Enclosed, hallowed, abounding in fire without matter,
A patch of earth offered up to light,
This spot delights me, overshadowed by torches,
Wrought of gilt, stone, and gloomy trees,
Where bountiful marble quivers on myriad shadows;
There upon my tombs slumbers the faithful sea!

Resplendent dog, keep the idolater at bay!
When all alone and smiling like a shepherd,
I graze long my mysterious sheep,
The white flock of my tranquil tombs,
Ward off the wary doves,
The futile dreams and the prying angels!

Once here, the future is languor.
The clear-cut insect scratches at the dryness;
All is scorched, decayed, borne away by the wind
Into who knows what austere essence...
Life is boundless, heady with absence,
And bitterness is sweet, and the mind clear.

The hidden dead rest easy in this earth
Warming them through and drying their mystery.
High Noon, motionless Noon
Pondering its very being and suited to itself...
Complete intelligence and perfect diadem,
In you I am the secret change.

You have but me to contain your fears!
My remorse, my doubts, and my limits
Are the defect in your great diamond...
Yet in their marble-bounded night,
An elusive people among the tree roots
Has gradually taken your side.

They have blended into a dense absence,
The red clay has drunk the pale-skinned race,
The gift of life has passed into flowers!

Où sont des morts les phrases familières,
L'art personnel, les âmes singulières ?
La larve file où se formaient des pleurs.   90

Les cris aigus des filles chatouillées,
Les yeux, les dents, les paupières mouillées,
Le sein charmant qui joue avec le feu,
Le sang qui brille aux lèvres qui se rendent,
Les derniers dons, les doigts qui les défendent,   95
Tout va sous terre et rentre dans le jeu !

Et vous, grande âme, espérez-vous un songe
Qui n'aura plus ces couleurs de mensonge
Qu'aux yeux de chair l'onde et l'or font ici ?
Chanterez-vous quand serez vaporeuse ?   100
Allez ! Tout fuit ! Ma présence est poreuse,
La sainte impatience meurt aussi !

Maigre immortalité noire et dorée,
Consolatrice affreusement laurée,
Qui de la mort fais un sein maternel,   105
Le beau mensonge et la pieuse ruse !
Qui ne connaît, et qui ne les refuse,
Ce crâne vide et ce rire éternel !

Pères profonds, têtes inhabitées,
Qui sous le poids de tant de pelletées,   110
Êtes la terre et confondez nos pas,
Le vrai rongeur, le ver irréfutable
N'est point pour vous qui dormez sous la table,
Il vit de vie, il ne me quitte pas !

Amour, peut-être, ou de moi-même haine ?   115
Sa dent secrète est de moi si prochaine
Que tous les noms lui peuvent convenir !
Qu'importe ! Il voit, il veut, il songe, il touche !
Ma chair lui plaît, et jusque sur ma couche,
À ce vivant je vis d'appartenir !   120

Zénon ! Cruel Zénon ! Zénon d'Élée !
M'as-tu percé de cette flèche ailée
Qui vibre, vole, et qui ne vole pas !

Where now are the familiar phrases of the dead,
Their personal ways and their singular souls?
The worm threads its way where tears once formed.

The shrill cries of tickled girls,
The eyes, the teeth, the moistened eyelids,
The charming breast dallying with the flame,
The blood gleaming upon yielding lips,
The final gifts, the fingers shielding them,
All goes to the earth and back into the game!

And you, great soul, do you still long for a dream
Free of these deceitful colours which
The waters and the gold light create for eyes of flesh?
Will you still sing when turned to thin air?
Come now! All fades away! My very presence is porous,
Holy impatience also dies!

Gaunt immortality, black and gilded,
Hideously laurelled comforter
Fashioning from death a maternal breast,
The lovely lie and the pious wile!
Who does not know, and who cannot refuse
This empty skull and this eternal grin!

Fathers buried deep in the ground, heads long uninhabited,
Who, beneath ponderous spadefuls, have become
The earth itself and who confuse our steps,
The true gnawing and irrefutable worm
Is not for you at rest in the tomb,
It lives on life, and it never leaves me!

Love, perhaps, or hatred of myself?
Its secret tooth is so close to me
That any name could suit it!
No matter! It sees, desires, dreams, and touches!
My flesh delights it, and even where I lie,
I live to be one with this living being!

Zeno! Cruel Zeno! Zeno of Elea!*
How you have pierced me with this fledged arrow
Which quivers, flies, and yet does not fly!

Le son m'enfante et la flèche me tue !
Ah ! le soleil... Quelle ombre de tortue 125
Pour l'âme, Achille immobile à grands pas !

Non, non !... Debout ! Dans l'ère successive !
Brisez, mon corps, cette forme pensive !
Buvez, mon sein, la naissance du vent !
Une fraîcheur, de la mer exhalée, 130
Me rend mon âme... Ô puissance salée !
Courons à l'onde en rejaillir vivant.

Oui ! Grande mer de délires douée,
Peau de panthère et chlamyde trouée,
De mille et mille idoles du soleil, 135
Hydre absolue, ivre de ta chair bleue,
Qui te remords l'étincelante queue
Dans un tumulte au silence pareil,

Le vent se lève !... Il faut tenter de vivre !
L'air immense ouvre et referme mon livre, 140
La vague en poudre ose jaillir des rocs !
Envolez-vous, pages tout éblouies !
Rompez, vagues ! Rompez d'eaux réjouies
Ce toit tranquille où picoraient des focs !

Ode secrète

Chute superbe, fin si douce,
Oubli des luttes, quel délice
Que d'étendre à même la mousse
Après la danse, le corps lisse !

Jamais une telle lueur 5
Que ces étincelles d'été
Sur un front semé de sueur
N'avait la victoire fêté !

Mais touché par le Crépuscule,
Ce grand corps qui fit tant de choses, 10
Qui dansait, qui rompit Hercule,
N'est plus qu'une masse de roses !

The sound gives me life, and the arrow slays!
Ah! the sun... What a tortoise-like shadow for
The soul to see Achilles motionless in full stride!

No, no!... Arise! Move into the unfolding years!
Break, my body, this thinking form!
Breathe in, my breast, the wind now stirring!
A freshness, exhaled by the sea,
Restores my soul... O briny potency! Let us run
To the waves and leap out brimming with life!

Yes! Mighty sea, blessed with wild furies,
Panther-like skin and chlamys rent with holes
By the sun's myriad idols,
Absolute hydra, intoxicated on your blue flesh,
Ever biting your gleaming tail
In a tumult akin to silence,

The wind is rising!... Let us try to live!
The boundless air opens and closes my book,
The wave's powdered plume dares dash up from the rocks!
Fly off, sun-dazzled pages!
Break, waves! With rapturous crests, shatter
This peaceful roof where spinnaker sails pecked!

Secret Ode

Superb the fall, sweet the end,
The struggles forgotten, what joy in
Stretching the smooth body
Upon the bare moss after the dance!

Never had such a glow
As these glimmers of summer
Upon a brow beaded with sweat
A victory to celebrate!

Yet touched by the Gloaming,
This great body which accomplished so much,
Which danced and overcame Hercules,
Is no more than a heap of roses!

Dormez, sous les pas sidéraux,
Vainqueur lentement désuni,
Car l'Hydre inhérente au héros   15
S'est éployée à l'infini...

Ô quel Taureau, quel Chien, quelle Ourse,
Quels objets de victoire énorme,
Quand elle entre aux temps sans ressource
L'âme impose à l'espace informe !   20

Fin suprême, étincellement
Qui, par les monstres et les dieux,
Proclame universellement
Les grands actes qui sont aux Cieux !

Le rameur

À André Lebey

Penché contre un grand fleuve, infiniment mes rames
M'arrachent à regret aux riants environs ;
Âme aux pesantes mains, pleines des avirons,
Il faut que le ciel cède au glas des lentes lames.

Le cœur dur, l'œil distrait des beautés que je bats,   5
Laissant autour de moi mûrir des cercles d'onde,
Je veux à larges coups rompre l'illustre monde
De feuilles et de feu que je chante tout bas.

Arbres sur qui je passe, ample et naïve moire,
Eau de ramages peinte, et paix de l'accompli,   10
Déchire-les, ma barque, impose-leur un pli
Qui coure du grand calme abolir la mémoire.

Jamais, charmes du jour, jamais vos grâces n'ont
Tant souffert d'un rebelle essayant sa défense :
Mais, comme les soleils m'ont tiré de l'enfance,   15
Je remonte à la source où cesse même un nom.

En vain, toute la nymphe énorme et continue
Empêche de bras purs mes membres harassés ;

Slumber beneath the starry steps,
Vanquisher, now slowly waning,
For the Hydra that dwells in the hero
Has spread itself to infinity...

O what Bull, what Dog, what Bear,
What honours of glorious victory
The soul imposes on formless space,
When it enters time drained of its riches!

Supreme the end, a twinkling
Proclaiming to the universe,
Through monsters and gods,
Heaven's almighty acts!

The Rower

For André Lebey

Arched against a great river, my endless strokes
Wrench me heavy-hearted from the smiling shores;
Soul of ponderous hands, clasping the oars,
The sky must yield to the blades' slow knell.

Hardened heart, eye drawn to the beauty I smite,
Letting rippling circles ripen all round me,
I strive with broad sweeps to break the gleaming realm
Of foliage and of fire I softly sing.

Trees I slide upon, plenteous and pristine silk,
Leaf-dappled waters, peacefully complete,
Cleave them, my boat, impose on them a crease
Which leaves no memory of this great calm.

Never, delights of day, never have your graces
Endured so much from a rebel trying his defence:
But, as suns have drawn me from childhood,
I return to the source where even names are no more.

The nymph's whole being, enormous and unrelenting,
Hinders in vain my harried limbs with her graceful arms;

Je romprai lentement mille liens glacés
Et les barbes d'argent de sa puissance nue.   20

Ce bruit secret des eaux, ce fleuve étrangement
Place mes jours dorés sous un bandeau de soie ;
Rien plus aveuglément n'use l'antique joie
Qu'un bruit de fuite égale et de nul changement.

Sous les ponts annelés, l'eau profonde me porte,   25
Voûtes pleines de vent, de murmure et de nuit,
Ils courent sur un front qu'ils écrasent d'ennui,
Mais dont l'os orgueilleux est plus dur que leur porte.

Leur nuit passe longtemps. L'âme baisse sous eux
Ses sensibles soleils et ses promptes paupières,   30
Quand, par le mouvement qui me revêt de pierres,
Je m'enfonce au mépris de tant d'azur oiseux.

Palme

À Jeannie

De sa grâce redoutable
Voilant à peine l'éclat,
Un ange met sur ma table
Le pain tendre, le lait plat ;
Il me fait de la paupière   5
Le signe d'une prière
Qui parle à ma vision :
—Calme, calme, reste calme !
Connais le poids d'une palme
Portant sa profusion !   10

Pour autant qu'elle se plie
À l'abondance des biens,
Sa figure est accomplie,
Ses fruits lourds sont ses liens.
Admire comme elle vibre,   15
Et comme une lente fibre
Qui divise le moment,

Slowly I shall sever myriad frozen bonds
And the silvery barbs of her bare potency.

These gentle purling waters, this river mysteriously
Lays my gilded days beneath a silken band;
Nothing more blindly frays the antique delight
Than the sound of steady, smooth flight.

Beneath the ringed bridges, the deep water bears me,
Vaults, echoing with swirling winds and murmuring night,
Glide above a brow crushed by their weariness,
But whose pride-filled bone is harder than their gate.

Their night slowly passes. Beneath them my soul
Lowers its perceiving suns and its flickering eyelids,
When, with a movement cloaking me in stone,
I plunge in contempt of this languid blue expanse.

Palm

For Jeannie

Scarcely veiling the splendour
Of its striking grace,
An angel lays upon my table
Soft bread and still milk;
With a flicker of his eyelid he makes
The sign of a prayer that
Speaks to my vision:
—Calm, calm, stay calm!
Feel the weighty palm
Bearing its abundance!

For as much as it may bend
Beneath its rich bounty,
Its form is fulfilled,
Its ponderous fruits are its bonds.
Marvel at how it sways,
And like a slow sinew
Cleaving the moment,

Départage sans mystère
L'attirance de la terre
Et le poids du firmament !   20

Ce bel arbitre mobile
Entre l'ombre et le soleil,
Simule d'une sibylle
La sagesse et le sommeil.
Autour d'une même place   25
L'ample palme ne se lasse
Des appels ni des adieux...
Qu'elle est noble, qu'elle est tendre !
Qu'elle est digne de s'attendre
À la seule main des dieux !   30

L'or léger qu'elle murmure
Sonne au simple doigt de l'air,
Et d'une soyeuse armure
Charge l'âme du désert.
Une voix impérissable   35
Qu'elle rend au vent de sable
Qui l'arrose de ses grains,
À soi-même sert d'oracle,
Et se flatte du miracle
Que se chantent les chagrins.   40

Cependant qu'elle s'ignore
Entre le sable et le ciel,
Chaque jour qui luit encore
Lui compose un peu de miel.
Sa douceur est mesurée   45
Par la divine durée
Qui ne compte pas les jours,
Mais bien qui les dissimule
Dans un suc où s'accumule
Tout l'arôme des amours.   50

Parfois si l'on désespère,
Si l'adorable rigueur
Malgré tes larmes n'opère
Que sous ombre de langueur,

Naturally decides between
The lure of the earth
And heaven's great burden!

This beauteous and limber arbiter
Between the shadow and the sun,
Imitates the wisdom and
The slumber of a sibyl.
All about this same place
The ample palm never wearies
Of greetings or farewells...
How noble and gentle it is!
How worthy it is to await
Only the hand of the gods!

The light gold it murmurs
Resounds at the air's gentle touch,
And with a silken mail
Burdens the desert's soul.
An undying voice which
It restores to the sandy wind,
Sprinkling it with seeds,
Acts as its own oracle, and
Prides itself on the miracle which
Sorrows sing to themselves.

Though unaware of its own
Presence between sand and sky,
Each resplendent day
Yields a little more honey.
Its sweetness is measured
By the divine duration
Not counted in days,
But instead conceals them
In a sap where all
Of love's aroma is stored.

If at times you despair,
If, despite your tears,
The delightful strictness works
Only in the guise of languor,

N'accuse pas d'être avare   55
Une Sage qui prépare
Tant d'or et d'autorité :
Par la sève solennelle
Une espérance éternelle
Monte à la maturité !   60

Ces jours qui te semblent vides
Et perdus pour l'univers
Ont des racines avides
Qui travaillent les déserts.
La substance chevelue   65
Par les ténèbres élue
Ne peut s'arrêter jamais,
Jusqu'aux entrailles du monde,
De poursuivre l'eau profonde
Que demandent les sommets.   70

Patience, patience,
Patience dans l'azur !
Chaque atome de silence
Est la chance d'un fruit mûr !
Viendra l'heureuse surprise :   75
Une colombe, la brise,
L'ébranlement le plus doux,
Une femme qui s'appuie,
Feront tomber cette pluie
Où l'on se jette à genoux !   80

Qu'un peuple à présent s'écroule,
Palme !... irrésistiblement !
Dans la poudre qu'il se roule
Sur les fruits du firmament !
Tu n'as pas perdu ces heures   85
Si légère tu demeures
Après ces beaux abandons ;
Pareille à celui qui pense
Et dont l'âme se dépense
À s'accroître de ses dons !   90

Do not accuse of miserliness
A Sage who is preparing
Such bountiful gold and authority:
Through the solemn sap
An everlasting hope
Rises to maturity!

These days that seem empty to you
And lost for the universe
Send forth eager roots that
Burrow into the arid soil.
The hair-covered clump
To the darkness assigned
Can never stop seeking
Within the earth's entrails
The deep water which
The treetops demand.

Patience, patience,
Patience in the blue heavens!
Every atom of silence
Holds the promise of ripened fruit!
The pleasant surprise will come:
A dove, the breath of wind,
The most delicate swaying,
A woman languidly leaning,
Will release that rain
Whereupon we sink to our knees!

May a people now fall,
Palm!... irresistibly!
May they wallow in the dust
Upon the fruits of heaven!
These lost hours have not been in vain
So light have you remained
After such beautiful yielding;
Like the thinker
Whose soul expends itself
In growing with its offering!

DOUZE POÈMES

La Jeune Fille

Je suis la jeune fille bleue
Et souple et rose et docte et si
Jolie avec toute une lieue
Marine à l'ombre du sourcil !

Voici ta plus fraîche pensée   5
Quand mon iris vraiment iris
Pour éphémère fiancée
Te laisse un regret d'oasis.

Tandis que tu songes d'écrire
Ce qu'a vu ton œil voyageur   10
S'il me voit rougissante rire,
Tu n'oublieras plus ma rougeur.

Et dans la braise et sous la lampe,
Sur la feuille où le doigt posé
Vainement tomba de la tempe,   15
Reviendra mon rire rosé.

Aux flammes se mêle la souple
Jeune fille vive qui sait
Encor mal garder une couple
De colombes dans son corset.   20

L'abeille spirituelle

Ô dieu démon démiurge ou destin
Mon appétit comme une abeille vive
Scintille et sonne environ le festin
Duquel ta grâce a voulu que je vive.

Ici dans l'or la muse a mis ce miel ;   5
Là dans le verre une clarté choisie
Tient froidement la lumière du ciel
Algèbre pure et glacée ambroisie.

TWELVE POEMS

The Maiden

I am the maiden,
Blue and lissom, rosy and learned,
Beauteous with my eyelid shading
A great league of ocean!

Here is your freshest thought
When my rainbow-coloured iris
For a fleeting bride-to-be
Leaves you yearning for an oasis.

Whilst you dream of writing
What your roaming eye has seen
If it glimpses me blushing as I laugh,
My flushed cheek will long remain with you.

And in the embers beneath the lamp,
Upon the page where the finger there placed
Fell vainly from the temple,
My rosy laughter will come again.

The lithe and lively maiden
Blends with the flames, not
Knowing still how to retain
A brace of doves in her corset.

Spiritual Bee

O god demon demiurge or destiny
My appetite like a lively bee
Shimmers and hums around the feast
With which your grace sought to sustain me.

Here the muse laid this honey in gold;
There in the glass a chosen clarity
Coldly holds the sky's radiance
Pure algebra and iced ambrosia.

Le libre amour du bel entendement
Ô difficile et trop légère abeille   10
Du même fil se croise et se dément,
Heurte la coupe et manque la corbeille.

Ce point sonore atome le très pur
Chargé de foudre et follement futile
Va-t-il porter la vie unique sur   15
Le plus beau songe et le plus inutile ?

Le diable au corps c'est le recul de Dieu
La flamme court fuyant la cendre pure
Chaque soleil n'est qu'un rien radieux
Qui fait pâlir son aurore future.   20

Où te poser bourdon de l'absolu
Instant toujours détaché de toi-même ?
Tout ce qu'il touche est sûrement élu
Indivisible angoisse du poème.

J'aime l'erreur qui tisse un long chemin   25
Dans une nuit non avare de mondes ;
La veille y brille avec son lendemain
Au même sein des ténèbres fécondes.

Béatrice

Le moindre pli de cette amour
Inflige la plus grande peine ;
Un instant fait noircir un jour,
Un soupir te rend incertaine,

Te fait paraître sans retour.   5
Et tu me sembles si lointaine
Quand au fond de cette fontaine
Où se reflète mon amour

Je crois voir d'assez tristes signes,
Des ombres de soleils insignes,   10
Et des reprises de tes yeux ;

Free love of beautiful understanding
O fussy and all too dizzy bee
Crosses its own path and belies itself,
Striking the bowl and missing the flowerbed.

This sonorous speck, atom most pure
Charged with lightning and wildly capricious,
Will it bring its distinct life to bear on
The most wondrous and pointless dream?

The devil who dwells in the body is God's retreat,
The spreading flame leaves but ash in its wake,
Each sun is no more than a glowing void
Making dawns yet to come turn pale.

Where will you alight, drone of the absolute,
Moment forever detached from yourself?
All that it touches is surely chosen
The poem's indivisible anguish.

I love the wandering that weaves its lengthy way
In a nocturnal plenitude of other worlds;
Evening glows there with its morrow
In the same bosom of bountiful darkness.

Beatrice

The slightest ripple in this love
Can inflict the greatest pain;
A moment casts a long shadow,
Uncertainty wells in your sigh,

Placing you beyond reach.
And you seem so remote
When at the bottom of this well
I glimpse in love's reflection

The faint trace of sorrow,
Shadows cast by memorable suns,
And renewal stirring in your eyes;

Et la douce amère parole
Par quoi se fane de mes cieux
La parfaite et pure corolle.

Le Philosophe

À peine m'eut-elle prédit
Sans parler, mais par l'œil immense,
Magnifiquement la démence
De mon désir approfondi

Que mon extase se perdit   5
Dans un sourire qui commence
Tel sur les mers l'or est semence
De soleils tombés de midi.

La splendeur à l'enfantillage
Touche par mille doigts dorés   10
Comme le dieu fait au feuillage ;

Trop de bonheur que vous aurez
Jeté du plus haut de votre âme
Brise en l'étincelle la flamme.

À chaque doigt

À chaque doigt sourd la goutte
Et tu trempes tes mains pour
Mieux feindre sur qui t'écoute
L'onde d'un premier amour

Né limpide flamme ou bulle   5
D'azur qu'on croit étranger
À tous les sus et sans nulle
Épaule à boire ou manger

Sans se pencher ton visage
Ou l'autre qu'on dirait tel   10
Vers ses sœurs du paysage
Que le vacarme immortel

Peur de la chèvre camuse
Inonde de cornemuse.

And the bittersweet words
Withering the pure and perfect
Corolla of my skies.

The Philosopher

No sooner had she predicted to me
Not in words, but in her boundless gaze,
The madness of my
Wonderfully deepened desire

Than my rapture melted
Into a budding smile
As gold spread on the seas is the seed
Of suns fallen from high noon.

Splendour lightly touches childishness
With its innumerable gilded fingers
Just as the god caresses the foliage;

Too much joy that you may
Cast from the pinnacle of your soul
Quenches the flame within the spark.

At Each Finger

At each finger a drop wells up
And you dip your hands
Better to feign on whoever listens to you
The ripple of a first love

Born a clear flame or a bubble
Of blue sky deemed foreign
To all those known and without a
Shoulder to eat or drink

Without leaning your face
Or the other that appears the same
Towards its sisters of the landscape
Which the eternal din

Dread of the snub-nosed goat
Floods with the skirl of bagpipes.

T'évanouir

T'évanouir—aile ou voilure
Par la brume bue au nadir
Et plus s'enfume la brûlure
Qu'est la mer pour y refroidir

Un vertige igné dont palpite   5
La ronde odeur d'onde et de pur
Vent de spire où se précipite
Ton vol de cheveux au sel sur.

Pense au plus délicieux gouffre ;
Crise du soir même—tu fus   10
Abondamment celle qui souffre
Aux grises roses de l'Infus

Sourire—comme au vague on glisse
Où meurt la lèvre humide hélice.

À la vitre d'hiver...

À la vitre d'hiver que voile mon haleine
Mon front brûlant demande un glacial appui
Et tout mon corps pensif aux paresses de laine
S'abandonne au ciel vide où vivre n'est qu'ennui.

Sous son faible soleil je vois fondre *aujourd'hui*   5
Déjà dans la pâleur d'une époque lointaine
Tant je sens que je suis vers ma perte certaine
Le Temps, le sang des jours, qui de mon âme fuit.

Passez, tout ce qui soit ! Seul, mon silence existe ;
Jusqu'au fond de mon cœur je le veux soutenir,   10
Et muet, feindre en moi la mort d'un souvenir.

Amour est le secret de cette forme triste ;
L'absence habite l'ombre où je n'attends plus rien
Que l'ample effacement des choses par le mien.

Vanishing

Vanishing, on wings or sails
Sucked down by the misty depths
All the more smoke-wreathed becomes the fire
Wrought by the cooling sea

A dizzying flame stirring
The swell's rolling fragrance and the
Swirling wind where your flowing locks
Plunge into the bitter brine.

Ponder the most delectable depths;
Evening's crisis itself—you were
She enduring the agonizing torment
In the grey roses of the Innate

Smile—as one glides to oblivion
Where the lip's smooth whorl dies.

At Winter's Window...

At winter's window veiled by my breath
My fiery brow seeks an icy support
And my entire pensive body so warmly languid
Yields to the empty sky where living is tedium.

Beneath its faint sun I see *this day* already melting
Into the mists of a bygone age
So deeply do I feel I am trailing to my definite end
Time, the lifeblood of days, oozing from my soul.

Pass by, all that is! Alone my silence lingers;
To the bottom of my heart I long to sustain it,
And silently feign a memory's demise within.

Love is the mystery of this sorrowful form;
Absence dwells in the shadow where I await
Only the broad erasure of things by my own.

À des divinités cachées

Des Néréides gîte,
Quand elles ont sommeil,
Grottes où l'onde agite
S'il existe un soleil,
Et vous montagnes, cave   5
En qui l'écume esclave
Des mers menant le choc
Ébranle l'ombre en butte
Aux bords que répercute
Sonorement le roc !   10

Sonnez trombes et trompes
Dans votre profondeur,
Fêtes d'Éros et pompes
Pures de l'impudeur !
Sonnez, sonnez, secrètes   15
Conques dans les retraites
De notre liberté !
Sonnez les beaux insultes
Et les tendres tumultes
Des membres concertés.   20

Tonnez, terre profonde
Sous les vulgaires pas ;
Ils marchent sur un monde
Que le ciel ne voit pas !
Mais nos étranges havres   25
Ne sont pas de cadavres
Mais pleins de dieux vivants
Et des mêmes déesses
De qui fuirent les tresses
Les voiles et les vents !   30

Sonnez, sonnez, Nuit creuse
Le temps retournera
Vers l'aube bienheureuse
D'un jour que l'on verra !
Ce jour de Janus même   35

To Hidden Divinities

Abode of the Nereids*
When they feel sleepy,
Caverns where the waters ponder
Whether the sun exists,
And you mountains, lofty vault
Where the captive foam
Leading the charge of the seas
Shakes the shadow exposed
To the edges which
The rock loudly echoes!

Sound, waterspouts, and horns
In your depths,
Eros' banquets and shameless
Pomps and vanities!
Sound, sound, mysterious
Conches in the sanctuaries
Of our liberty!
Sound the fine insults
And the gentle tumult
Of limbs acting in unison.

Thunder, depths of the earth,
Beneath the vulgar footsteps;
They tread upon a world
Unseen by the heavens!
Yet our strange havens
Brim not with corpses
But with living gods
And the same goddesses
Whose tresses with
Veils and winds took flight!

Sound, sound, hollow Night
Time shall turn back
Towards the blessed dawn
Of a day we shall behold!
That day of Janus himself

Nouant le diadème
Sur ma double raison
Dira le droit des tombes
À laisser les colombes
Poindre de leur prison !   40

Odelette nocturne

Écoute la nuit...
Tout devient merveille :
Le silence éveille
Une ombre de bruit...

Une ombre de voix   5
N'est-ce point la mienne
Dont l'âme te vienne
Si loin que je sois ?

Oh ! ne doute point :
C'est moi, c'est moi-même   10
Le même qui t'aime
Si proche de loin,

Se parle de toi,
Le drap sur la bouche,
Blotti dans sa couche   15
Et seul avec soi.

Il n'y a plus rien
Qu'une peine tendre
Et le mal d'attendre
On ne sait quel bien.   20

J'implore tout bas
Dans la nuit obscure
La claire figure
Que tu ne vois pas ;

J'implore si fort,   25
Tout est si tranquille,
Qu'à travers la ville
Où tout fait le mort

Tying the diadem
To my dual reason shall
Proclaim the right of the tombs
To allow the doves
To emerge from their prison!

Little Night Ode

Listen to the night...
All becomes wonder:
Silence stirs
A ghostly sound...

A ghostly voice
Is it not mine
Whose soul comes to you
Far away though I am?

Oh! doubt not:
It is me, it is indeed me
I, the one who loves you,
So near from far away.

Inner words, engaging with you,
The sheet veiling his mouth,
Curled up in bed
And alone with himself.

Nothing lingers
But a tender pain
And the agony of waiting
For an unknown gain.

Softly I beseech
In the black of night
The glowing face
You cannot see;

So strongly I beseech you,
All is so still,
That over the city where
All is silent as the grave

Une ombre de voix
Qui sera la mienne   30
Dans l'âme te vienne
Si loin que je sois.

Fragment

...les morts n'ont point de ces retours étranges
Ils reviennent peut-être en de faibles esprits ;
Mais le tien, mais le mien, jamais ne sont repris
Que d'un vivant retour de leur soif de vendanges.

Celle qui sait le goût des choses que tu manges   5
M'a retiré des mains leurs délices sans prix ;
J'ai vu s'évanouir comme il m'avait surpris
Tout l'amour qui le cède au vain orgueil des anges.

Le cœur n'est pas plus pur pour vieillir plus amer ;
L'un et l'autre chacun le regard sur la mer   10
Voient le même regret dans la diverse écume...

Silence

Il ne reste de nous ce soir qu'un grand silence
Vers l'ombre va pencher l'implacable balance ;
Bientôt de ce beau jour que j'ai tant attendu
Dans le creux de ma main l'or tiède aura fondu.
La puissance du soir à la fin s'est montrée.   5
Un grand silence touche à plus d'une contrée !
Le temps qui disparut n'est plus si loin de nous
Ni la mort qui s'éveille et baise nos genoux,
Se fait plus familière avec cette âme sombre.
Nos plus doux souvenirs mordent nos cœurs dans l'ombre   10
Où les faveurs se font d'implacables refus
Ô quel soupir arrache à celui que je fus
Des temps délicieux les présences funèbres...

A ghostly voice
Which will be mine
Comes to your soul
Far away though I am.

Fragment

...the dead do not mysteriously return
They come back perhaps in weak spirits;
But yours, or mine, are never taken back
Save for a renewed thirst for the wine harvest.

She who knows the taste of the things you eat
Took their priceless delights from my hands;
I watched ebb in wonder-stricken surprise
All the love which yields to the angels' vain pride.

The heart is none the purer, becoming embittered by age;
One and the other staring out to sea
Glimpse the same regret in the eddying spume...

Silence

All that remains of us this evening is a great silence
The unrelenting scales will tilt towards the shadows;
The warm gold of this splendid day which I long awaited
Will soon have melted in the palm of my hand.
Evening's mighty mantle has finally descended.
A boundless silence breathes on many a land!
Time long since vanished is no longer so far from us
Or death, which awakens and kisses our knees,
Is no more a stranger to this gloomy soul.
Our fondest memories gnaw at our hearts in the shadows
Where kind acts turn to blank refusals
O what a sigh wrenches from him I once was
The mournful presence of a glorious yesteryear...

Aux vieux livres

Gardiens, profonds témoins, purs et puissants Pénates,
   Conservateurs des dons,
Tombes où sont réduits à leurs vains aromates
   Les dieux que nous perdons,

Ors devant qui le temps pleure pour qu'on délivre,   5
   Armés d'un doigt pieux,
De l'immortel ennui de n'être plus qu'un livre
   Un mort harmonieux,

Longtemps j'ai détesté, foule dense et dorée,
   L'insupportable faix   10
Que place au front vivant la montagne laurée
   Des monuments parfaits !

Quel poids resplendissant sur l'âme vierge, ô Maîtres,
   Que vos temples parlants !
Delphes définitive aux masses hexamètres,   15
   Antres étincelants,

Marbres tout murmurants d'âmes récompensées
   Car elles ont construit
Leur auguste demeure à de pures pensées
   Soustraites à la nuit.   20

Charmes, mesures d'or, odes nettes et grecques
   Splendeur des vieux soleils
Qui se couchent dans l'or mort des bibliothèques
   Pour de riches sommeils,

Telle qu'on le répand de la Belle enchantée   25
   Qui close tant de jours
Se plut à tant dormir pour n'être point tentée
   À de viles amours.

Hélas, ce long dormir à la mort s'appareille
   Tant le réveil sursoit !   30
Des barbares naissants vous n'aurez plus l'oreille
   Si longue qu'elle soit.

To Old Books

Guardians, wise observers, pure and powerful Penates,
 Custodians of offerings,
Tombs where the gods we have forsaken
 Are reduced to their faint essences,

Gildings before which time yearns for some
 Devout finger to release them
From the eternal tedium of being no more than
 A lifeless and harmonious book.

I have long scorned, golden serried ranks,
 The unbearable burden
Placed on the living brow by the mountain wreathed
 In perfect monuments!

How your talking temples, O Masters, are such a dazzling
 Burden on the virgin soul!
Delphi measured in plenteous hexameters,
 Gleaming caves!

Marble resounding with murmurs of souls rewarded
 For having built
Their noble abode for thoughts distilled and
 Drawn from night.

Charms, golden measures, plain Greek odes
 Glow of ancient suns
Setting in the lifeless gold of libraries
 For sleep's rich gains.

Thus it is said of the enchanted Beauty
 Who, long secluded from the world,
Chose to sleep rather than be enticed
 By vile lovers.

Alas, this long slumber resembles death
 So delayed is the waking!
You shall not have the ear of newly fledged barbarians
 However long it may be.

Déjà le Cygne cède, et dans la nuit sonore
    S'envolera demain.
Le parfum de Platon lentement s'évapore   35
    Du souvenir humain.

The Swan already yields, and will on the morrow take flight
    Into the deep echoing night.
Plato's sweet scent slowly fades
    From human memory.

DERNIERS VERS DE CIRCONSTANCE

Heure

L'HEURE me vient sourire et se faire sirène :
Tout s'éclaire d'un jour que jamais je ne vis :
Danseras-tu longtemps, Rayon, sur le parvis
    De l'âme sombre et souveraine ?

Voici L'HEURE, la soif, la source et la sirène.   5

Pour toi, le passé brûle, HEURE qui m'assouvis ;
Enfin, splendeur du seul, ô biens que j'ai ravis,
J'aime ce que je suis : ma solitude est reine !
Mes plus secrets démons, librement asservis
Accomplissent dans l'or de l'air même où je vis   10
Une sagesse pure aux lucides avis :
    Ma présence est toute sereine.

Voici L'HEURE, la soif, la source et la sirène,

Danseras-tu longtemps, rayon, sur le parvis,
Du soir, devant l'œil noir de ma nuit souveraine ?   15

La distraite

Daigne, Laure, au retour de la saison des pluies,
Présence parfumée, épaule qui t'appuies
Sur ma tendresse lente attentive à tes pas,
Laure, très beau regard qui ne regarde pas,
Daigne, tête aux grands yeux qui dans les cieux   5
    t'égares,
Tandis qu'à pas rêveurs, tes pieds voués aux mares
Trempent aux clairs miroirs dans la boue arrondis,
Daigne, chère, écouter les choses que tu dis...

LATER OCCASIONAL VERSE

Hour

The HOUR comes to me smiling, then changes into a siren:
Light I have never seen illuminates all:
Will you dance for long, Sunbeam, on the concourse
    Of my sovereign and gloomy soul?

Here comes the HOUR, the thirst, the spring, and the siren.

For you, the past burns, HOUR appeasing me;
At last, solitary splendour, O bounty I have purloined,
I adore what I am: my solitude is queen!
My innermost demons, freely enslaved
Attain in the gold-suffused air where I dwell
A pure wisdom giving wise counsel:
    My presence is so serene.

Here comes the HOUR, the thirst, the spring, and the siren,

Will you dance for long, sunbeam, on the concourse
Of evening, in my sovereign night's dark gaze?

The Absent-Minded One

Deign, Laura, now that the rainy season has come again,
Perfume-suffused presence, shoulder resting
Upon my languid affection attuned to your every step,
Laura, resplendent gaze, gazing at nought,
Deign, face with your all-embracing glances leading you
    astray in the heavens,
Whilst, with dreamy steps, your feet condemned to the puddles
Tread lightly in the mire's glassy waters,
Deign, beloved one, to listen to the things you say...

Sinistre

Quelle heure cogne aux membres de la coque
Ce grand coup d'ombre où craque notre sort ?
Quelle puissance impalpable entre-choque
Dans nos agrès des ossements de mort ?

Sur l'avant nu, l'écroulement des trombes   5
Lave l'odeur de la vie et du vin :
La mer élève et recreuse des tombes,
La même eau creuse et comble le ravin.

Homme hideux, en qui le cœur chavire,
Ivrogne étrange égaré sur la mer   10
Dont la nausée attachée au navire
Arrache à l'âme un désir de l'enfer,

Homme total, je tremble et je calcule,
Cerveau trop clair, capable du moment
Où, dans un phénomène minuscule,   15
Le temps se brise ainsi qu'un instrument...

Maudit soit-il le porc qui t'a gréée,
Arche pourrie en qui grouille le lest !
Dans tes fonds noirs, toute chose créée
Bat ton bois mort en dérive vers l'Est...   20

L'abîme et moi formons une machine
Qui jongle avec des souvenirs épars :
Je vois ma mère et mes tasses de Chine,
La putain grasse au seuil fauve des bars ;

Je vois le Christ amarré sur la vergue !...   25
Il danse à mort, sombrant avec les siens ;
Son œil sanglant m'éclaire cet exergue :
UN GRAND NAVIRE A PÉRI CORPS ET BIENS !...

Disaster

What hour knocks on the hull's ribs
The shadows' great blow where our destiny creaks?
What impalpable force rattles
The bones of the dead in our tackle?

Upon the empty bow, thunderous cloudbursts
Wash away the smell of living and wine:
The sea hauls up and digs tombs once more,
The same water hollowing and filling the ravine.

Hideous man, his heart capsizing within,
Strange drunkard adrift upon the sea
Whose nausea bound to the ship
Wrenches from the soul a yearning for hell,

Total man, I quiver and gauge,
Mind all too lucid, attuned to the instant
When, in a flicker of light,
Time shatters like an instrument...

Cursed be the swine who rigged you,
Rotten ark where the ballast swarms!
In your gloomy holds, all created things
Beat your lifeless timbers as they drift East...

The abyss and I form between us a machine
Juggling with scattered memories:
I see my mother and my bone china cups,
The blowsy harlot in the doorway of sleazy bars;

I see Christ bound to the yardarm!...
He dances himself to death, foundering with his flock;*
His bloodshot eye illuminates this epigraph for me:
A GREAT SHIP PERISHED WITH CREW AND CARGO!
ALL HANDS...

Colloque

(POUR DEUX FLÛTES)

*À Francis Poulenc,
qui a fait chanter ce colloque*

D'une Rose mourante
L'ennui penche vers nous ;
Tu n'es pas différente
Dans ton silence doux
De cette fleur mourante ;   5
Elle se meurt pour nous...
Tu me sembles pareille
À celle dont l'oreille
Était sur mes genoux,
À celle dont l'oreille   10
Ne m'écoutait jamais ;
Tu me sembles pareille
À l'autre que j'aimais :
Mais de celle ancienne,
Sa bouche était la mienne.   15

B

Que me compares-tu
Quelque rose fanée ?
L'amour n'a de vertu
Que fraîche et spontanée...
Mon regard dans le tien   5
Ne trouve que son bien :
Je m'y vois toute nue !
Mes yeux effaceront
Tes larmes qui seront
D'un souvenir venues !...   10
Si ton désir naquit
Qu'il meure sur ma couche
Et sur mes lèvres qui
T'emporteront la bouche...

Colloquy

(FOR TWO FLUTES)

For Francis Poulenc,
who made this colloquy sing

The weariness of a dying
Rose leans towards us;
You are no different
Suffused in sweet silence
From this wilting flower;
It is languishing for us...
You remind me of
She whose ear
Lay upon my knees,
Of she whose ear
Never listened to me;
You remind me of
She whom I loved:
But this former one's
Mouth was mine.

B

Why compare me to
Some withered rose?
Love has virtue only when
Spontaneous and fresh...
My gaze finds in yours
All that it seeks:
I see there myself laid bare!
My eyes will wipe away
Your tears as they
Well up from a memory!...
Should your desire awaken,
Let it expire upon my bed
And upon my lips which will
Bear your mouth away...

La caresse

Mes chaudes mains, baigne-les
Dans les tiennes... Rien ne calme
Comme d'amour ondulés
Les passages d'une palme.

Tout familiers qu'ils me sont,   5
Tes anneaux à fraîches pierres
Se fondent dans le frisson
Qui fait clore les paupières,

Et le mal s'étale tant,
Comme une dalle est polie,   10
Une caresse l'étend
Jusqu'à la mélancolie.

Équinoxe

ÉLÉGIE

To look...

Je change... Qui me fuit ?... Ses feuilles immobiles
        Accablent l'arbre que je vois...
Ses bras épais sont las de bercer mes sibylles :
        Mon silence a perdu ses voix.

Mon âme, si son hymne était une fontaine   5
        Qui chantait de toutes ses eaux,
N'est plus qu'une eau profonde où la pierre lointaine
        Marque la tombe des oiseaux.

Au lit simple d'un sable aussi fin que la cendre
        Dorment les pas que j'ai perdus,   10
Et je me sens vivant sous les ombres descendre
        Par leurs vestiges confondus.

Je perds distinctement Psyché la somnambule
        Dans les voiles trop purs de l'eau
Dont le calme et le temps se troublent d'une bulle 15
        Qui se défait de ce tombeau.

The Caress

Bathe my warm hands
In yours... Nothing soothes
Like the loving touch
Flowing from a passing palm.

Familiar though they be,
Your fine bejewelled rings
Melt in the quiver
Softly closing my eyes,

And sorrow spreads,
Just as a paving stone is polished,
A caress stretches it
To the point of melancholy.

Equinox

ELEGY

To look...*

I am changing... Who flies from me?... Its motionless leaves
    Burden the tree in my gaze...
Its sturdy limbs are weary of lulling my sibyls:
    My silence has shed its voice.

If my soul's hymn were once a fountain
    Singing with all its burbling waters,
It is now but gloomy depths where the distant stone
    Marks the birds' resting place.

On a natural bed of sand as fine as ash
    The footsteps I have left behind quietly slumber,
And I feel my being slip beneath the shadows
    Along the trails of blended footprints.

I lose all sight of the sleepwalker Psyche*
    In the diaphanous veils of water
Whose tranquillity and time are disturbed by a bubble
    Breaking free from this tomb.

À soi-même, peut-être, Elle parle et pardonne,
    Mais cédant à ses yeux fermés,
Elle me fuit fidèle, et, tendre, m'abandonne
    À mes destins inanimés.   20

Elle me laisse au cœur sa perte inexpliquée,
    Et ce cœur qui bat sans espoir
Dispute à Perséphone Eurydice piquée
    Au sein pur par le serpent noir...

Sombre et mourant témoin de nos tendres annales,   25
    Ô soleil, comme notre amour,
L'invincible douceur des plages infernales
    T'appelle aux rives sans retour.

Automne, transparence ! ô solitude accrue
    De tristesse et de liberté !   30
Toute chose m'est claire à peine disparue ;
    Ce qui n'est plus se fait clarté.

Tandis que je m'attache à mon regard de pierre
    Dans le fixe et le dur 'Pourquoi ?',
Un noir frémissement, l'ombre d'une paupière   35
    Palpite entre moi-même et moi...

Ô quelle éternité d'absence spontanée
    Vient tout à coup de s'abréger ?...
Une feuille qui tombe a divisé l'année
    De son événement léger.   40

Vers moi, restes ardents, feuilles faibles et sèches,
    Roulez votre frêle rumeur,
Et toi, pâle Soleil, de tes dernières flèches,
    Perce-moi ce temps qui se meurt...

Oui, je m'éveille enfin, saisi d'un vent d'automne   45
    Qui soulève un vol rouge et triste ;
Tant de pourpre panique aux trombes d'or m'étonne
    Que je m'irrite et que j'existe !

To herself, perhaps, She speaks and forgives,
  But yielding to her closed eyes,
Loyal, she flees me and, loving, abandons me
  To my lifeless fate.

She leaves her mysterious loss in my heart,
  And this heart hopelessly beating
Vies with Persephone for Eurydice* bitten
  By the black serpent on her innocent breast...

Mournful and dying witness of our tender past,
  O sun, just like our love,
The unwavering softness of hellish sands
  Summons you to the shore of no return.

Autumn, translucency! O solitude deepened
  By sorrow and release!
All things make sense to me once departed;
  That which is no more becomes perfectly clear.

While I bind myself to my stony gaze
  In the relentless and harsh 'Why?',
A dark quiver, an eyelid's shadow
  Flutters between myself and me...

O what an everlasting and natural absence
  Has swiftly drawn to a close?...
A falling leaf has riven the year
  With its delicate event.

Flaming remnants, weak and withered leaves,
  Roll your frail murmuring towards me,
And you, pale Sun, with your last few arrows,
  Pierce this time's slow ebb...

Yes, I awake at last, seized by an autumn wind
  Whipping up a dreary red whirl;
So startled by purple panic amid the golden cloudbursts
  That it rouses my being and I feel life's breath within!

Job

J'ai râclé jusqu'au sang l'abominable ulcère ;
Mais enfin rejetant le radieux tesson—
Vers le ciel, je redresse, éclairé d'un frisson
Job noir, l'immonde Job qu'un linge sale serre.

Le dégoût monte en moi de mon mal nécessaire.　　　5
Ma bouche a trop mâché la menteuse chanson
Mon cœur se lève, las d'une antique leçon :
Ils vont enfin vomir une rancœur sincère !

Peut-être effarouchés par ce vrai mouvement,
Les maux mystérieux d'une âme qui se ment,　　　10
La pourpre épouvantable et la lèpre candide,

Vont-ils s'évanouir devant ma vérité ?
Puisqu'à nier l'horreur de mon destin sordide
Je n'ai connu qu'injure et que sévérité !

Neige

Quel silence, battu d'un simple bruit de bêche !...

Je m'éveille, attendu par cette neige fraîche
Qui me saisit au creux de ma chère chaleur.
Mes yeux trouvent un jour d'une dure pâleur
Et ma chair langoureuse a peur de l'innocence.　　　5
Oh ! combien de flocons, pendant ma douce absence,
Durent les sombres cieux perdre toute la nuit !
Quel pur désert tombé des ténèbres sans bruit
Vint effacer les traits de la terre enchantée
Sous cette ample candeur sourdement augmentée　　　10
Et la fondre en un lieu sans visage et sans voix,
Où le regard perdu relève quelques toits
Qui cachent leur trésor de vie accoutumée
À peine offrant le vœu d'une vague fumée.

Job

I scraped the abominable ulcer until it bled;
Now finally rejecting the gleaming shard—
I stand against the sky, illuminated by a shiver
Dark and vile Job, swathed in a filthy cloth.

Disgust wells up from my inherent evil.
My mouth has too long chewed the deceitful song
My heart rises up, weary of the ancient lesson:
They will at last spew out true wrath!

Perhaps startled by this true movement,
Will the mysterious sorrows of a soul lying to itself,
The dreadful purple and the innocent scourge

Vanish when faced with my truth?
For having spurned the vileness of my wretched fate
I have endured nothing but cruelty and insult!

Snow

What silence, shattered only by the stroke of a spade!...

I awake, greeted by this mantle of fresh snow which
Seizes me in the heart of my warm glow.
My eyes behold a pale, stark light
And my languid flesh dreads such purity.
Ah! while I slept softly, how many snowflakes must
The dark heavens have shed the night through!
What a pristine desert fallen silently from the gloom
Came to blanket the features of the enchanted earth
Beneath this white expanse so furtively deepened
And melting it into a place without face or without voice,
Where the absent gaze picks out a few roofs
Concealing the treasure of everyday life which
Scarcely promises a thin wisp of smoke.

Insinuant II

Folle et mauvaise
Comme une abeille
Ma lèvre baise
L'ardente oreille.

J'aime ton frêle   5
Étonnement
Où je ne mêle
Qu'un rien d'amant.

Quelle surprise...
Ton sang bourdonne.   10
C'est moi qui donne
Vie à la brise...

Dans tes cheveux
Tendre et méchante
Mon âme hante   15
Ce que je veux.

Le Sonnet d'Irène

PAR MONSIEUR DE SAINT AMBROYSE 1644

De ses divers désirs combien qu'Elle se vante,
Pour mon cœur enchanté Son dire est un détour ;
Elle n'ayme qu'un seul, Elle ayme dans l'Amour
Une personne rare, et supresme et sçavante.

Vainement se plaist-Elle à Se feindre mouvante   5
Et de trop de regards le divin quarrefour ;
Cette beauté n'est point pour les galants d'un jour
Qui porte un corps si pur d'éternelle vivante !

Vous m'avez beau parler d'une trouppe d'amants,
Vous parer de désirs comme de diamants,   10
Et me vouloir au cœur placer plus d'une flèche,

Beguiler II

Fierce and frenzied
Like a bee
My mouth kisses
The passionate ear.

I adore your frail
Wonder
Which I infuse with
The hint of a lover.

What a surprise it is...
Your blood hums:
It is I who breathe
Life on the gentle wind...

In your tresses
My loving and spiteful
Soul stalks
What I desire.

Sonnet for Irene

BY MONSIEUR DE SAINT AMBROISE 1644

Of the many desires She may vaunt,
Her word is a distraction for my enchanted heart;
She loves but one, She loves in Love
A unique, supreme, and wise being.

'Tis conceit if She fancies feigning her own movement
And the divine attention of bounteous wooing glances;
She is no beauty for the fleeting swains
Embodying so purely a living eternity!

'Twas in vain you spoke to me of a troupe of gallants,
Adorning you with desires as though with diamonds,
And in vain you sought to pierce my heart with many an arrow,

J'en souffre, Irène d'or, mais j'en souffre sans foy,
Instruit qu'en chaque aurore, ô Rose toute fraîche,
Tu ne vis qu'en moy seul et ne Te plays qu'en moy.

L'oiseau cruel

L'oiseau cruel toute la nuit me tint
Au point aigu du délice d'entendre
Sa voix qu'adresse une fureur si tendre
Au ciel brûlant d'astres jusqu'au matin.

Tu perces l'âme et fixes le destin   5
De tel regard qui ne peut se reprendre ;
Tout ce qui fut tu le changes en cendre,
Ô voix trop haute, extase de l'instinct...

L'aube dans l'ombre ébauche le visage
D'un jour très beau qui déjà ne m'est rien :   10
Un jour de plus n'est qu'un vain paysage,

Qu'est-ce qu'un jour sans le visage tien ?
Non !... Vers la nuit mon âme retournée
Refuse l'aube et la jeune journée.

À l'aurore

À l'aurore, avant la chaleur,
La tendresse de la couleur
À peine éparse sur le monde,
Étonne et blesse la douleur.

Ô Nuit, que j'ai toute soufferte,   5
Souffrez ce sourire des cieux
Et cette immense fleur offerte
Sur le front d'un jour gracieux.

Grande offrande de tant de roses,
Le mal vous peut-il soutenir   10
Et voir rougissantes les choses
À leurs promesses revenir ?

I suffer from it, golden Irene, but I suffer without fear,
Knowing that in each sunrise, O all fresh Rose,
You live in no one but me and take pleasure in me alone.

The Cruel Bird

All night long the cruel bird held me
On the sharp point of the joy of hearing
Its voice sent forth with a gentle fury
To the sky ablaze with stars till morning.

You pierce the soul and set the fate
Of such a gaze that cannot be withdrawn;
You change all that was to ashes,
O voice all too loud, ecstasy's instinct...

Dawn in the shadows outlines the face
Of a glorious day that already leaves me cold:
One more day is but an empty landscape,

What is a day without your face?
No!... My soul turned back towards night
Spurns dawn and the youthful day.

At Dawn

At dawn, before the heat of day,
The gentleness of the colours,
Scarcely strewn upon the world,
Rouses and inflames pain.

O Night, so deeply endured,
May you suffer heaven's smile
And this vast flower offered up
On the brow of a gracious day.

Great offering of many a rose,
Can sorrow sustain you and
Watch these blushing things
Honour their promises?

J'ai vu se feindre tant de songes
Sur mes ténèbres sans sommeil
Que je range entre les mensonges   15
Même la force du soleil,

Et que je doute si j'accueille
Par le dégoût, par le désir,
Ce jour très jeune sur la feuille
Dont l'or vierge se peut saisir.   20

Chanson à part

Que fais-tu ? De tout.
Que vaux-tu ? Ne sais,
Présages, essais,
Puissance et dégoût...
Que vaux-tu ? Ne sais...   5
Que veux-tu ? Rien, mais tout.

Que sais-tu ? L'ennui.
Que peux-tu ? Songer.
Songer pour changer
Chaque jour en nuit.   10
Que sais-tu ? Songer
Pour changer d'ennui.

Que veux-tu ? Mon bien.
Que dois-tu ? Savoir,
Prévoir et pouvoir   15
Qui ne sert de rien.
Que crains-tu ? Vouloir.
Qui es-tu ? Mais rien !

Où vas-tu ? À mort.
Qu'y faire ? Finir,   20
Ne plus revenir
Au coquin de sort,
Où vas-tu ? Finir.
Que faire ? Le mort.

I have seen so many feigned
Dreams in my wakeful gloom
That I class as a lie
Even the sun's potency,

And know not if I greet,
Out of disgust or of desire,
This day's birth upon the leaf
Whose virgin gold may be held in hand.

A Special Song

What do you do? Anything.
What are you worth? Don't know.
Portents, attempts,
Power and disgust...
What are you worth? Don't know...
What do you want? Nothing, yet all.

What do you know? Tedium.
What can you do? Dream.
Dream of turning
Each day to night.
What do you know? To dream
To leave boredom behind.

What do you want? My own good.
What must you do? To know,
To foresee and be able,
Which is to no avail.
What do you fear? To wish.
Who are you? Why nothing!

Where are you going? To death.
Why so? To end,
To never return
To devilish fate.
Where are you going? To end.
What for? To be dead.

'Il est vrai, Je suis sombre'

Il est vrai, Je suis sombre. Et misérablement
Las de moi-même, et las de ces aurores sombres
Où l'âme fume et songe et compulse ses ombres
...Je sens peser sur moi la fatigue d'un ange.

'It is true, I am gloomy'

It is true, I am gloomy. And wretchedly
Weary of myself, and weary of these gloomy dawns
Where the soul smoulders, dreams, and consults its shadows
...I feel the lassitude of an angel weighing upon me.

QUATRAINS ET DÉDICACES
DE TOUTE ÉPOQUE

Vers pour Mme de R...

Plongerai-je l'éclair secret dedans ? que n'ai-je
Rêvé de lourds baisers—marchant dans cette neige
Dont le vent d'or m'aère allégeant mon Été
De blanc crêpe et touchant de bulles ma peau d'ombre
Par cet intime jeu de s'y être jeté ?   5
Ô mon front vois de l'onde accourir le pur nombre !

Ambroise, au Jardin Botanique...

Pour André Gide

Ambroise, au Jardin Botanique
Avec toi-même a devisé...
Alas ! quel broyeur mécanique
A nos moments pulvérisé !

Sur cette tombe inoffensive   5
(Il n'y avait personne dedans)
Nous rîmes !—La rose gencive
Éclatait encore de dents !

Mais les Terrestres Nourritures,
Le citron, les choses à l'ail,   10
Les purges et les confitures
Ont eu raison du bel émail.

Finissons par la chose triste :
Il me faut demain mercredi
Ouvrir largement au dentiste   15
Ma bouche qui l'avait prédit.

Le Temps est fait d'un tas de choses,
C'est un Océan qu'on a bu !

QUATRAINS AND DEDICATIONS
OF ALL PERIODS

Verse for Mme de R——

Shall I plunge the secret thunderbolt therein? what
Ponderous kisses have I not dreamed of—treading upon this snow
Whose gilded wind airs me, lightening my Summer
With white crêpe and brushing my shadowy skin with bubbles
By this intimate game of having leapt in?
O brow of mine, behold the water's pure number rushing forth!

Ambroise, in the Botanic Garden...

For André Gide

Ambroise,* in the Botanic Garden
Chatted with yourself...
Alas! what mechanical grinder
Crushed these times we spent!

Upon this innocuous tomb
(There was no one within)
We laughed!—Then the rosy gum
Still gleamed with teeth!

But the Fruits of the Earth,*
Lemon, garlic-flavoured things,
Purgatives and jams
Took a heavy toll on the shiny enamel.

Let us finish on a sad note:
Tomorrow Wednesday I must
Open wide for the dentist
My mouth which had predicted it.

Time is fashioned from many things,
It is an Ocean that has been drunk!

De mille merdes et de roses
Monte dans l'âme le rebut !   20

À Gênes

Odoriférantes
Sentes où l'on sent
Tant d'herbes et cent
Drogues différentes,

Où, narine errante,   5
Tu fends les encens
Que cède aux passants
L'ombre incohérente...

Connais-tu ce coin ?
—Je n'ai pas besoin   10
De pupille glauque !

Ni bruit ni couleur
Ne valent la rauque
Friture en chaleur.

Pour votre Hêtre 'suprême'

À M.A.G.

Très noble Hêtre, tout l'été,
Qui retins la splendeur esclave,
Voici ton supplice apprêté
Par un ciel froidement suave.

Cent fois rappelé des corbeaux,   5
L'hiver te flagelle et t'écorche ;
Au vent qui souffle des tombeaux
Les flammes tombent de ta torche !

Ton front, qui cachait l'infini,
N'est plus qu'une claire vigie,   10
À qui pèse même le nid
Où l'œil perdu se réfugie !

From myriad roses and filth
The dross rises in the soul!

In Genoa

Sweet-scented
Paths redolent of
Bounteous herbs and endless
Intoxicating fragrance

Where, wandering nose,
You pierce the incense
Wafting from the hazy shadow
To the passer-by...

Do you know this spot?
—I have no need
Of a bluish-green eye!

No sound or colour
Can match the sizzle
Of hot fried fish.

For Your 'Towering' Beech Tree

For M.A.G.

Most noble Beech, you who kept
Majesty enslaved all summer long,
Now your torment is prepared
By a sky coldly serene.

Summoned time and again by the crows,
The winter flogs and flays you;
On a wind gusting from the tombs
Flames tumble from your torch!

Your brow that concealed infinity
Is no more than a bare lookout post,
Even a nest is now ponderous, there
Where the bewildered eye takes refuge!

Tout l'hiver, le regard oiseux,
Trahi par la vitre bossue,
Sur la touffe où furent les œufs   15
Compose un songe sans issue !

Mais—ô Tristesse de saison,
Qui te consumes en toi-même,
Tu ne peux pas que ma raison
N'espère en le Hêtre Suprême !   20

Tant de Grâce et de Vénusté !
Se peut-il que toute elle meure,
France, où le moindre nid resté
Balance une fière demeure ?

Mille oiseaux chanteront plus d'un   25
Souvenir d'atroce tangage,
Quand reverdira par Verdun
Sauvé, notre illustre Langage !

Quatrain à Adrienne Monnier (1917)

D'autres préfèrent la prairie
Mais les plus sages vont nier
La rose, dans ta librairie
Ô Mademoiselle Monnier

Dédicace à Léon-Paul Fargue

Hèle-moi ce 3-mâts barque
Ébène et sombre pavois !
   'La Parque'
A rugi le porte-voix...

Sous la barre, il prend le largue   5
S'il cède au souffle savant
   Si Fargue
Me le campe au lit du vent !

Paris le 17 avril 1917

All winter long, the idle gaze,
Blurred by the embossed window,
On the clump where the eggs once lay
Crafts a fruitless dream!

Yet—O seasonal Gloom,
Consuming you within,
You cannot prevent my reason
From believing in the Towering Beech!

So much Grace and Beauty!
Can it be that all is dying,
France, where the smallest remaining nest
Rocks a proud dwelling place?

Myriads of birds will sing out their
Memories of the dreadful pitching and tossing,
When, after Verdun* saved,
Our glorious Language will once again turn green!

Quatrain for Adrienne Monnier (1917)

Others prefer the meadow
But the wisest will decline
The rose, in your bookshop
O Mademoiselle Monnier.

Dedication to Léon-Paul Fargue

Hail this three-master
Ebony and dark masthead flags!
    'The Fate'
Roared the loudhailer...

Beneath the helm, she takes to the open sea*
If she holds the learned course
    If Fargue
Settles her in the wind's eye!

Paris 17 April 1917

Vers à Miss Natalie Clifford Barney

Quoi ! C'est le chemin des Vignes
Qu'à la faveur des hivers
Vous prenez pour fuir mes vers ?
Mais quoique de vous indignes

Les voici, chœur acharné   5
À chanter pour Miss Barney !

                30 décembre 1917

Vers à Natalie Clifford Barney

Toujours, même dans le Maine,
Elle est close dans son flacon
Cette Natalie inhumaine...
(Qui considère *as a bad job*
De ne pas être ru' Jacob.)   5

Sonnet à Mme Lucien Mühlfeld

Vous qui logez à quelques pas
De ma littéraire cuisine,
Belle dame, bonne voisine,
Voici mes fruits qui ne sont pas

Dans la laque ni le lampas,   5
Ni de Boissier fruits de l'usine,
Mais ce sont fruits de Mnémosyne
Qui sait confire ses appas.

Croquez, mordez les rimes qu'offre
Le sonnet ou bizarre coffre,
Non ouvré par les fils du Ciel ;   10

Et choisissez dans une gangue
De mots collés selon leur miel
La noix fondante sur la langue !

Verses for Miss Natalie Clifford Barney

What! You're taking the road of the Vineyards*
Under the cover of winter
To flee my verses?
But unworthy of you though they be

Here they are, dogged choir
Ready to sing for Miss Barney!

                                30 December 1917

Verses for Natalie Clifford Barney

As ever, even in Maine,
She is enclosed in her vial
The inhumane Natalie...
(who thinks it *a bad job*
Not to be on the rue Jacob.)

Sonnet for Mme Lucien Mühlfeld

You who live a stone's throw away
From my literary kitchen,
Lovely lady, kind neighbour,
Here are my fruits that are neither

In lacquer nor in silk lampas,
Nor those from the Boissier* factory,
But they are fruits of Mnemosyne*
Who knows how to preserve her charms.

Crunch, sink your teeth into the rhymes
Offered by the sonnet or strange box,
Not finely carved by Heaven's sons;

And choose within a coating of words
Whose honeyed sweetness binds them
The melting centre in the mouth!

'Mon vieux cadran, je regrette tes heures'

Mon vieux cadran, je regrette tes heures,
Et la longue Pallas,
Fine, grise, et favorable aux demeures
D'où je reviens, hélas !

S'ouvre sans moi la rose secouée   5
De ce jardin mouvant
Sur qui, grande eau de délices douée,
Tu souffles si souvent.

'Le Temps, ce vil adversaire'

Le Temps, ce vil adversaire
De ma chair, de mes cheveux,
N'a pour vous de nécessaire
Que le retour de nos vœux.

Jadis, près d'une fontaine,   5
(Arthur, comme vous savez)
Cette Parque trop lointaine
Sut les dons que vous avez.

Ô ma Parque, pur visage,
J'avais fait les hymnes tels   10
Qu'ils soient d'immortel usage
Pour la lèvre de mortels !

Mais à peine deux années
Sur ces charmes ont couru
Que ces grâces sont fanées,   15
Son sourire disparu !

Elle prend d'une momie
L'horrible immortalité—
Mais vos grâces, chère amie,
Sont d'une autre qualité.   20

'Old dial of mine, I long for your hours'

Old dial of mine, I long for your hours,
And long Pallas,*
Fine, grey, and suitable to dwellings
Whence, alas, I return!

The shaken rose now opens without me*
In this changing garden
Upon which, great water blessed with delights,
You breathe so often.

'Time, this vile enemy'

Time, this vile enemy
Of my flesh and of my hair,
Is of no significance to you
Other than to return our wishes.

Once, near a fountain
(Arthur, as you know)
This far too distant Fate
Once knew the talents you possess.

Ah, my Fate,* pure face,
I had crafted hymns
As has long been the custom
For the mouth of mortals!

Yet scarcely two years
Have flown by on this charm
Than its appeal has faded,
Its smile vanished!

It takes its hideous immortality
From a mummy—
But your charm, dear friend,
Is of a different quality.

Quatrain à Valéry Larbaud

Ma soif n'est pas peu piquante,
Ô Viñes et V. Larbaud,
De boire le soleil beau
Vobiscum, en Alicante.

Dédicace à Anna de Noailles

Noailles, tout le feu qui n'est point dans ces vers,
C'est que vous l'avez pris pour votre seul usage ;
Ces Charmes n'ont d'espoir, par vos mains entre'ouverts,
Que dans les chauds regards de votre clair visage.

'Esprits subtils qui traversent les murs'

Esprits subtils qui traversent les murs
Pour nous jeter la rose inimitable
Ces frais œillets, surprise délectable
Ne tombent point de vos jardins obscurs.
Je sais la main qui fit sur cette table   5
Où je me brise aux pensers les plus durs
Pleuvoir ces fleurs, paraître ces dons purs,
D'une très douce amitié véritable.
Une autre main que je ne puis saisir
Frappe celui qu'elle avait su choisir   10
Il n'est de maux qui ne me viennent d'elle
Tant qu'à la fois elle offense le sort
Et qu'il me montre, à moi, une infidèle,
La claire main qui vient fleurir ma mort.

'Sur le bord des cieux'

Sur le bord des cieux
Béatrice est triste
Sur le bord des cieux
Pleurez mes chers yeux.

Quatrain for Valéry Larbaud

My thirst is more than a little whetted,
O Viñes* and V. Larbaud,
To drink the beautiful sun
With you, in Alicante.

Dedication to Anna de Noailles

Noailles, you have taken for your sole use
All the fire missing from these verses;
These Charms, half-open in your hands, hold promise
Only in the loving glances of your bright countenance.

'Light spirits crossing the walls'

Light spirits crossing the walls
To throw us the inimitable rose
These fresh carnations, delightful surprise,
Fall not from your shaded gardens.
I know the hand which, upon this table
Where the harshest thoughts crush me,
Makes these flowers rain and these true gifts appear,
Of a very true and caring friendship.
Another hand I cannot grasp
Strikes the one she had chosen
All my heartache comes from her
While at once she scorns fate
And it shows me an unfaithful woman,
The clear hand that lays flowers upon my death.

'On the edge of heaven'

On the edge of heaven
Beatrice is sorrowful
On the edge of heaven
Weep, dear eyes of mine.

Adieu tous les dieux !   5
Quels sont les plus tristes,
Les miens ou tes yeux
Les bruns ou les bleus ?

Sur le bord des cieux
Des cieux améthyste   10
Le plus doux des dieux
Me ferme les yeux.

'De vos oisives campagnes'

De vos oisives campagnes
La grandeur et la douceur
Là-bas furent mes compagnes
L'une épouse, et l'autre sœur.

Ô langueur, or immobile   5
Le temps simple s'immolait
Le jour pur mourait tranquille
Sur les toits de la Graulet.

Je voyais, noirs de mystères
Sur mon front se refermant   10
Ces beaux arbres de vos terres
Qui grandissent en dormant.

Juillet 1922

Petites choses

AU-DESSOUS D'UN PORTRAIT

Que si j'étais placé devant cette effigie
Inconnu de moi-même, ignorant de mes traits,
À tant de plis affreux d'angoisse et d'énergie
Je lirais mes tourments et me reconnaîtrais.

SUR UN ÉVENTAIL

Tantôt caprice et parfois indolence
L'ample éventail entre l'âme et l'ami

Farewell all the gods!
Which eyes are sadder
Yours or mine
The brown or the blue?

On the edge of heaven
Amethyst heaven
The gentlest of the gods
Closes my eyes.

'The splendour and serenity'

The splendour and serenity
Of your languid countryside
Were my companions there
One a spouse and the other a sister.

O languor, motionless gold
Unhurried time surrendered itself
The beauteous day gently ebbed
Upon the roofs of La Graulet.

On your land I saw those majestic trees,
Wreathed in the mysterious gloom
Descending on my brow,
Growing as they sleep.

Small Things

INSCRIPTION BENEATH A PORTRAIT

What if I were placed before this effigy
Unknown to myself, unaware of my features,
By so many dreadful lines of anguish and vigour
I would read my torment and recognize myself.

ON A FAN

Sometimes whim, sometimes idleness
The ample fan between soul and friend

Vient dissiper ce qu'on dit à demi
Au vent léger qui le rend au silence.

...Voici la porte refermée
Prison des roses de quelqu'un ?...
La surprise avec le parfum
Me font une chambre charmée...

Seul et non seul, entre ces murs,   5
Dans l'air les présents les plus purs
Font douceur et gloire muette...
J'y respire un autre poète
                Madrid, Miércoles 21 de Mayo 1924

Vers pour Charles-Adolphe Cantacuzène

À qui par la grippe alité
Trouverait la saison méchante,
Charles Cantacuzène chante
Quelque rose réalité.

Il se trouve sans nul malaise   5
Jusque dans le Père Lachaise ;
Et cette muse danserait

Dans les plus sombres atmosphères...
La mort même n'a de secret
Pour tel subtil chargé d'affaires.   10
                                            1918

HYPOTYPOSE

Kant accuse ici-bas une si fauve haine
        (L'écho répond : Cantacuzène)
Qu'il est si doux de se fondre à la fine syrinx,

Diplomate discret, mais fantasque larynx
Soufflant au frac brodé l'âme syracusaine   5
        (L'écho redit : Cantacuzène).

Comes to dispel what was half said
To the gentle wind which restores it to silence.

TO JUAN RAMÓN JIMÉNEZ
WHO SENT ME SUCH BEAUTIFUL ROSES . . .

...Now the door is closed once again
A prison of roses from someone?...
Scent and wonder blend
To create an enchanted room...

Alone, yet not alone, within these walls,
In the air gifts so pure
Beget tenderness and hushed glory...
Here I breathe in another poet
                    Madrid, Wednesday 21 May 1924

Verses for Charles–Adolphe Cantacuzène

To he confined to bed with flu and
Enduring the frightful season,
Charles Cantacuzène sings of
Some rosy reality.

He feels no malaise
Not even in Père Lachaise;*
And this muse would dance

In the darkest circumstance...
Even death holds no secrets
For such an artful diplomat.

                                        1918

HYPOTYPOSIS*

Kant highlights here below a hate so savage
        (The echo replies: Cantacuzène)
That it is nice to melt into the slender syrinx,*

Discreet diplomat, yet capricious larynx
Giving breath to the Syracusan soul's embroidered dress coat
        (The echo repeats: Cantacuzène)

Quatrain à Tristan Derème

Tristan, votre cœur est de bronze.
Je compte plus de jours que de biens je n'acquis
Depuis le jour où je naquis
Trente octobre soixante et onze.

Quatrain à Renée Vautier

Que me fait le temps nouveau,
Quand de l'une ou l'autre année,
Il n'est point d'heure qui vaut
De respirer sans Renée !

Quatrain à Mme M.B.

Sur cette page, afin d'y retenir
Un peu de moi qui deviens souvenir
Et tels propos dans l'heure consumée,
Voici ma main, qui parle par fumée...

Souvenir de Marrault, Septembre 1939

Quel souvenir fait à demi
D'inquiétudes et de charmes !
Tout pour le calme et pour l'Ami,
Mais le ciel roule des bruits d'armes...
Marrault, les bois, le salon clair,   5
Nos regards sur la paix dorée...

Mais au cœur la poigne de fer
Et dans l'âme l'ombre abhorée.
Ô ce septembre auprès de vous,
Sur le bord bleu d'une ère noire,   10
Mélange étrange, amer et doux,
Chers habitants de ma mémoire !

                              P.V. ce jour de Noël 40

Quatrain for Tristan Derème

Tristan, yours is a heart of bronze.
I can count more days than goods I have acquired
Since the day I was born
Thirtieth October seventy-one.*

Quatrain for Renée Vautier

How little the calendar renewed matters to me,
When from one year to the next,
There is not an hour worth
Breathing without Renée!

Quatrain for Mme M.B.

To preserve upon this page
A little of me slowly turning into memory
And some words in the hour expended,
Behold my hand which speaks by smoke...

A Memory of Marrault, September 1939

What a memory,
Half anxiety and half delight!
All given to peacefulness and to Friends,
But the sky is rumbling with the clamour of arms...
Marrault, the woods, the bright living room,
Our gaze upon that golden serenity...

But an iron fist has lodged in the heart
And a despised shadow in the soul.
O this September by your side,
On the blue verge of a dark time,
Such a strange blend, bittersweet,
Beloved dwellers of my memory!

P.V. this Christmas Day 40

APPENDIX

PRINTED here is the poem 'Ma Nuit' ('My Night') to which Nadal refers
in his introduction to *Douze poèmes* (p. xi) in 1959 and which he erroneously described as a version of 'The Slumbering Woman' of *Charmes*.
Although sharing the same theme, it is in effect a wholly distinct piece
inspired by Jeannie and written shortly after his marriage in 1900. It was
reworked in 1913 and again in 1916–17 along with the other older poems
that Valéry was preparing for the *Album de vers anciens*. The redrafted version took on a more erotic tone, similar to other poetic evocations of the
sleeping woman. It subsequently appears on all the lists of poems drawn up
by Valéry for *Charmes* between 1917 and 1921—which makes it the only
remaining poem written prior to *The Young Fate*. It was finally eliminated,
still unfinished, in 1921.

Ma nuit

Ma nuit, le tour dormant de ton
flanc pur amène
Un tiède fragment d'épaule pleine,
peu

Sur ma bouche, et buvant cette
vivante, dieu
Je me tais sur ma rive opposée à
l'humaine.

Toute d'ombre et d'instinct amassée
à ma peine,
Chère cendre insensible aux
fantômes du feu,
Tu me tiens à demi dans le pli de
ton vœu
Ô toujours plus absente et toujours
plus prochaine.

Et ce bras mollement à tes songes
m'enchaîne
Dont je sens m'effleurer le fluide
dessin

My Night

My night, the slumbering curve of
your smooth side
Rises to a warm crest of firm
shoulder, almost

Caressing my mouth, and drinking
in this divine being,
I fall silent upon my shore facing
the living.

All shadow and instinct piled upon
my pain
Beloved ashes impervious to the
fiery spectres,
You half hold me in the fold of
your longing
O ever more absent and ever
nearer.

And this arm gently binds me to
my dreams
Brushed lightly by the flowing

De fraîcheur descendue au velours d'une haleine

Jusqu'à la masse d'ambre et d'âme de ton sein
Où perdu que je suis comme dans une mère
Tu respires l'enfant de ma seule chimère.

Freshness borne on a velvety breath

To the breast's bounteous amber concealing your soul
Where, nestled like I am as if within a mother,
You inhale the child of my only chimera.

EXPLANATORY NOTES

EARLY POEMS 1887–1892

From the summer of 1889, Valéry, then a student in the University of Montpellier, began submitting his first sonnets to *Le Courrier libre*, *La Revue indépendante*, *La Plume*, *La Conque*, and *L'Ermitage*, the last being the only review which he occasionally purchased. Most of the poems were sent in advance to Gustave Fourment and Pierre Louÿs, early critics of his work who, in the abundant letters exchanged between the writers in the period 1887–92, commented on them in candid and sometimes very harsh terms, noting corrections and suggesting changes therein. It was Louÿs who first showed the verses to Mallarmé, verses which Valéry himself described as 'poor, lame and counterfeited efforts' (André Gide, Pierre Louÿs, and Paul Valéry, *Correspondances à trois voix, 1888–1920*, ed. Peter Fawcett and Pascal Mercier (Paris: Gallimard, 2004), 208). The early influences of Hugo and particularly of the Decadent and Symbolist poets whom Valéry had been reading from his mid-teens, are evident in theme and style. The close imitation of Baudelaire—immediately perceptible in the titles and rhyming patterns of sonnets such as 'The White Cats' and 'The Swan' from the late 1880s—is gradually supplanted by the emerging presence of Mallarmé in the following years. Valéry's particular interest in Gothic architecture, mysticism, Catholic iconography, and liturgical celebration is reflected in the imagery of this early verse. The order of poems here follows the chronology of their composition.

A VENETIAN WOMAN'S LAST WILL

The poem was sent to Gustave Fourment in a letter dated 'Tuesday February 1887'. In January of the following year, he wrote an almost identical version entitled 'A Venetian Woman's Desire', with an epigraph from Shakespeare's Sonnet 13 from 'The Passionate Pilgrim'. The poem was first published in Paul Valéry and Gustave Fourment, *Correspondance 1887–1933*, ed. Octave Nadal (Paris: Gallimard, 1957), 224.

AN HOUR'S GLOOM

Dated 27 September 1887, the poem was not published until 11 September 1954 by Henri Mondor in *Le Figaro littéraire*. Three years later, an almost identical version (dated 26 December 1887) was published in Valéry and Fourment, *Correspondance 1887–1933*, ed. Nadal, 226. The themes of pain, disgust, sorrow, and despair, as well as the imagery (vultures) and tone, are reminiscent of Baudelaire's Spleen poems in *The Flowers of Evil*.

THE VOICE OF THINGS

Dedicated to Gustave Fourment, the manuscript of the poem bears the date 24 November 1887. Like 'A Venetian Woman's Last Will', it was published seventy years later in Valéry and Fourment, *Correspondance 1887–1933*, ed. Nadal, 226.

DREAM

This is Valéry's first published poem, which, according to Julien-Pierre Monod, was written on 11 February 1899. Happening upon it on Valéry's table, his brother Jules, then professor of law at the University of Montpellier, sent it without his knowledge to the *Petite Revue maritime* in Marseilles on 15 August. A note held at the Bibliothèque nationale indicates Valéry's delight at its publication: 'Today 16 August '89 I received the *Petite Revue de Marseille* where for the first time my *Rêve* is printed. / Go ahead' (*Notes anciennes*, N.a.fr. 19113, fo. 134). During this same summer Valéry discovered the poetry of Mallarmé and Huysmans's *A rebours*. Informed by Baudelaire's sensuous imagery, the poem depicts the imaginary flight to the expanse of the open sea.

1 *I dream a splendid and peaceful port*: an early typographical error resulted in 'port' being published as 'fort' in Paul Valéry, *Œuvres*, ed. Jean Hytier (Paris: Gallimard, Bibliothèque de la Pléiade, 1957–60), i, 1576, and which has been corrected in the Jarrety edition (Valéry, *Œuvres*, ed. Michel Jarrety, 3 vols. (Paris: Le Livre de Poche, 2016) volume 1, p.54. The evocation of the port in this opening quatrain is undoubtedly that of Genoa with its stately Renaissance and Baroque palaces ('Palazzi dei Rolli') where Valéry spent several summers with his mother's family.

16 *lanterns*: an early version of the original poem incorrectly used the word 'flots' (waves) instead of 'falots' (lanterns).

MOONRISE

A version of this sonnet, bearing the date 'Monday 23 July '89', was sent two months later to Karl Boès (born Charles Pottier, 1864–1940), director of the review *Le Courrier libre* where it was published on 1 October (no. 4, p. 6), accompanying the following letter:

> Sir, herewith some poems written in the provinces by someone who lives in the provinces far from the inferno of Paris. I do not know what way the wind is blowing up there, if young people are Symbolists, analysts, or neo-Christian, and I have not tried to satisfy any school programme. I am a believer in the short and concentrated poem, a brief closed evocation through sonorous and full verse. I cherish, in verse and prose, the very profound and deceitfully knowledgeable theories of Edgar Poe, I believe in the almighty power of rhythm and in the suggestion of the attributive adjective. I prefer Mallarmé to Verlaine and Joris Karl (Huysmans) to all the others. And when I write poetry, it is my fantasy that I follow.
> I am very grateful to you in advance for publishing my work.
> Yours sincerely
> P.V.
> M. Paul Valéry
> Student in Law,
> 3 rue Urbain-V
> Montpellier
> (Valéry, *Lettres à quelques-uns* (Paris: Gallimard, 1952), 9)

One month after their first fortuitous meeting in Palavas at a banquet on the occasion of the 600th anniversary of the University of Montpellier, Valéry sent a copy of the poem, along with 'For Night' ('Pour la nuit'), to Pierre Louÿs (spelt Louis up to 1890) on 2 June 1890 (Gide, Louÿs, and Valéry, *Correspondances à trois voix, 1888–1920*, 184–5). Unaware that it was already in print, Louÿs advised him not to submit it for publication, pointing out the likeness to Hugo's poem 'Religio' (ibid. 199). In October 1890, Valéry sent the poem to Fourment who in a long and particularly harsh analysis criticized its lack of originality and the similarity of some imagery to that used by Baudelaire and Alfred de Vigny (Valéry and Fourment, *Correspondance 1887–1933*, ed. Nadal, 78–81).

7 *Thurifer*: the altar server appointed to carry the thurible in which incense is burned during the religious ceremony.

12 *Then, She appeared! immense white host*: an echo of Hugo's poem 'Religio' from Book 6 (poem XX) of *Les Contemplations*: 'La lune à l'horizon montait, hostie énorme'. Valéry began reading Hugo's work after the death of the writer in May 1885. In a letter to Pierre Louÿs on 22 June 1890, he remarked: 'I began at 14 with *Les Orientales*. I continued with *Notre-Dame [de Paris]* which plunged me into Gothic ecstasy from which I have yet to fully emerge' (Gide, Louÿs, and Valéry, *Correspondances à trois voix, 1888–1920*, 210).

SOLITUDE

Octave Nadal states that the sonnet was written in the summer of 1887, when Valéry was 15 years old. Nadal, who found the piece in the envelope of a letter sent to Fourment from Genoa (Valéry and Fourment, *Correspondance 1887–1933*, 34–5), gave it to Henri Mondor who published it in *Le Figaro littéraire* on 11 September 1954. The poem appeared in the *Mercure de France* on 1 April the following year. Valéry dedicated it to Fourment whom he met in October 1884 at the lycée in Montpellier where he had moved that autumn, but their friendship did not properly mature until early 1887. Michel Jarrety has cast doubt over the accuracy of Nadal's date, positing that Valéry did not commonly use the fourteen-line rhyming scheme of the sonnet until early 1889 (*Œuvres*, ed. Jarrety, i. 266). Moreover, an almost identical version of the sonnet, dated 2 September of this same year, is held in the Bibliothèque nationale. With its references to beauty ('le beau') and voluptuousness, the lexicon of the poem is reminiscent of Baudelaire's *The Flowers of Evil* which Valéry began reading in January. The inspiration is most certainly the character Des Esseintes of Huysmans's *A rebours* which Valéry discovered in the summer of 1889.

THE IMPERIAL MARCH

This sonnet first appeared in *Le Courrier libre* (no. 16) on 1 November 1889, with a few variants from a version dated 17 September. Valéry sent a slightly modified version of the poem, along with 'Mystical Flower', to Pierre Louÿs on

22 June of the following year (Gide, Louÿs, and Valéry, *Correspondances à trois voix, 1888–1920*, 211).

THE WHITE CATS

There are three (almost identical) versions of this sonnet. The first, dated 26 September 1889, was sent by Valéry, along with 'Mirabilia sæcula', to Fourment in October (Valéry and Fourment, *Correspondance 1887–1933*, ed. Nadal, 213–14); a second (written the same day) is held at the Bibliothèque nationale; a third (written in October) was sent to Louÿs on 15 June 1890 (Gide, Louÿs, and Valéry, *Correspondances à trois voix, 1888–1920*, 195). In a later letter (ibid. 261) to Valéry, Louÿs draws his attention to an obvious affinity with Baudelaire's sonnet 'The Cat' (*Flowers of Evil*). In his return letter of 2 November 1889 (sent to the Minimes military barracks in Montpellier where Valéry had just begun his twelve-month military service), Fourment undertakes a detailed, and somewhat unfavourable, analysis of the poem, highlighting various flaws in style and expression therein (Valéry and Fourment, *Correspondance 1887–1933*, ed. Nadal, 85–7). Dedicated to Albert Dugrip, a school friend from Sète and future lawyer, the poem was first published in Pierre-Olivier Walzer, *La Poésie de Valéry* (Geneva: Cailler, 1953), 43.

MEAL

A similar version of the poem entitled 'Sonnet / Le Saltimbanque' in the Bibliothèque nationale is dated 30 September 1889. This regular octosyllabic sonnet first appeared in the *Petite Revue maritime* in Marseilles on 13 February 1890. An almost identical version is published in Walzer, *La Poésie de Valéry*, 24.

MIRABILIA SÆCULA

The title of this sonnet is a Latin term meaning 'wonderful century', or 'wondrous age'. Dated 1 October 1889, it was sent along with 'The White Cats' to Fourment who commented on both poems in his return letter of 2 November. His remarks relate primarily to rhyming details (Valéry and Fourment, *Correspondance 1887–1933*, ed. Nadal, 87). The poem was first published by Octave Nadal in 1957 (ibid. 214). An almost identical version of the sonnet, written the same day, is held at the Bibliothèque nationale.

THE CHURCH

Although the manuscript of the poem is dated 3 October 1889, Valéry quotes the last quatrain in a letter sent to Fourment in August from the town of Le Vigan in the Var (Valéry and Fourment, *Correspondance 1887–1933*, ed. Nadal, 68). It was first published by Nadal in 1957 (ibid. 211). The theme and imagery reflect Valéry's fascination with the liturgy and religious architecture. In a letter to Albert Dugrip of 21 September 1890, he writes:

> As regards churches, I was at the Cathedral this morning doing a bit of liturgy. I adore my old and austere Cathedral and I love High Mass, like that today. A sombre and pallid light scarcely comes through the obscure stained

glass. Very few people. The organ by itself fills the cavity of vaults. How far away it seems! From another century! How it transports you back to the first ones, the symbolism of rites, the candles counted, the three officiating priests attentive to the mysterious signs; and the incense, and the ancient and traditional chalice of the dalmatics! What a pure work of art the Mass is. (Valéry, *Lettres à quelques-uns*, 23–4)

THE DIVINE ADULTERER (ANCIENT SCENE, AD 30)

Valéry wrote three versions of this sonnet, dated 3 October 1889, and sent it, along with 'Rape', to Louÿs on 13 July of the following year (Gide, Louÿs, and Valéry, *Correspondances à trois voix, 1888–1920*, 239). Expressing his liking for the poem, and particularly its title, Louÿs predicts in his reply that Valéry, who considered sending it to *L'Ermitage* in September 1890 (ibid. 313), would be regarded as one of the foremost poets if he were to move to Paris (ibid. 243–4). In a letter of 16 April 1891, he states that he intended sending it on Valéry's behalf to *La Conque* (Gide, Louÿs, and Valéry, *Correspondances à trois voix, 1888–1920*, 443), but the poem was not published until 1953 in Walzer, *La Poésie de Valéry*, 35.

FRIEND'S ADVICE

Valéry composed several versions of this sonnet on 5 October 1889. Two are held at the Bibliothèque nationale: one dedicated to Albert Dugrip and the other to Eugène Bonnet, a school friend from Montpellier. Henri Mondor published a version in *Les Nouvelles littéraires* on 26 July 1945—six days after Valéry's death, and on the eve of his burial in Sète. The version reproduced here was first published in Walzer, *La Poésie de Valéry*, 27.

THE SWAN

Valéry wrote three versions of this sonnet, dated 5 October 1889. In a letter to Valéry on 9 November, Fourment offered a detailed and harsh commentary that opens with the pointed reminder of its similarity to Baudelaire's poem of the same title in *The Flowers of Evil*. The sonnet was first published in Valéry and Fourment, *Correspondance 1887–1933*, ed. Nadal, 214–15.

THE SEA

Like several of the previous sonnets from the period 1887–9, this one, dated 10 October 1889, was first published sixty-eight years later in Valéry and Fourment, *Correspondance 1887–1933*, ed. Nadal, 216. Fourment devotes an entire letter of detailed commentary on the poem, which he sent to Valéry on 24 October (ibid. 90–3).

SPIRITUAL RENAISSANCE

The poem was composed on 11 October 1889 and dedicated to Paul Verlaine (1844–1896) whose collection of poems *Les Amies* and *Fêtes Galantes* Valéry bought that year. In the late 1890s, he greatly admired the Symbolist poet's verse which he transcribed in a notebook at the end of 1889. Although Valéry never knew Verlaine, he recounts having seen the bohemian poet, drunken and bedraggled, late one night in October 1891. He sent the poem to Fourment who undertook an exceptionally long analysis of the poem which he dubs a 'neo-Christian piece' in a letter dated 4 January 1890 (Valéry and Fourment, *Correspondance 1887–1933*, ed. Nadal, 93–100). Two almost identical versions, dated 7 and 11 October 1889, are held at the Bibliothèque nationale. The poem was published by Nadal in 1957 (ibid. 216–18).

  9 *The golden-armoured goddesses*: reference to Athena, Olympian goddess of wisdom and war, often depicted clad in armour.

 10 *Fauns*: half-human and half-goat creatures in Roman mythology. Mallarmé's poem 'Afternoon of a Faun' ('L'Après-midi d'un faune') was published in 1876, on which Debussy based his symphonic poem of the same name in 1894.

 16 *Phoebe*: Titan goddess, daughter of Uranus and Gaia. Her name signifies brightness and is associated with the moon.

SOUTHERN PORT

Dated 22 October 1889, the poem was first published in Henri Mondor, *Précocité de Valéry* (Paris: Grasset, 1957), 109. Similar to 'The Ship', the imagery and tonality are reminiscent of the voyage poems in Baudelaire's *The Flowers of Evil* which Valéry had recently acquired. The port is most likely Valéry's native Sète where he spent his early years observing the vessels and fishing boats docked at the quays and which he later evoked in the famous essay 'Mediterranean Inspirations'.

THE SHIP

Dated 6 November 1889, the sonnet was not published until 1953 in Walzer, *La Poésie de Valéry*, 23. The theme of the distant sea voyage, the evocation of fragrance ('parfum', 'odeur') and exotic scents, as well as the lexical references to 'vessel' and 'tropical swells', reflect the contemporaneous reading and influence of Baudelaire.

MYSTICAL FLOWER

Valéry wrote several versions of this sonnet in early November 1889 and sent it to Pierre Louÿs on 22 June 1890 (Gide, Louÿs, and Valéry, *Correspondances à trois voix, 1888–1920*, 210–11). In a letter dated 28 September, he states that he sent the sonnet which he described as 'the least clumsy, the *lightest*' (ibid. 313) of his poems, to *La Revue indépendante*; for whatever reason, it appeared, not in the journal, but in the *Bulletin de l'Association générale des étudiants de Montpellier* on 1 January 1891. The combination of mystical, liturgical, and sensuous elements creates a Symbolist or Parnassian ambience. One variant of note pertains to the final line of the poem which in the version used here (and like that in Gide, Louÿs, and Valéry, *Correspondances à trois voix, 1888–1920*, 211) refers to the third person, unlike Hytier's version which reads 'my face' (Valéry, *Œuvres*, ed. Hytier, i. 1583).

4 *Angelus*: a devotion in the Roman Catholic Church commemorating the Incarnation which is recited in the morning, at noon and at evening, accompanied by the bell announcing the prayers.

FOR NIGHT

Dated 29 April 1890, the poem appeared in *La Revue indépendante* 17/8 (October 1890), 48. Pierre Louÿs sent the poem to Gide in June (Gide, Louÿs, and Valéry, *Correspondances à trois voix, 1888–1920*, 203–4) and subsequently to Mallarmé, which he explains in a letter to Valéry on 15 October:

> I wrote to the poet you-know-who [Mallarmé] on Sunday to ask him what day would suit to hear the verse of one of my friends; and having heard back I brought him over your sonnet 'For Night' which is unquestionably your 'Broken Vase' (said without any insulting comparison for the sonnet). He read it slowly, read it again, assessed it, and said in a low voice: 'Ah, it's really good. [. . .] He's a Poet, there's not a shadow of a doubt about it . . . [. . .] Great musical subtlety' [. . .] Turning to me: 'Have you any others?' I had only that one and this was a good thing, I think. You can send him some others yourself. It would be much better. Send to: Stéphane Mallarmé, 89 rue de Rome, and copy for him 'The Young Priest' with another of your sonnets of your choosing: 'Cemetery' for example, or 'Myriam'. (Ibid. 325)

A slightly modified version appeared in the *Bulletin de l'Association générale des étudiants de Montpellier* in January 1892, signed 'D' for Doris (pseudonym used by Valéry).

DO YOU RECALL?

Written on 5 May 1890, this mystical sonnet on the theme of fraternal love is the first poem dedicated to Fourment (1869–1940), whose cherished friendship it appears to celebrate. Jules Véran (1868–1960), journalist and author of books on Romance languages, published a version in *Les Nouvelles littéraires* on 1 May 1952 and Nadal in Valéry and Fourment, *Correspondance 1887–1933*, 93–100 in 1957.

7 *Dreamers fleeing the Eternal Ennui*: an echo of the line 'ce séjour de l'éternel ennui' in Baudelaire's prose poem 'La chambre double' from *Le Spleen de Paris*.

RAPE: BRONZE OF THE SECRET MUSEUM

Valéry wrote the sonnet on 11 July 1890 and submitted it, along with 'The Young Priest', to a competition organized by the literary review *La Plume* (founded by the novelist and poet Léon Deschamps, 1864–99) which published the entries in a supplement on 15 November. When the results were announced in January of the following year, the poem was ranked in fifteenth place.

1 *In the resonant and rare metal of Corinth*: Corinthian bronze was the most highly prized metal by the ancients, and referred to in the Bible and by various Greek and Roman authors.

THE YOUNG PRIEST

Dated 14 July 1890 and sent, along with 'Myriam', to Louÿs on 20 July. In the competition run by *La Plume* (see previous note), the sonnet received an 'honourable mention' and was ranked eighth. As suggested by Louÿs to whom he dedicated it, Valéry sent it to Mallarmé in October 1890, thereby initiating his first contact with 'le Maître' (for the letter, see Introduction, p. xvi). In his reply, Mallarmé wrote, 'You certainly possess the gift of subtle analogy, with adequate music, and that is everything. I have said this to our friend M. Louis; and I repeat it here before your two short and rich poems' (*Paul Valéry vivant* (Marseille: Cahiers du Sud, 1946), 62). Louÿs also showed the sonnet to the journalist and writer Rodolphe Darzens (1865–1938). With minor variants, it was published in *La Conque* on 1 June 1891. Valéry wrote a prose version under the same title but the original manuscript of the poem has been lost. Valéry's interest in ecclesiastical traditions and liturgical celebration is evident in several poems of this time.

MYRIAM

Written on 17 July 1890, the sonnet was published in Walzer, *La Poésie de Valéry*, 41. Valéry sent the poem, along with 'The Young Priest', to Louÿs on 20 July, with the following question: 'Myriam is Mary. Here future mother of God. But is this comprehensible??' (Gide, Louÿs, and Valéry, *Correspondances à trois voix, 1888–1920*, 254). In another letter written ten days later, he solicits once again his friend's opinion: 'In your next letter (soon) tell me frankly what you think of "Myriam", because I do not know what to think. It's a bit vague. . .' (ibid. 265). While liking the poem, Louÿs makes the following observation: 'I defy anyone to guess the real meaning. Myriam, in contemporary poetic slang, means Mary Magdalene, and, if you do not state that it's Mary, mother of Jesus, this won't be known' (ibid. 267).

VOLUPTUOUS BATHER

The poem was written on 23 July 1890, followed by another version on 23 September, and sent to Louÿs three days later, with the enjoinder: 'Herewith, as usual, some verse. I am hoping they're not too obscure' (Gide, Louÿs, and Valéry, *Correspondances à trois voix, 1888–1920*, 310–11). Valéry wrote the sonnet 'Bathed', which shares the same theme, two years later.

THE WRETCHED POET'S LAST THOUGHT

The poem (like 'Spiritual Renaissance': see note on p. 19 and p. 21) is dedicated to Paul Verlaine. The two versions of this sonnet were written in early August 1890, one published by Henri Mondor in the review *Arts et Lettres* in April 1946, and the other by Walzer in *La Poésie de Valéry*, 25.

SPLENDOR

Taking its title from the Latin *splendere* meaning brilliance or lustre, this sonnet was written in early August 1890 and appeared in *L'Ermitage* in January 1891.

It is dedicated to Karl Boès, director of the review *La Plume* from 1900 to 1905 and of *Le Courrier libre*. On the advice of his friend Albert Dugrip, Valéry first contacted Boès on 23 September 1889 and sent him 'Moonrise' and 'The Imperial March'.

2 *ciborium*: covered metal receptacle used to hold the host for the Eucharist.

ON THE WATER

This sonnet was composed on 24 August 1890. The manuscript is held at the Bibliothèque nationale, along with an almost identical version entitled 'Pudeur sur l'eau' ('Modesty on the Water') dated 19 September and which Valéry sent to Louÿs two days later (Gide, Louÿs, and Valéry, *Correspondances à trois voix, 1888–1920*, 297). Although Louÿs wished to publish the poem in *La Conque*, it did not appear until 1953 in Walzer, *La Poésie de Valéry*, 25.

BASILICA

Dated 26 August 1890, the sonnet was sent to Louÿs on 2 December (Gide, Louÿs, and Valéry, *Correspondances à trois voix, 1888–1920*, 349); in his reply, Louÿs highly commended the poem and Valéry's talent:

As for you, you bowl me over. How, eighteen months ago, at sixteen and a half, were you able to write lines of verse like those that you have sent me? And I would not dare send you *one* of my old pieces! I love the entire second quatrain, and the two last lines but above all *'the pure Sun weaver of impalpable halos'* which is an exquisite image. (Ibid. 352)

The mystical tone and religious imagery are reminiscent of poems such as 'Moonrise' and 'Mystical Flower' which evince lexical similarities.

FAIR MAIDEN IN A NIGHTDRESS

Written on 28 August 1890, this sonnet was sent to Louÿs on 26 September (Gide, Louÿs, and Valéry, *Correspondances à trois voix, 1888–1920*, 311). It was published, along with 'Do You Recall?', by Jules Véran in *Les Nouvelles littéraires* on 1 May 1952.

SMALL SONNET

Written on 1 September 1890, the manuscript is held in the Bibliothèque nationale. Valéry sent the poem a week later to Louÿs (Gide, Louÿs, and Valéry, *Correspondances à trois voix, 1888–1920*, 275), who praised its 'adorably rhymed nine-syllable lines' (ibid. 280).

TOGETHER

The manuscript of the second version (of three) of this sonnet is dated 11 September 1890. Dedicated to Louÿs, the poem, along with 'The Friendly Wood' which Valéry dedicated to Gide, was published in the eleventh and final issue of *La Conque* in April 1892, three months after its due date (Gide, Louÿs, and Valéry, *Correspondances à trois voix, 1888–1920*, 557). Having received a copy, Valéry wrote to his friend the following month, describing his two sonnets as 'childlike' (ibid. 598). The theme is the poet's spiritual journey through the mystical night to a spiritual communion conveyed by the liturgical imagery. The medieval atmosphere is further conveyed with the archaic French spelling 'Saint Thrésor' (*trésor*) and allusions to the Gregorian chant.

APPEASING DEATH THROES

Written on 13 September 1890, the poem was sent, along with 'The Young Priest', to Mallarmé on 19 October and two days later to Louÿs (Gide, Louÿs, and Valéry, *Correspondances à trois voix, 1888–1920*, 298). (See Mallarmé's complimentary remarks in the note on 'The Young Priest', p. 282.) The sonnet, published in *La Conque* on 1 June 1891, is reminiscent of the poetry of Verlaine which Valéry was reading at this time.

CEMETERY

This sonnet was most likely written in September 1890 (a previous version dated 2 September is held at the Bibliothèque nationale) and sent to Louÿs on 5 October 1890 (Gide, Louÿs, and Valéry, *Correspondances à trois voix, 1888–1920*, 321), a few weeks before the end of Valéry's military service. Louÿs recommended he send it to Mallarmé, but Valéry wrote on 19 October that he considered it 'too clumsy and much too *casual*' (ibid. 326). The poem was not published until 1953 in Walzer, *La Poésie de Valéry*, 40. It bears a thematic resemblance to 'The Graveyard by the Sea' and shares some of the same imagery of the later poem.

BEING BEAUTEOUS EMERGING FROM THE SEA

Valéry wrote this sonnet in early October 1890 and sent it to Louÿs (Gide, Louÿs, and Valéry, *Correspondances à trois voix, 1888–1920*, 358–9) on 9 December, a week after its publication in the *Bulletin de l'Association générale des étudiants de Montpellier*. The poem, with minor modifications, reappeared in *L'Ermitage* in June 1891, but Valéry expressed dissatisfaction to Gide in a letter from the same month: 'the sonnet is less than average. Louis himself and Régnier have criticized it' (André Gide and Paul Valéry, *Correspondance 1890–1942*, ed. Peter Fawcett (augmented edn., Paris: Gallimard, 2009), 103). Later, he envisaged including the poem in the *Album de vers anciens* but the version that became known as 'Birth of Venus' would be entirely rewritten and modified. The theme shows a certain affinity with Leconte de Lisle's 'Hélène' (*Poèmes antiques*), one of his many poems inspired by Greek legend and myth.

UNCERTAIN VIRGIN

A first version of the sonnet (the manuscript of which has been lost) was sent to Louÿs on 11 November 1890, five days before the end of his year of military service (Gide, Louÿs, and Valéry, *Correspondances à trois voix, 1888–1920*, 397–8). In the accompanying letter, Valéry refers to this sentimental poem evoking the poet looking longingly at a virgin as 'mediocre verse' (ibid. 338). Published in *La*

Conque on 1 April 1891, the sonnet is scarcely distinguishable from another entitled 'You who shed...' ('Toi qui verses...'), which was written at the end of 1889,
but not published until 1 May 1952 in *Les Nouvelles littéraires* and five years later
in Valéry and Fourment, *Correspondance 1887–1933*, ed. Nadal, 227.

TO ALCIDE BLAVET

Valéry dedicated the sonnet to his friend Alcide Blavet, poet of the Félibrige,
the Provençal movement founded in 1854 by Frédéric Mistral to promote the
culture, language, and customs of the south of France. Dated 7 December
1890, the poem was first published in July 1934 in the Félibre review *Calendu*
and then by Jules Véran in *Les Nouvelles littéraires* on 1 May 1952, along with
'Fair Maiden in a Nightdress' and 'Uncertain Virgin'.

10 *Bacchantes*: group of priestesses, known as maenads, who were followers of
Bacchus (also called Dionysus), the god of wine and the grape harvest.

RETURN OF THE CONQUISTADORS

In a letter to Louÿs on 21 December 1890, Valéry announced his intention to
write a poem for José-Maria de Heredia with the following subject: 'Return of
the conquistadors of true Poetry, victorious clarions can be heard at sea, here
are the galleys whose sails stand out against the setting sun, here at the bow is
the victorious J. M. de H. whose sonorous name would splendidly close the
piece by rhyming with *irradiate*' (Gide, Louÿs, and Valéry, *Correspondances
à trois voix, 1888–1920*, 367). Valéry sent the sonnet to Louÿs on 7 January 1891
(ibid. 380–1) and, ten days later, to Heredia who, remarkably, never received the
poem, as Louÿs confirmed to Valéry in a letter of 2 January 1892 (ibid. 549).
The poem, along with the letter to Louÿs, was not published until 1975 in
Cahiers Paul Valéry 1 – Poétique et poésie (Paris: Gallimard, 1975), 23–7.

4 *wyverns*: legendary dragon-like creatures, often represented in heraldry
with a serpent's head, large wings, and a forked tail.

10 *Palos*: Palos de la Frontera in Huelva whence Christopher Columbus and
the three ships departed for the New World on 3 August 1492.

14 *Heredia*: José-Maria de Heredia (1842–1905), Cuban-born Parnassian
poet and member of the Académie française. Heredia's mastery of the sonnet was an important influence, before Baudelaire, on the young Valéry
who read his work in the late 1880s. It is likely they were introduced to
each other on Valéry's first visit to Mallarmé in October 1891.

'TO THE EAST SWEEPS THE SEA...'

This undated poem was most likely composed in 1891. It is one of the few
examples of free verse from this period.

REFLECTIONS ON THE APPROACH OF MIDNIGHT

The sonnet was sent in one of Valéry's early letters to Gide in February 1891
with the following description: 'Here are a few verses which are not yet finished

and may never be. . . . They play around with vague words, plus a scent, not yet music, even less than nothing' (Gide and Valéry, *Correspondance 1890–1942*, ed. Fawcett, 59). The poem was published for the first time in 1955 by Robert Mallet in the first edition of the correspondence (p. 51) between the two writers.

YOUR PORTRAIT

Valéry sent the poem to Louÿs on 14 February 1891 as an expression of his appreciation for a signed photograph he had recently received from him. In the letter he tells Louÿs that he had wanted to write a full sonnet but, being short on time, asked him to make do instead with two quatrains, dubbed 'eight monsters', which are 'still in a bit of a rough state and unworthy—what!?—of the Model' (Gide, Louÿs, and Valéry, *Correspondances à trois voix, 1888–1920*, 403).

BATHYLLUS OF LESBOS...

Valéry sent the poem to Gide on 8 November 1891 who judged it to be 'quite appalling' (Gide and Valéry, *Correspondance 1890–1942*, ed. Fawcett, 181–2) and, three days later, to Louÿs (Gide, Louÿs, and Valéry, *Correspondances à trois voix, 1888–1920*, 531–2) to whom he described it as an 'impromptu sonnet, written by chance'. It was published in 1955 by Robert Mallet in the first edition of Gide and Valéry, *Correspondance 1890–1942*, 136.

Bathyllus is a woman here, but the historical Bathyllus was a male youth from Samos of whom the Greek lyric poet Anacreon (582–485 BC) was deeply enamoured and whom he immortalized in his odes.

INTERLUDE

Published in *L'Ermitage* in September 1892, although most probably written the year before, since Louÿs alludes to the sonnet (dubbing it playfully 'Petticoat' ('Jupon'), in reference to the last line) in a letter of 21 November 1891 (Gide, Louÿs, and Valéry, *Correspondances à trois voix, 1888–1920*, 539).

ARION

The epigraph is taken from Vergil's pastoral poems *Bucolics* or *Eclogues* which Valéry translated between 1942 and 1944 at the behest of Dr Roudinesco: '*Sit Tityrus Orpheus | Orpheus in silvis, inter delphinas Arion*', 8.55–6, 'Que le hibou s'égale au cygne et que Tityre | Veuille être Orphée aux bois, Arion aux Dauphins!' (Valéry, *Œuvres* ed. Hytier, i. 268–9). (English translation: 'Let Tityrus be Orpheus, Orpheus in the forest, Arion among the dolphins.')

In the famed myth by fifth-century historian Herodotus, Arion the musician was dispossessed of his fortune on his return to Corinth from Sicily. The crew offered him the choice to either kill himself and be buried on land, or to hurl himself into the sea. Allowed to perform one last song, Arion then threw himself overboard and was left by the ship's crew to his ignominious fate. A dolphin drawn by the music carried him back to Corinth to the astonishment of the crew.

Valéry sent the sonnet to Louÿs on 31 January 1892 (Gide, Louÿs, and Valéry, *Correspondances à trois voix, 1888–1920*, 560). It appeared in *La Wallonie* in

January–February and in *La Syrinx* the following month, in the form of an octet and a six-line stanza. In a letter to Gide, Valéry describes it as 'really bad! Experimental sonnet' (Gide and Valéry, *Correspondance 1890–1942*, ed. Fawcett, 206).

THANK YOU

Sent to Fourment in April 1892, the sonnet was published in 1957 in Valéry and Fourment, *Correspondance 1887–1933*, ed. Nadal, 21. The manuscript of the poem, identical to another in the Valéry collection at the Bibliothèque nationale, has been lost.

BALLET

The sonnet was written in 1892 and published posthumously in Henri Mondor, *Les Premiers Temps d'une amitié: André Gide et Paul Valéry* (Monaco: Éditions du Rocher, 1947), 111. (I have added this text to the Select Bibliography as a source of material). It was included in a small anthology of ten poems entitled *P. A[mbroise] Valéry, Ses Vers*, offered to Gide that spring, in which it was the sole unpublished piece.

ME IN PARIS

Unlike most of Valéry's sonnets which are based on the structure of two quatrains and two triplets, this sonnet uses the Elizabethan sonnet (three quatrains and a couplet). This undated poem, written after he moved permanently to Paris in March 1894, evokes the experience of the newly arrived provincial who contemplates the capital he had imagined and the one he encounters.

THE YOUNG FATE

The genesis of this long poem predates the Great War. Exhorted by Gide from October 1911 to publish an anthology of his old verse (Gide and Valéry, *Correspondance 1890–1942*, ed. Fawcett, 696), and then by Gaston Gallimard, Valéry began retouching some poems of adolescence. While reworking 'Helen, the sad queen' (first published in *La Conque*) at the end of 1912, he decided to add a final piece which he conceived as a valedictory work. In a notebook, he began sketching out some fragments of the new poem entitled 'Helen' (written in Greek), including the line: 'Who weeps there, if it's not the simple wind, at this hour?' On the first two manuscript pages which bear the name of the eponymous heroine from classical mythology, some of the key motifs are already present: the maritime setting, the tear as manifestation of pure emotion, the starry night and solitude of being, awakening to self-consciousness, desire, and the key to the poem's modulated form embodied in the word 'curves'. While the indeterminate subject matter of this new creation was germinating, the conception of its form was very precise, as he said in a revealing letter to Albert Mockel from 1917, the year of the work's publication:

In 1913, when I was asked to bring together my old verse, though ashamed of the small number, and ashamed even more by the size of them—I had the idea of composing a piece of thirty to forty lines; I pictured an opera recitative in the manner of Gluck; almost one phrase, long and for contralto. I tried out a few alexandrines. Then along came the war. [. . .] I found at the time that the way to resist thinking about events and to counter the consuming matter of helplessness was to impose a difficult game on myself; to make endless toil for myself, laden with conditions and clauses, entirely bound by strict observances. Poetry became a private charter. I adopted the most classical restrictions. Furthermore, I imposed on myself continuous harmony, the most precise syntax, the careful selection of words, individually sorted, evaluated, and picked. (Valéry, *Lettres à quelques-uns*, 123)

The original modest ambition of composing a work of thirty or forty lines swelled, after five years' toil and several hundred pages of manuscripts, to 512 verses. The syllabic metre that Valéry used was the centuries-old alexandrine verse (twelve syllables or six iambic feet) with an obligatory medial caesura (dividing the line into two hemistichs) arranged in rhyming couplets. The principal formal challenge was how to accommodate the single speaking consciousness of the poem. To this end, Valéry turned to the recitative, a style of vocal writing, normally for a single voice, that imitates the natural rhythms of spoken language—which he had admired in Gluck's opera *Alceste*: 'J[eune] P[arque]. In the Memoirs of this poem, don't overlook the role of the old operatic forms—Gluck and occasionally W[agner]. I wanted to compose recitative, interspersed with melodies—and I was consumed by the idea of changes of tone. This completely outweighed any obsession with the subject' (*Cahiers*, 29 vols. (Paris: CNRS, 1957–61), xxii. 533; references to the *Cahiers* in these notes are to this edition unless otherwise stated). The poem is a dramatic construction in two acts, structured like two panels of a diptych, and comprising sixteen episodes of varying length which he likened to a hydra that could be cut into coils or parts. He later remarked that the transition or modulation between these components caused him infinite difficulty. Valéry conceived the philosophical poem as 'a depiction of a series of psychological substitutions' of the soul and the transformation of consciousness in the course of a night to morning. Divided between her former 'Harmonious' self and her present 'Mysterious' self, the Fate awakens to a heightened awareness of her corporeal Self ('MOI', always capitalized), which is the central theme in the work. As he later noted, the poem is fundamentally the representation of lucidity and self-consciousness, and specifically the physiological feeling of consciousness and the functioning of the body: 'I endeavoured to bring out in monologue (in *La Jeune Parque*) what appeared to me the substance of the living being, and physiological life inasmuch as this life can be perceived by the self, and expressed *poetically*' (*Cahiers*, xviii. 93). After five years' labour, the long symbolic poem was published on 30 April 1917. Numerous readings took place in the summer following its publication, notably in the salons of Jeanne Mühlfeld, Arthur Fontaine, and Mme Aurel (Mme Alfred Mortier), as well as at the head office of the *NRF*, rue Madame, which contributed to its rapid renown. The work is dedicated to Gide but Louÿs, who followed its genesis and encouraged Valéry during its long evolution, was privately aggrieved. Valéry commented extensively on *The Young Fate* in various essays; numerous letters to, among others, Gide, Louÿs, and Fontainas; and his private *Notebooks* (*Cahiers*, vi. 544).

The collection of manuscripts and notes of the poem are held at the Bibliothèque nationale, and the final manuscript draft at the Bibliothèque Jacques Doucet. The latter collection is the result of the efforts of Julien-Pierre Monod (1879–1963), Swiss banker and grandfather of Jean-Luc Godard, who met Valéry in November 1924 and became an intimate friend, amanuensis, and confidant. Nicknamed by Valéry his 'ministre de la plume' ('minister of the quill'), Monod, who proposed looking after the writer's banking affairs in 1925, began fervently purchasing and collecting all types of material, including eight pages of the manuscript of *The Young Fate* which he acquired in March 1926.

Summary: In the prelude devoted to the disarray of wakening consciousness, the Fate emerges from a voluptuous dream featuring a serpent (a powerful symbol of concupiscence), and goes to the seashore. Standing on a rock above the sea in the darkness immediately preceding dawn, the anguished protagonist, on the verge of tears, asks questions of her existence and addresses the stars. She is bitten by the serpent which is a reminder of her sentient body and conscious self. He is not just the tempter of desire and pleasure but also the symbol of lucidity and rationality. Though entranced and beguiled by the snake's charms and mysteries, she spurns his approach. This encounter brings about a scission or duality of self from which another inner self ('sister') emerges, one that is ruled by the intellect and resists her own sensibility. In the following sequence, the former naïve ('Harmonious') self becomes aware of its mortality and turns in on itself and to memory. Her deep anguish before dawn induces the temptation to suicide at the end of the first act. She expresses weariness of life and willingness for her own mortality, but feels torn between the allure of Darkness and that of Day.

In the second diurnal act, this new 'Mysterious' self awakens, surprised to find herself still alive, yet lucid with her inner tensions quietened. With this self-recognition, she wonders if she should not have fulfilled the temptation to end her life. She succumbs to sleep again, dreams, and awakens. Spring is near and, as the first light of dawn appears, she sees the islands which she addresses and her impulse to live prevails. (Louÿs proposed 'Islands' as a possible title and Valéry designed a cover for the work bearing the word.) This new sense of destiny and a surge in vital impulses bring her back from the precipice of despair and death. Now possessed by life, she reflects on what saved her: falling asleep and the absence of consciousness. She goes to the cliff edge, offering herself to the sun whose brightness now warms her. The poem concludes with the Fate's joyful yet bitter acceptance of life and her rebirth, which rises to an exultation of the light and senses against the symbolic backdrop of the radiant sea and the invigorating wind.

0.8–0.9 *Did Heaven create . . . serpent's lair*: quotation from *Psyché*, Act III, scene 2, a *tragédie-ballet* written by Pierre Corneille, Molière, and Philippe Quinault in 1671, the music of which was composed by Jean-Baptiste Lully.

35 *I saw me seeing myself, sinuous, and gilding*: similar to the famous line at the
    end of Valéry's early prose work *The Evening with Monsieur Teste*, which
    was published in December 1896: 'I am being, and seeing myself; seeing
    me see myself, and so forth.'

83 *More versatile, O Thyrsus, and more treacherous than they*: Valéry later con-
    fided that he took this line from the play *La Pisanelle* (1913) by the Italian
    poet and politician Gabriele D'Annunzio (1863–1938). The thyrsus is
    a staff wrapped entwined with ivy or vine leaves and surmounted by a pine
    cone, associated with the wine god Bacchus (Dionysus).

241 *To the heart-rending departures of splendid archipelagos*: an echo of Rimbaud's
    'Drunken Boat' (*Illuminations*): 'I have seen sidereal archipelagos.'

268 *The embittered multitude of impotent Manes*: Fontainas reproached Valéry
    for this line which he found excessive; in his reply on 22 May 1917, Valéry
    agreed: 'I do not like it at all. It belongs to one of three passages that were
    literally improvised in my hasty weariness to finish it' (Paul Valéry and
    André Fontainas, *Correspondance 1893–1945*, ed. Anna Lo Giudice (Paris:
    Éditions du Félin, 2002), 223).

304–5 *Gently bear me . . . Gently bear me*: these lines were written in 1898 on
    the death of Mallarmé and are included here largely unaltered.

364 *lustra*: plural of *lustrum*, a period of five years when the population census
    performed in Rome was followed by a lustration or ceremonial purifica-
    tion of the people.

429 *Swan-God*: allegory of Apollo to whom the bird was sacred. Seven swans
    flew around the island of Delos when he was born and his chariot was
    drawn by swans when he travelled.

ALBUM OF EARLY VERSE

Pressed by Gide and Gaston Gallimard in 1912, Valéry began working intermittently on these early poems up to 1916, after which *The Young Fate* took precedence. He submitted the volume to Gide on 14 September 1917, but halted its
publication as he contemplated for a time publishing both old and new verse in
one volume. In 1920, he finally decided on the title *Album de vers anciens*, undoubtedly influenced by Mallarmé's 1885 anthology of a similar name. Taking Louÿs's
advice not to restrict himself to one publisher, Valéry opted to publish the collection, not with Gallimard/*NRF* who had just published 'The Graveyard by the
Sea' in June, but with Adrienne Monnier's new series, the 'Cahiers des Amis des
Livres'. Valéry met the editor and influential literary figure in 1917 and frequented
her famous Left Bank bookshop at 7 rue de l'Odéon, opposite Sylvia Beach's
Shakespeare and Company. It is not surprising that the decision to publish the
collection with Adrienne Monnier's Maison des Amis des Livres irritated Gaston
Gallimard who, having waited for eight years, expressed his displeasure in a letter
to Valéry in October 1920, a month before the publication of the *Album*. The first
edition comprised fifteen poems, including eleven sonnets, and the short prose
piece 'The Lover of Poems'. With the exception of 'View' and 'The Friendly

Wood', the dominant metre is the alexandrine. Moreover, Valéry made very few additional changes to the seven poems which had already been lightly retouched for the anthology *Poètes d'aujourd'hui, 1880–1900* by Adolphe Van Bever and Paul Léautaud (Paris: Société du Mercure de France, 1900). The second edition of 1926 saw further significant modifications to poems like 'Birth of Venus' and 'Episode'; 'The Vain Dancers' was completely rewritten in 1931 while 'Anne', 'Semiramis', and 'Summer' were augmented. Of the twenty-one poems included in the final edition of the *Album*, eleven were written and published in reviews between 1890 and 1892; two poems ('Summer' and 'View') appeared in *Le Centaure* in 1896; 'Valvins' the following year; 'Anne' in 1900; 'The Lover of Poems' in 1906; 'Distinct Fire' in the first edition of 1920 with four more titles added to the 1926 edition. In the editor's note of the 1920 and 1933 versions, Valéry refers to the earlier publication of the poems in reviews but makes no mention of them being redrafted or retouched:

> Nearly all of these small poems [. . .] were published between 1890 and 1893, in a few reviews that have since disappeared. *La Conque, Le Centaure, La Syrinx, L'Ermitage, La Plume* were once kind enough to accept these endeavours, which led their author rather promptly to a genuine and prolonged abandonment of poetry. Two unfinished pieces, abandoned around 1899, as well as a page of prose to do with the art of poetry, but which does not profess to instruct or to proscribe anyone, have been added. (*Œuvres*, ed. Jarrety, i. 434)

THE SPINNER

The poem is written in terza rima, the Italian stanzaic form (tercets aba bcb cdc) used by Dante in *The Divine Comedy*, which is most likely the inspiration here. Referring to the poem in a letter to Gide dated 15 June 1891, Valéry expressed his intention to publish it in *La Conque* (Gide and Valéry, *Correspondance 1890–1942*, ed. Fawcett, 117) where it appeared on 1 September. It was published two months later in *Entretiens politiques et littéraires* by Francis Vielé-Griffin (1864–1937), in *La Wallonie* (January–February edition) the following year, and in the anthology *Poètes d'aujourd'hui* by Bever and Léautaud in 1900 (p. 348). The poem was included in the small anthology *P. A[mbroise] Valéry, Ses Vers* that Valéry dedicated to Gide and which Henri Mondor published in *Les Premiers Temps d'une amitié* in 1947. The poem was inspired by Gustave Courbet's painting *La Fileuse endormie* in the Musée Fabre in Montpellier which Valéry frequented in his adolescence and described in 'Le Musée de Montpellier' in 1939.

0.1 *Lilies... neither do they spin*: the Latin epigraph is taken from Matthew 6:28: 'Consider the lilies in the field, how they grow: they toil not, neither do they spin.' (Quotations from the Bible are taken from the Authorized Version.)

HELEN

In a letter to Gide dated 5 April 1891, Valéry announced that he was 'working on a large fresco evoking antiquity, Helen' (Gide and Valéry, *Correspondance*

1890–1942, ed. Fawcett, 94). The sonnet, sent to Louÿs on 18 April, was published under the title 'Helen, the sad queen' in *La Chimère* in August, signed 'M. Doris' (Valéry's pseudonym); in *La Conque* in October; and then in the anthology *Poètes d'aujourd'hui* by Bever and Léautaud in 1900 (p. 345). The version published in the *Album* in 1920 showed very few changes from the original.

ORPHEUS

The poem first appeared in prose form which Valéry integrated as the concluding two paragraphs of the essay 'Paradox on the Architect' in *L'Ermitage* in March 1891. On Louÿs's initiative, it was published as a sonnet, under the current title, in *La Conque* on 1 May. Having been significantly reworked for publication in *Les Fêtes* in 1913, it was omitted from the first edition of the *Album* in 1920, and appeared in its current form in the second edition in 1926. As a traditional figuration of The Poet for the Symbolist poets, Orpheus had held a special place in Valéry's personal pantheon since his youth. In early 1901, he discussed a collaboration based on the myth with Debussy that would combine mime and dance, anticipating a direction taken by the Ballets Russes. In the summer of that year, Valéry, accompanied by Julie and Ernest Rouart, attended the production of Gluck's opera *Orphée et Eurydice* and was particularly moved by Acts 1 and 4. According to the myth, Orpheus, the legendary musician, married Eurydice who died from a snakebite while fleeing a satyr. Overwhelmed with grief, he travelled to the underworld where Hades, so impressed by his lyre playing, allowed him to bring Eurydice back to the world of the living on condition he would not look back. However, as he approached the exit, Orpheus looked back in delight at Eurydice who then disappeared. He was later slain and dismembered by the maenads.

BIRTH OF VENUS

The poem was written in early October 1890 and published under the title 'Celle qui sort de l'onde' ('Being Beauteous Emerging from the Sea') on 1 December in the *Bulletin de l'Association générale des étudiants de Montpellier*. Valéry returned to the sonnet while composing *The Young Fate* during a holiday in Perros-Guirec in Brittany in 1913, extensively reworking the original sonnet up to 1917.

7 *Thetis*: in Greek mythology, a Nereid or sea nymph who married Peleus and bore the legendary Achilles.

FAERY

When published in *L'Ermitage* for the first time in April 1890 and when Valéry sent it to Louÿs on 30 August (Gide, Louÿs, and Valéry, *Correspondances à trois voix, 1888–1920*, 274), the poem was entitled 'White'. It was renamed 'Faery' when it appeared in the review *Les Fêtes* on 15 January 1914. Having been reworked in 1915 and 1916, the 'Faery' of the *Album* is markedly different from the original written thirty years before. The poem is typically Symbolist in terms of its imagery and ambience, evoking the enchanted night of the virgin girl, ethereal and magical in the moonlight.

SAME FAERY

Written in 1926 and published in *Quelques vers anciens* (Maestricht: A.A.M. Stols). The same year, it appeared with some variants in the second edition of the *Album* entitled 'Faery (Variant)'. In his essay 'Fragments of Memory of a Poem', Valéry alludes to this practice of variations on the same poem: 'It has sometimes happened that I published different versions of the same poem: some of them have even been contradictory, and I have been roundly criticized for it. Yet no one has told me why I should have abstained from these variations' (*Œuvres*, ed. Michel Jarrety, iii. 782).

BATHED

The sonnet was sent to Louÿs on 18 April 1892 (Gide, Louÿs, and Valéry, *Correspondances à trois voix, 1888–1920*, 583–4) and published in *La Syrinx* (no. 8) in August. The version published in the anthology *Poètes d'aujourd'hui* by Bever and Léautaud in 1900 (p. 348), like that in the *Album*, varies very little from the original. The measure of Mallarmé's influence on Valéry can be discerned in this sonnet, which was inspired by 'Ballet' and whose last two lines share identical rhymes and imagery.

  5 *Beauty blossoming forth by the rose and the pin!*: almost identical line used in the early sonnet 'Bathyllus of Lesbos' (stanza 2, line 3); see p. 47.

IN THE SLEEPING WOOD

Originally entitled 'La Belle au bois dormant', it was published by Louÿs in *La Conque* on 1 November 1891 without Valéry's consent, about which he expressed his annoyance in a letter to Gide a week later (Gide and Valéry, *Correspondance 1890–1942*, ed. Fawcett, 180). The Félibrige (literary association of Provençal writers with whom Valéry became associated in his youth) published a translation of it in Provençal in the review *La Cigale d'or* on 15 June 1891, which Gide mentions in a letter of 29 June (ibid. 134). The poem under the new title was extensively revised between 1913 and 1916 before its inclusion in the *Album*.

CAESAR

The sonnet was sketched out in the manuscript notebook 'Cahier II' of *Charmes* in early 1919 when Valéry was working on that collection. Not deeming it worthy of inclusion, it then featured on the list of poems for the *Album* that he drew up in September 1920 while staying with Catherine Pozzi in the Dordogne, but it did not appear until the 1926 edition and again in *Quelques vers anciens* (Maestricht: A.A.M. Stols) the same year.

THE FRIENDLY WOOD

Valéry sent the sonnet to Louÿs on 21 December 1890, describing its theme as a 'suggestion of Friendship' (Gide, Louÿs, and Valéry, *Correspondances à trois voix, 1888–1920*, 368–9). Having initially been rejected for publication in *La Conque* by Louÿs who considered it 'too intimate for indifferent people' (ibid. 530), the poem, along with 'Together', appeared in the review under the title 'Interlude—The Friendly Wood' in April 1892. Although dedicated to Gide, to whom it was offered a few days after their first meeting in Montpellier in December, the evocation of the evening walk in the first verse suggests it is more likely a reminiscence of Valéry's teenage friendship with Gustave Fourment. On learning of Fourment's death on 21 November 1940, Valéry noted in his *Notebooks*:

> My oldest friend, and one of the most important for me between '87 and
> '92. He alone in the beginning, then Charles Auz[*illion*] were my sole
> confidants back then [. . .] And strolling in the evening, in the moonlight.
> We ended up knowing each other so well that all we could say to one another
> was what we were utterly determined not to say, and we would spend hours
> together, walking without speaking. (*Cahiers*, xxiv. 30)

THE VAIN DANCERS

Written in 1892, this poem was published in *La Conque* on 1 July 1891 and then in *La Syrinx* in December. A slightly modified version was included in the 1931 edition of the *Album* and a new radically transformed one in 1942, three years before Valéry's death. Only three lines of this last version remain unaltered from the early sonnet (see *Œuvres*, ed. Jarrety, i. 1768-9).

A DISTINCT FIRE...

The sonnet was first published in the *Album* in 1920. A sketch of the poem was written in a notebook from 1898 (*Cahiers*, i. 202), constituting one of the very rare verse poems (about five in total) to be found in the 26,000 pages of the *Notebooks*. Valéry worked on this poem up to 1900 and then again in 1913 and 1915–16. The theme here is that of the descent into sleep and the retreat into oneself, reminiscent of the unfinished prose story *Agathe*, also written in early 1898, which narrates the internal transformations of the subject disconnected from all external stimuli. Both works are in effect a precursor to *The Young Fate*.

NARCISSUS SPEAKS

Valéry sent one version of the poem (of which there are three), dated 28 September 1890, to Louÿs on 19 November (Gide, Louÿs, and Valéry, *Correspondances à trois voix, 1888–1920*, 345) but, dissatisfied with the piece, he requested that it not be published in *La Conque*. He then sent it to his friend in February 1891 and it appeared in the review on 15 March. As he explained to Louÿs, he wished to achieve 'an almost purely musical poetry, as much in ideas as in form. My "Narcissus" is a weak endeavour lacking in boldness' (ibid. 408). This version was reprinted with minor variations in the anthology *Poètes d'aujourd'hui* by Bever and Léautaud in 1900 (p. 346-7). Valéry reworked the poem in 1913 and again in August–September 1917 when he began writing the 'Fragments of Narcissus' which later appeared in *Charmes*. The sonnet here constitutes the inaugural work on the theme of Narcissus which is a central motif for Valéry who treated it in different forms, notably a prose piece in 1890 ('The Funereal Smile'); the 'Fragments of Narcissus', published in 1919; and the libretto *Cantata of Narcissus* (*Cantate du Narcisse*), written in 1938 at the request of Germaine Tailleferre (1892–1983), a member of the group of composers known as 'Les Six'.

0.1 *To appease the manes of Narcissus*: the epigraph is taken from the Latin inscription—Valéry inverted the first two words—on the supposed tomb in the Botanical Garden in Montpellier of Elizabeth Young, the step-daughter of the English poet Edward Young who mentions it in his long dramatic monologue entitled *The Complaint* or *Night Thoughts in Life, Death and Immortality* (1742–5). The poem, which deals with the various bereavements in Young's life (those of his wife, his stepdaughter and her husband), became immensely successful across Europe. Elizabeth died in Lyons, where she is buried, and not in Montpellier.

EPISODE

The poem was first published in the first issue of *La Syrinx* in January 1892, the same month that Valéry sent it to Louÿs (Gide, Louÿs, and Valéry, *Correspondances à trois voix, 1888–1920*, 552) who published it in *La Conque* in April under the title 'Fragment', a title it kept when it appeared in the anthology *Poètes d'aujourd'hui* by Bever and Léautaud in 1900 (p. 349). Slightly modified, the poem was retitled 'Episode' for the *Album* in 1920.

VIEW

Written around 1891, it was first published in *Le Centaure* in 1896. The poem comprises a single sentence on the pattern of an Elizabethan sonnet: three quatrains and a final rhyming couplet in heptasyllabic lines which Valéry uses very rarely.

7 *To the sheer wall of a sea*: this line is a variant of 'the sea is *upright* at the horizon' in the essay 'Introduction to the Method of Leonardo da Vinci', published on 5 August 1895.

VALVINS

The poem, evocative of the language in Mallarmé's 'The Afternoon of a Faun', was one of the twenty-three poems included in an anthology compiled by Albert Mockel to celebrate the Symbolist poet and presented to him on 23 March 1897. The poem followed the pattern of the Elizabethan sonnet and was devoid of punctuation. A punctuated version was published in *La Coupe* in February 1898, and Valéry adopted the traditional French sonnet for the *Album*.

Valvins was the country residence of Mallarmé, situated near Fontainebleau on the Seine, where he sailed his little yawl ('yole'). In the 1900 anthology *Poètes d'aujourd'hui* by Bever and Léautaud (p. 351), Valéry included a dedication 'To S.M.' ('S.M.' was written on the skiff's sail) which was removed from the version that appeared in the *Album*. Mallarmé occasionally took visiting writers and artists boating on the Seine, including Berthe Morisot (the aunt of

Valéry's future wife, Jeannie Gobillard) who purchased a house nearby and represented the skiff in an oil painting in 1893. Valéry last visited Mallarmé at Valvins on 14 July 1898, just two months before Mallarmé's sudden death on 9 September. Valéry relates his memories of the residence in the essay 'Last Visit to Mallarmé' ('Dernière visite à Mallarmé') which was published in *Le Gaulois* on 17 October 1923.

SUMMER

The poem appeared in the first edition of *Le Centaure* in March 1896 along with 'View'; these were the first verses that Valéry had published since the 'Crisis in Genoa' which had brought about a renouncement of poetry four years earlier. His decision to contribute to the review was most likely the result of a convenient opportunity, since Louÿs, Gide, André Lebey, and Régnier were on the editorial committee with its editor-in-chief Henri Albert. The review was short-lived and published only two issues. The sonnet appeared in the anthology *Poètes d'aujourd'hui* by Bever and Léautaud in 1900 (p. 350). Valéry dedicated the sonnet to the poet Francis Vielé-Griffin whom he befriended in 1894 at the salon of the writer Rachilde (pseudonym of Marguerite Eymery, 1860–1953) which was held at the offices of the *Mercure de France*. In 1942, Valéry reworked the poem for the new edition of *Poésies*, adding six new stanzas to the existing eleven. It is this enlarged and definitive version which I have translated here.

PROFUSION OF EVENING, ABANDONED POEM

Composed in 1899, this poem was significantly reworked between 1915 and 1917 and appeared for the first time in the 1926 edition of the *Album*. It is one of the most revised and redrafted poems of the collection, with numerous name changes on the abundant manuscripts, which explains the title 'abandoned poem' and the incomplete date '189...' that Valéry added at the end of the final edition. The complex prosodic structure comprises twelve sections separated by an asterisk with each one having an individual rhyming pattern. Inspired by the Mediterranean sky, the poem shares similar imagery, ideas, and vocabulary with 'The Graveyard by the Sea'. It is a transcendental meditation on the sacred element of space, exploring the eye's encounter with the setting sun in this seaside expanse and the inner response in language of the contemplative self. The poem is dedicated to Paul Claudel whom Valéry had met at Mallarmé's famous literary salon (which were held on Tuesday evenings and known simply as 'les mardis') at the rue de Rome on his first visit to Paris in the early 1890s. Their relationship had a chequered history with disagreements on many issues, but they grew close in the interwar years. In 1942, Valéry sent a copy of *Poésies* to Claudel who particularly liked 'Profusion of Evening', and then promised to dedicate it to him in the next reprint, which he did in 1944.

ANNE

In 1900 Karl Boès, director of *Le Courrier libre*, wrote to Valéry requesting unpublished poems and, although having abandoned verse, the writer sent him the six-stanza 'Anne' which appeared in *La Plume* on 1 December. A shortened version (five stanzas) was published in the *Recueil pour Ariane ou Le Pavillon dans un parc* in 1912. Valéry worked on the poem intermittently between 1913 and 1917, adding new stanzas in 1913 and 1915, bringing the total to nine for the version that appeared in the *Album* in 1920 and a further four stanzas for the second edition in 1926.

Written in tandem with *The Young Fate*, the poem is thematically reminiscent of the prose tale *Agathe*. Valéry dedicated 'Anne' and 'The Rower' in *Charmes* to the poet and future Socialist deputy André Lebey (1877–1938) whom he had met in 1895. Through his friendship with André, Valéry was appointed personal secretary to his uncle Édouard Lebey, president of the Havas Agency in 1900, a position he held until 1922.

22 *golden ratio*: the golden ratio (Greek letter phi), referred to as the 'divine proportion' given its frequency in natural forms such as shells and plants, is a mathematical ratio, approximately 1:618, and considered to be the most pleasing to the eye.

SEMIRAMIS' AIR

Composed in the summer of 1918, the poem was reworked during 1919 and again in early 1920. It was published under the title 'Semiramis (fragment of a very old poem)' in *Les Écrits nouveaux* in July. For the second edition of the *Album* published by Stols in 1926, Valéry added three more stanzas (22, 23, and 24) to the poem which he renamed 'Semiramis'. It featured in the 1922 and 1926 editions of *Charmes*, before being definitively withdrawn.

It was inspired by Degas's mythological painting *Semiramis Building Babylon* (Musée d'Orsay, 1861), which Valéry admired in Degas's studio where it was kept until the painter's death on 26 September 1917. In Greek legend, Semiramis married King Ninos upon whose death she became queen of Assyria and oversaw the building of Babylon. Degas's grandiose canvas depicts her, accompanied by her attendants, on the bank of the Euphrates, surveying the construction of the city on the opposite side. The painting was acquired by the Musée du Luxembourg in the first auction of Degas's extensive art collection at the Galerie George Petit on 6–8 May 1918 which Valéry attended. The theme of Semiramis had an enduring appeal for the writer who wrote a melodrama of the same name in 1934 which was set to music by Arthur Honegger. In the poem, the Assyrian queen is addressed by dawn and goes to the parapet to greet the sun with which she seeks communion. She then turns her attention to the activity in her kingdom below where the city is being constructed. She exults in her own pride and power, yet knows she is dependent on the toil of the populace, who despise the lonely sovereign, to achieve her ambition of architectural and personal triumph.

The poem is dedicated to Camille Mauclair (1872–1945) whom Valéry met at Mallarmé's salon during his first stay in Paris in the autumn of 1891. Mauclair, a writer and art critic, wrote numerous works on Mallarmé. In 1941, Mauclair described Valéry as 'the poet laureate of the Masonic Republic', in what was an attempt by the extreme right to discredit him. Unlike his friend André Lebey, Valéry was never a Freemason. The dedication to Mauclair was consequently dropped for the 1942 edition of the *Album*.

92 *my hanging gardens*: the Hanging Gardens of Babylon were one of the Seven Wonders of the Ancient World described by various classical authors. Thought to have been constructed at Nineveh (close to modern-day Mosul in Iraq) and not in fact at Babylon, their location has always remained elusive.

THE LOVER OF POEMS

This prose piece concerning the art of poetry was published in the *Anthologie des poètes français contemporains* (Paris: Delagrave, 1906, 57) by Dutch writer and journalist Gérard Walch (1865–1931) who wrote in his editorial note to the volume: 'At our request, M. Paul Valéry wanted to explain both himself and his art to our readers. To this end, we are publishing here a typical page that he sent to us. It constitutes an unusual literary document' (*Œuvres*, ed. Hytier, i. 1575-6).

CHARMS

In 1930, Valéry told the philosopher Alain (pseudonym for Émile Chartier, 1868–1951) that *Charmes* was born of *The Young Fate*. The genesis of many of the poems can in fact be traced back to its manuscripts and notebooks, including 'The Graveyard by the Sea', the first sketch of which can be found on a manuscript page of the great poem in 1916. The true beginning of the volume was to emerge the following year with the publication of *The Young Fate*, even if Valéry had yet no clear project in mind. In August 1917, he sent a list of poem titles for the *Album de vers anciens* to Gaston Gallimard who had been patiently requesting them for five years. In a curt retort, the publisher dismissively said he wanted the texts not the titles. In a period of intense creativity, Valéry set about reworking various sonnets of youth, most of which went into the *Album*, but also many new poems which no longer used the alexandrine. From October, Valéry included only his recent verse on the list of pieces for *Charmes*, excluding thereafter the poems of youth.

Valéry deliberated on what he would do with the new poems composed in the autumn of 1917, and copied them into a new notebook ('P.V. Small Poems MCMXVII'), drawing up an early list of what would become a new volume. Work stagnated until the following spring but the German advance on Paris and the threat of bombardments forced Édouard Lebey to head for Normandy. Valéry resided with his ailing boss at the Château de l'Isle-Manière, near the town of Avranches in the Manche department in Normandy, from 25 June to 8 October. The tranquillity of the estate allowed him to work intensively on the poems of the volume in what proved to be a period of exceptional creativity:

I endeavoured to compose 'The Pythia' and a few other pieces in a countryside planted with the most beautiful trees that I have ever seen;

near to Avranches; watered by a tiny river [. . .] Beneath my window there
were copses of very tall copper beech trees, raised groups of huge lime trees
[. . .] whose foliage bowing to the ground completely hid the massive forms.
(*Œuvres*, ed. Hytier, i. 1655)

Valéry continued to work on the poems between 1919 and 1921, publishing
about twenty of them in reviews such as *Les Écrits nouveaux*. The death of
Lebey in February 1922 and the resultant search for new employment brought
a new sense of urgency to complete the twenty-one poems under the title
Charmes which was published on 25 June. ('Charms' derives from *carmina*,
Latin for song, and is taken from Book 1 of Ovid's *Metamorphoses*: 'Ad mea
perpetuum deducite tempora carmen' ('Carry down my perpetual song from
the beginning of the world to my own time'); the epigraph 'deducere carmen'
appeared in the manuscript notebook 'Cahier III' in December 1919). In a letter sent to Jacques Doucet to whom he offered the manuscript the following
month, he wrote: 'These are all the poems I have written since "The Young
Fate", in other words since 1917, and I called them *Charmes*, which, in my
mind, simply means Poems. The etymology, and an old meaning of this word,
allows it perhaps to be still used with this sense.' (Unpublished letter, dated
6 July 1922, held at the Bibliothèque Jacques Doucet (VAL MS 1128.) The order
of the poems long preoccupied Valéry who saw the work as an architecturally
unified whole, which is attested by the numerous lists drawn up in the manuscripts. It was this aspect that Gide disliked as well as the mix of long and
shorter poems. While some critics tended to insist excessively on the intellectual, philosophical, and abstract nature of *Charmes*—Paul Souday saw him as
'the most intellectual of poets'—Valéry was most irritated by the frequent
comparison with Mallarmé, not only by critics but also by writers like Régnier
whom he met in October 1891 on his second visit to the rue de Rome.

Two further editions appeared in February and December 1926 and then in
Poésies in 1929 and 1942. *Charmes* was translated into German by Rilke, a friend
and fervent admirer of Valéry, in 1924.

DAWN

Valéry composed this poem, originally entitled 'The Spiritual Garden', along
with 'Palm' at the end of March 1917, a few weeks after finishing *The Young
Fate*. He sent it to Louÿs on 29 March under the title 'In the Spiritual Morning'
(Gide, Louÿs, and Valéry, *Correspondances à trois voix, 1888–1920*, 1224–5).
When it was published in the *Mercure de France* on 16 October, Louÿs acclaimed
it as 'an abyss of sheer amazement' (ibid. 1377). It appeared in 1920, along with
'Palm' and 'The Pythia', in the volume *Odes* where the order of the stanzas was
modified. Valéry dedicated the poem to Paul Poujaud (1856–1936), a highly
cultured lover of music and a friend of composers such as Gabriel Fauré and
Paul Dukas, whom he met in 1919 and who occasionally corrected his verse.
The poem is a reflection on the waking consciousness, incipient language after
sleep, and the return to lucidity at dawn—the pre-eminent moment of the Pure
Self ('Moi pur') and a central theme in Valéry's poetics which he explored in
many of the prose aubades of the *Cahiers*.

TO THE PLANE TREE

The poem was written in the summer of 1918 during Valéry's stay with his employer Édouard Lebey at the Château de l'Isle-Manière, surrounded by enormous trees. The ten-stanza poem appeared in the August–September issue of the review *Les Trois Roses*. Valéry reworked the poem in March 1919 and again at the end of the year, adding a further ten stanzas, before finally removing two. The version published by the *NRF* in January 1921 comprised eighteen stanzas. The motif of the tree appears recurrently in Valéry's opus: in the *Dialogue of the Tree* and in several poems ('Palm') as well as being the subject of numerous meditations, biological reflections, and watercolours in the *Notebooks*.

65 *Dryads*: in Greek mythology, lesser deities or nymphs who live in trees, specifically in oak trees (Gk: *drys* = oak).

CANTICLE OF THE COLUMNS

Valéry began the poem in late October 1918 under the working title 'Round Dance of the Columns' and then 'Small Hymn of the Columns' which, by November, comprised thirteen stanzas of ten-syllable lines. It appeared under the definitive title in March 1919 in the first issue of the Surrealist review *Littérature*, founded by André Breton, Louis Aragon, and Philippe Soupault with whom Valéry developed close relations at the end of the war. The thematic correlation of music and architecture in the poem links it to the myth of Orpheus the musician-poet which had held a fascination for Valéry since his youth. As he wrote in a notebook, architecture, together with ornament, was his 'first love' (*Cahiers*, vi. 917) and he devoted numerous works to it: the essay 'Paradox on the Architect' in 1891 which culminates in a sonnet about Orpheus becoming an architect, the Socratic dialogue *Eupalinos, or the Architect* in 1920, the melodrama *Amphion* in 1928, as well as many theoretical reflections in the *Notebooks*. The column is the symbol Valéry chose for the graphic emblem of the cover of *Charmes*. The manuscripts and notebooks contain numerous sketches of the ionic capital with its characteristic twin volutes or spiral scrolls.

49 *golden ratio*: see note to p. 297.

THE BEE

Written in January 1919 under the title 'The Tip' ('La Pointe'), and sent to Louÿs the same month (Gide, Louÿs, and Valéry, *Correspondances à trois voix, 1888–1920*, 1419), it was published in the *NRF* on 1 December. The poem, reworked for *Charmes* in early 1922, is dedicated to the novelist Francis de Miomandre (1880–1959) whose article on *The Young Fate*—sent to Valéry in May 1917—initiated a friendship between them. The erotic tension in the poem stems from the analogy fruit–woman to which the bee is attracted. The somnolent girl implores the bee to sting her and thereby engender physical and intellectual revivification.

POETRY

Begun in September 1917, and reworked under various titles ('The Childminder', 'Reproach', and 'The Source') in late 1918–19 and again in June 1921, the poem appeared in *La Revue de France* on 15 July. Valéry revised the piece in early 1922 before its publication in *Charmes*. Contemporaneous with the beginning of the passionate encounter with Catherine Pozzi, the poem engages directly with the source of poetic inspiration, creation, and transcendence.

THE FOOTSTEPS

Conceived on 20 October 1918, the poem was initially entitled 'Psyké' (Gk: 'soul') and then 'Approach of Psyche', most likely inspired by Jean de La Fontaine's (1621–95) *Loves of Cupid and Psyche* (1669), a short romance interspersed with verse written a year after the famous *Fables*, which Valéry had read during the summer. The poem, comprising four octosyllabic quatrains, was reworked in March 1919 under the title 'Nocturne'. It appeared under its definitive title in the review *Feuillets d'art* in November 1921, but was again redrafted in February–March 1922 for *Charmes*. The poem is an expression of imminence and poised expectancy distilled in the image of the footsteps, a synecdoche for the lover's eagerly anticipated approach in the darkness. Valéry expressed his surprise in the *Notebooks* in 1944 that 'an intellectual meaning' (*Cahiers*, xxviii. 427) was being ascribed to this 'small purely *sentimental* poem' and that it was being interpreted as a 'symbol of "*inspiration*"!'

THE GIRDLE

The genesis of the poem, using the pattern of an Elizabethan sonnet or 'quatorzain', dates back to late 1917, and was sketched out in May of the following year. Valéry reworked it intermittently in the years up to 1922 when it was published in *Les Écrits nouveaux* on 3 March. The poem personifies sunset as a female figure, and echoes the poet's changing mood to loneliness just before its imminent disappearance into the 'shroud' of darkness (an image reminiscent of Baudelaire's poem 'Recueillement') expressed in the final couplet.

THE SLUMBERING WOMAN

Begun in May 1918, the poem was reworked in January–February 1920 and published in *L'Amour de l'art* in June. Valéry revised it in early 1922 when preparing the poems of *Charmes*. The sonnet subsequently appeared in *Quelques vers et un peu de prose* (Paris: Renouard) in 1924 and *Vers et prose* (Paris: *NRF*) in 1926. The theme of the sleeping woman is a constant in Valéry's poetics and appears in several poems: 'In the Sleeping Wood', 'A Slumbering Girl II', 'Anne', 'My Night', *The Young Fate*, and in the prose poem *Alphabet*.

It is dedicated to Lucien Fabre (1889–1952), engineer, writer, and winner of the Prix Goncourt in 1908. Valéry wrote a foreword for his volume of poems *Connaissance de la déese* published by the *NRF* in 1924.

FRAGMENTS OF NARCISSUS

While reworking the early 'Narcissus Speaks' in August–September 1917, Valéry began sketching out some verses of a new poem on the theme of consciousness composed in alexandrines, but which he never managed to complete despite numerous attempts over the years. What he envisaged, as he wrote years later, was 'a work that would be almost the counterpart of *The Young Fate*, far simpler in form and not presenting any comprehension difficulties, with all effort going into the very harmony of the language' (*Paul Valéry vivant*, 290). Narcissus, who occupies a pre-eminent place in Valéry's poetics and his philosophical system, embodies the binary nature of consciousness—in other words, the self being aware of its double self. Valéry elucidated the conception of Narcissus in an interview with Frédéric Lefèvre:

> It [Narcissus] is the confrontation between man such as he sees himself—in other words as perfectly general and universal awareness, since his awareness embraces all objects—and his image as a defined and particular being, restricted to a time, to a face, to a race, and to a host of real or potential conditions. In some way, it's the opposition between a whole and one of its parts and the type of tragedy that results from this inconceivable union. (*Entretiens avec Paul Valéry* (Paris: Le Livre, 1926), 358)

This acute inner consciousness is reminiscent of Monsieur Teste. In October 1918, Valéry returned to the poem, having read the poetry of La Fontaine over the course of the summer. A long extract of the new poem together with verses from 'Narcissus Speaks' were published in *La Revue de Paris* on 15 September 1919. In 1921, Valéry composed the prelude and the finale that was to remain unfinished. With work on the poem at a standstill, and unable to complete it, he published segments in various reviews. The three sections appeared in their entirety in 1926 under the title *Narcisse* (Stols) and the following year in *Études pour Narcisse* (Éditions des Cahiers libres).

The first part (the longest of the three scenes which details the natural setting) constitutes a monologue by Narcissus who has arrived at the water just as night is falling and apostrophizes the nymphs not to awaken for fear they will disturb the tranquil image of the pool. In the second part, the youth addresses the fountain which has borne witness many times to the passion of lovers and the dissolution of their amorous drama. Opening with an invocation to the body as the object of its own physical desire, the third fragment returns to the monologue and to the theme of self-directed love symbolically embodied by Narcissus and the duality of self. Narcissus realizes the unbridgeable distance between himself and his double and fatally kisses the beloved image of his own unattainable self which he thereby shatters.

0.1   *Why did I see something?*: epigraph taken from Ovid's *Tristia* (*Sorrows of an Exile*), 2.103.

10   *Napaeae*: in Greek mythology, nymphs who inhabit valleys and glens.

94   *Echo*: a mountain nymph or oread besotted with Narcissus who spurned her after which only remnants of her voice remained.

88 *The most beauteous of mortals can cherish only himself*: line taken from La Fontaine's poem 'Adonis': 'le plus beau des mortels, l'amour de tous les yeux'. Valéry had been reading the poem during his stay at the Château de l'Isle-Manière in the summer of 1918. Two years later, the writer Jean-Louis Vaudoyer requested a preface to a book on La Fontaine's poem which Valéry wrote ('On the subject of *Adonis*') in September at Catherine Pozzi's residence of La Graulet near Bergerac (Dordogne) where he also wrote some verses of the 'Fragments'.

THE PYTHIA

In Greek mythology, the Pythia was a priestess of Apollo at Delphi on Mount Parnassus who delivered the oracles from the gods in a fevered state induced by vapours rising from the earth. The name, signifying Delphi, derives from the verb *pythien* (to rot), which refers to the decomposing carcass of the serpent Python that once guarded the mount before being slain by Apollo who claimed the site for himself.

As Valéry remarked in an interview with Frédéric Lefèvre, the origins of 'The Pythia', conceived in October 1917 (according to an entry dated 2 January 1923 in Gide's *Journal*), can be traced back to 'a discussion on the eight-syllable line with Pierre Louÿs' (*Entretiens avec Paul Valéry*, 276); the allusion here is to line 5 of the first stanza: 'Pallid, deeply wounded'. Finished in November 1918 and reworked in January, the poem caused Valéry considerable difficulty during his stay at the Château de l'Isle-Manière in the summer of 1918. Like other pieces in *Charmes*, 'The Pythia' was composed under the cloud of the Great War. In a letter to Valéry on 13 November 1918, Louÿs states that he received the poem 'on the day when France took back Alsace and Lorraine' (Gide, Louÿs, and Valéry, *Correspondances à trois voix, 1888–1920*, 1407). Valéry dedicated it to Louÿs who wrote on 8 January 1919: 'Your "Pythia" will forever remain a unique ode in your work [. . .] I thank you for giving it to me' (ibid. 1416). It first appeared in *Les Écrits nouveaux* in February 1919 and in the volume *Odes* in July 1920, along with 'Palm' and 'Dawn'. In a text of the *Notebooks* from 1937, Valéry compares it to *The Young Fate*: 'I tried to keep to the intention of expressing the physiological feeling of consciousness; the functioning of the *body*, inasmuch as it is perceived by the Self, acting as a *basso continuo* to incidents or ideas—Since an idea is merely an incident' (*Cahiers*, xx. 250).

0.2 *At these words, she [Dido] fell silent and her face grew pale*: taken from *Aeneid*, 4.499, the epigraph first appeared in the edition of *Poésies* in 1933. Valéry noted the quotation in a manuscript copybook of *Charmes* in the Bibliothèque nationale (N.a.fr. 19010, fo. 35).

118 *empyreuma*: (Gk: *empureuein* = to set on fire) the pungent smell given off by burnt organic matter.

120 *neumes*: (Gk = notation) system of graphic symbols indicating pitch, used in medieval church music, such as Gregorian chant, and at the origins of musical notation.

THE SYLPH

The poem was sketched out in July 1918 and published in *Intentions* in January 1922. Valéry reworked it in February–March for *Charmes*. First postulated by the Swiss physician and forefather of medicine Paracelsus (Theophrastus Bombastus Von Hohenheim, 1493–1541), the sylph is a mythological air spirit according to his classification of the Earth's elements (undines: water; salamanders: fire; gnomes: earth). The brevity of the poem, whose cohesion is built around the vocalic repetition of *i* and *u*, is evocative of the light movement of this elemental of air. The sylph symbolizes here that which eludes the mind and the fleeting source of poetic inspiration.

THE BEGUILER

Written in September 1917 and published, together with 'The Caress', in *Les Écrits nouveaux* (no. 8) in June 1918. Valéry reworked it in February–March 1922 for *Charmes*. It was one of the poems most admired by the Surrealist poet Louis Aragon (1897–1982) whom Valéry met around 1919.

DEATH BRUSHES HER LIGHTLY

Written in July 1918, the poem was reworked in early 1921 for *Charmes*. It was published in the magazine *L'Œil de bœuf* in April of that year and in *Vers et prose* in January 1926. Valéry considered it one of the less important pieces of the collection.

SKETCH OF A SERPENT

In a letter to André Fontainas in March 1922, Valéry explained the burlesque origin of the 'Serpent', one of the key pieces of the collection, which was published by the Éditions de la *NRF* in July of the previous year: 'This poem was originally a jokey ballad, written to torment P[ierre] L[ouÿs] in 1915. [. . .] Found in 1917 or '18 in a notebook, the theme was deemed to be worthy of a fresh look' (Valéry and Fontainas, *Correspondance 1893–1945*, ed. Lo Giudice, 271). In addition to changing its title several times, he 'eliminated ¾ of the ballad' (which he described as a 'comic, blasphemous, and slightly smutty monologue' (Gide, Louÿs, and Valéry, *Correspondances à trois voix, 1888–1920*, 1193)), as well as its jocular tone by the autumn of 1918. He subsequently added numerous stanzas and reworked the poem, all written in octosyllables, in early 1922 before its publication in *Charmes*. It is dedicated to Henri Ghéon (born Henri Vangeon, 1875–1944), a Catholic writer who was a close friend of André Gide and with whom he founded the *NRF*. The symbolism of the snake as a force of intelligence, knowledge, and sexual awareness holds a special place in Valéry's iconography. The snake entwined about a key was his personal insignia and features as an artistic motif and colophon in his *Notebooks*.

52 *He who reigns in Heaven*: satirical allusion to Bossuet's *Funeral Oration for Henrietta-Maria of France, Queen of Great Britain*.

74 *Gehenna*: valley of the damned in the afterlife; originally a valley where children were sacrificed by the Israelites near Jerusalem.

239 *beryl*: a green or aquamarine mineral.

POMEGRANATES

Drafted in October 1917, the octosyllabic sonnet was reworked in 1918–19 and published in *Rythme et synthèse* in May 1920. The poem was revised and modified in early 1922 before it appeared in *Charmes*. The bursting fruit, revealing its secret richness, induces the poet to reflect on his own innermost essence and on the experience of the creative mind.

LOST WINE

This octosyllabic sonnet was drafted in October 1917 and reworked on several occasions before its publication in *Les Feuilles libres* in February 1922, and then in *Charmes* later that year. The image of a drop of wine diffused in clear water to which it imparts momentarily a rosy tint suggests the germ of poetic creation and radiance. It is borrowed from Henri Poincaré's interpretation (in *La Valeur de la science* from 1905) of Carnot's principle of irreversible processes in thermodynamics; the models from this particular branch of physics, which Valéry studied from the early 1890s, served as analogies in his own research on the functioning of the human mind. This same image of a drop of wine in clear water is evoked in a prose poem, 'Song of the Master Idea', published in *Mélange* in 1939.

INTERIOR

Written in 1916, the poem was originally part of another poem, 'L'Heure et la Femme', which Valéry split into 'Intérieur' and 'Heure', the latter being omitted from *Charmes*. 'Interior', the shortest piece in the collection, was reworked between 1916 and 1919 and finally completed in 1922. Using imagery of transparency and refraction, the poem evokes the dreamy movements of consciousness upon which the almost imperceptible feminine presence scarcely intrudes.

THE GRAVEYARD BY THE SEA

This twenty-four-stanza poem, widely regarded as Valéry's best-known verse and among the most celebrated in the French language, is the only work in which he invested some of himself and of his own experience. The context for this personal yet universal monologue on mortality is the cemetery of Sète overlooking the sea at the Golfe du Lion; it treats, as he wrote in the essay 'Au sujet du "Cimetière marin"', 'the simplest and most constant themes of my affective and intellectual life, just as they had imposed themselves on my adolescence and were associated with the sea and light of a certain place on the shores of the Mediterranean' (*Œuvres*, ed. Jarrety, ii. 285). At the beginning of the poem, the poet reflects on being and non-being at high noon from the vantage point of the cemetery overlooking the sea. From the rapt contemplation of the motionless sea and light, his mood moves from quietude and anxiety to an acceptance of mortality and realization that he is the element of change therein. Prompted by the rising wind, he responds to the call of the now-dynamic sea breaking on the rocks at the end of the poem.

The elegiac meditation was conceived during the composition of *The Young Fate* in 1916, but was not begun until October/November of the following year under the title 'Mare nostrum' (meaning 'our sea', the Roman designation for the Mediterranean to which Valéry alludes in his celebrated autobiographical essay 'Mediterranean Inspirations'). In 1918, the poem then entitled 'The Graveyard by the Sea' comprised ten stanzas to which he added four in March 1919 and a further ten in the spring of 1920. The poem was first published separately by the *NRF* on 1 June 1920, and then by the Émile-Paul Frères in August, before appearing in *Charmes* in June 1922.

At the request of Gustave Cohen (1879–1958), Valéry wrote the essay 'Au sujet du "Cimetière marin"' for the 1933 edition published by Gallimard, which illuminates the origins and the philosophical concept underpinning the poem. Its genesis can be traced back to a decasyllabic rhythm that obsessed Valéry. He gives the following account of what prompted him to use the form, which is rarely used in modern poetry:

> I have said that 'The Graveyard by the Sea' first came into my head in the form of a composition of six-line stanzas comprising ten syllables. This position allowed me to spread quite easily in my work what it required in perceptible, emotional, and abstract terms in order to convey the contemplation of a certain *self*, transcribed into the poetic realm (*Œuvres*, ed. Jarrety, ii. 287).

The introduction of Zeno's philosophical arguments was intended to counterbalance the human and sensual tonality of the preceding stanzas.

0.1–0.2 *Do not aspire . . . the realm of the possible*: Valéry read the ancient Greek lyric poet Pindar (*c*.522–*c*.438 BC) in 1919 and noted the quotation in a notebook, but it was not included until the 1926 edition of *Charmes*. Camus used the same quote as an epigraph for *The Myth of Sisyphus*.

121 *Zeno of Elea*: Greek philosopher and mathematician (*c*.495–*c*.430 BC) who devised several paradoxes purporting to show that motion was impossible since duration and distance (space and time) are infinitely divisible. By the time Achilles reaches the tortoise, it has already advanced. In the arrow paradox, Zeno postulates that, for movement to occur, an object must change position, but the arrow at every moment is at rest in space and is thus motionless.

SECRET ODE

Conceived in April 1917 and written later that year, the poem was retouched in December 1919 before its publication in *Littérature* in February. There are numerous manuscript versions of the piece about which Valéry wrote to the philosopher Alain in 1930: 'I am surprised you like "Secret Ode", which I believed I alone could like a little. It's a type of natural child. Of unknown parents. Hence the title' (*Lettres à quelques-uns*, 184). The poem celebrates the triumph of the poet after a long struggle in language and of the creative human spirit universally, embodied in the mythological figure of Hercules, and with echoes, as some critics have suggested, of the Armistice in 1918.

THE ROWER

Begun in Paris in May 1918 and reworked at the Château de l'Isle-Manière, the poem was published in the *Mercure de France* in December and dedicated to his friend André Lebey. In a letter to his wife seeking her opinion on the piece, Valéry referred to it as 'obviously, too obviously, an exercise with or against various difficulties' (*Œuvres*, ed. Hytier, i. 41). Several reflections in his *Notebooks* (*Cahiers*, vii. 72) confirm the technical problems he had with the use of the alexandrine. The theme of the poem is the struggle against natural forces, rigour, and the elegance of movement, with echoes of time and death.

PALM

Written contemporaneously with 'Dawn' (with which it originally formed a single piece) in March 1917, the poem was augmented and reworked during that year with some additions in May of 1918 and 1919. Dedicated to his wife Jeannie, it was published along with 'Dawn' and 'The Pythia' by the *NRF* in June 1919 and in *Odes* in 1920, before appearing again, slightly modified, in *Charmes* in 1922. This biblical-like parable celebrates poetic creation in the guise of the Angel of the Annunciation who comes to bestow the gift of creativity, which will yield fruit for the pensive mind. The tree, one of the pre-eminent natural objects in Valéry's poetics, is the supreme embodiment of time and space, standing between two realms (its roots in the maternal earth and its crown in the heavens) on which its fruitful abundance depends.

TWELVE POEMS

Compiled by Octave Nadal from the manuscripts in Valéry's study in the rue de Villejust after his death, this collection *Douze poèmes* was published by Bibliophiles du Palais in 1959 in an ornate volume with thirteen lithographs by Jean Cocteau (1889–1963) whom Valéry befriended around 1919. The poems appeared in the November issue of the *Mercure de France* that same year with an introduction by Nadal. The selection is based on his personal choice, and chosen from different periods: two are poems from Valéry's youth, six were conceived and written during the work on *Charmes*, and four post-publication. The poem 'Ma nuit' is printed in the Appendix, pp. 273–4.

THE MAIDEN

The poem was sketched out on a manuscript page of one of the notebooks of *The Young Fate* ('*JP* MS II', held at the Bibliothèque nationale) in April 1917. To these initial ten lines Valéry added a few more stanzas in October of the following year. The finished poem of five octosyllabic quatrains featured on the earliest lists of pieces drawn up by Valéry to be included in *Charmes* but was subsequently eliminated.

SPIRITUAL BEE

The poem, composed of decasyllabic quatrains, is one of several versions that Valéry wrote between October 1918 and January of the following year, under the titles 'The Bee' and 'Ambroisie' (see *Œuvres*, ed. Jarrety, i. 929-31), the latter published, both by Nadal in 1957, in the *Cahiers du Sud* and in Valéry and Fourment, *Correspondance 1887–1933*, ed. Nadal, 228-9. It featured on the lists of poems he intended to include in *Charmes* before eliminating it in favour of an entirely new poem 'The Bee', written in January 1919. The spiritual bee here is a metaphor for the creative poetic mind.

BEATRICE

Written for Catherine Pozzi, this undated octosyllabic sonnet was composed during the period of their relationship from 1920 to 1928. Beatrice is one of the code names that Valéry used in the *Notebooks* for Pozzi, along with the more common 'K', 'Karin', or 'CK'. (Beatrice Portinari was Dante's muse and inspiration for *The New Life* and *The Divine Comedy*.) Aside from a rough draft entitled 'Poèmes de Béatrice' held at the Bibliothèque Jacques Doucet (VAL MS 1816), there is no complete manuscript of the sonnet. In his letters to Pozzi from November 1921 and early 1922, Valéry refers to working on a project named 'Beatrice', most likely a poem (Catherine Pozzi and Paul Valéry, *La Flamme et la cendre: Correspondance*, ed. Lawrence Joseph (Paris: Gallimard, 2006), 220, 224, and 304).

THE PHILOSOPHER

The germ of this octosyllabic sonnet is to be found on two pages of 'The Pythia' (in the manuscripts and a notebook pertaining to *Charmes*) and most likely intended for that poem, but Valéry developed it as a separate piece. Composed between October 1917 and October 1918, the location of the original manuscript transcribed by Nadal is unknown.

AT EACH FINGER

One of the two poems of youth in *Douze poèmes*, this Elizabethan sonnet (or quatorzain) dates from September 1892. A similar version entitled 'Pastorale', held at the Bibliothèque nationale, was dedicated to Valéry's friend and neighbour in Montpellier, Pierre Féline.

VANISHING

This second poem of the collection from 1892 was written in the form of an Elizabethan sonnet. There are two versions of the poem in the dossier of early verse ('Vers anciens II') in the Bibliothèque nationale. The complicated syntax reflects the influence of Mallarmé.

AT WINTER'S WINDOW...

Written for the novelist Jean Voilier (pseudonym for Jeanne Loviton, 1903–96) in 1938. Valéry first met her around 1925, but only became intimately involved with her in early 1938 when she was then 34 years old and he almost 67. Valéry also dedicated the libretto *Cantate du Narcisse*, written that same year, to her.

TO HIDDEN DIVINITIES

Begun in October 1917, along with 'The Caress', 'Disaster', 'Colloquy (*for two flutes*)' and 'In Genoa', and reworked in November, this poem consisting of four ten-line stanzas of hexasyllables was originally called 'Grottes' ('Caves'), then 'Grotesque' and 'Hymne Grotesque'. The theme of caverns/cavities underpins the entire poem whose erotic tone was informed by the relationship with Catherine Pozzi. In the autumn of 1920, Valéry intended including it in the *Album of Old Verse*. It features on lists of poems for the collection, but judging it to be unsatisfactory, he eliminated it at that point. The title of the final existing manuscript is 'Odelette to Hidden Divinities'.

 1 *Nereids*: a group of fifty sea nymphs of the god Nereus in Greek mythology.

LITTLE NIGHT ODE

Comprising eight quatrains of pentasyllables, the poem was written around 1940. Its theme is that of separated lovers and, like 'At Winter's Window...', it was dedicated to Jean Voilier. After its publication by Nadal, it subsequently appeared in *Plaisir de France* in December 1965.

FRAGMENT

The poem is undated but is thought to have been composed around 1940.

SILENCE

The first fragments dating from March 1919 are to be found in a manuscript notebook 'P.V. 1918' of *Charmes* and it featured on the lists of poems to be included therein, but was soon eliminated. In a different manuscript notebook, Valéry reworked the poem (along with another unfinished version) and completed it in June 1921. Its sombre tone, tinged with bitterness, transposes the torment and turbulence of the relationship with Catherine Pozzi, whose code name 'K' appears on the manuscript. In a letter to Pozzi on 22 November 1921, Valéry refers to this 'occasional poem' by its first line 'All that remains of us' (Pozzi and Valéry, *Correspondance*, 219).

TO OLD BOOKS

Valéry began writing the poem in a manuscript notebook of *Charmes* in the summer of 1918 and included it that autumn on the lists of poems to be included in the collection. The idea for the theme of old books came most likely from the large library in the Château de l'Isle-Manière which Valéry used regularly in the course of his three-month stay with Édouard Lebey. The poem was reworked in January 1919 but eliminated from the list in March.

LATER OCCASIONAL VERSE

In the definitive version of *Poésies* from 1942, Valéry brought the number of unpublished poems to twelve in a section entitled 'Pièces diverses'. The poems are from two different eras, notably those from the period 1917–20 ('Snow'; 'Disaster'; 'Colloquy (*for Two Flutes*)'; 'Hour'; 'Beguiler II'; 'The Absent-minded One'; 'Equinox'; 'The Caress') and those after 1935 ('The Cruel Bird'; 'At Dawn'; 'A Special Song'; 'The Philosopher and "The Young Fate"'). The 'Pièces diverses', along with the poems published in *Mélange* in 1939, those by Octave Nadal in 1959, as well as other unpublished verse and miscellaneous fragments, are contained in the manuscript notebook 'Charmes II' (N.a.fr. 19008) in the Bibliothèque nationale. Many of them are deeply personal in nature, inspired by Jeannie, close friends, or intimate moments of his relationship with Catherine Pozzi.

HOUR

The poem was sketched out in the manuscript notebook 'Charmes II' during the composition of *The Young Fate* into which he envisaged incorporating it. The poem was initially linked to 'Interior' before they were split into two discrete pieces after the fourth draft. Valéry reworked 'Hour' in 1917 and 1919. He placed it on the list of poems for *Charmes*, but subsequently removed it in 1920 and then for a time considered including it in the *Album de vers anciens*. It appeared in the 'Pièces diverses' of *Poésies* in 1942. This meditation celebrates the calm and peace of night before the incipient light of dawn, Valéry's preferred moment of the day and the subject of many prose poems.

THE ABSENT-MINDED ONE

This poem was sketched out in the *Notebooks* (*Cahiers*, vi. 666) in July 1917 at Gide's country residence at Cuverville in Normandy. It featured on all the lists of poems to be included in *Charmes* but its composition, which involved over ten drafts, caused Valéry endless problems and was eventually eliminated. It appeared in *Mélange* in 1939. The feminine figure evoked here is reminiscent of that of 'Interior'.

DISASTER

When the poem first appeared in *Mélange* in 1939, Valéry stated in the preface that it was a poem of youth, but it was actually written in 1909 under the title 'Shipwreck' ('Naufrage') and reworked on 4–5 October 1917. He had Edgar Allan Poe's novel *The Narrative of Arthur Gordon Pym on Nantucket* (1838) in mind when he composed it, as attested by the reference to the eponymous protagonist in the original manuscript. Valéry disliked the piece, written when Jeannie was seriously ill in 1909, and which he felt was too personal. Consequently, he eliminated it from the list of poems to be included in *Charmes*, and only published it at the request of Julien-Pierre Monod.

26 *He dances himself to death, foundering with his flock*: inversion of the story of Christ calming the storm and walking on the water in Matthew 14:24–33 and in Mark 6:47–51: 'And when even was come, the ship was in the midst

of the sea, and he [Jesus] alone on the land.' Valéry inscribed the epigraph 'Erat navis in medio mari' ('The ship was in the midst of the sea') from the biblical narrative at the top of the manuscript page of the 1909 version.

COLLOQUY (*FOR TWO FLUTES*)

The earliest rough draft of the poem dates from late 1916 with the first version called 'Canzone' written in early October 1917 on the back of a manuscript page of 'In Genoa'. Although Valéry considered including the poem in the *Album de vers anciens* and then in *Charmes*, it did not appear until June 1939 in the *NRF* under the title 'Colloque (Old piece, intended to be set to music)', and that same year in *Mélange* with the dedication to Francis Poulenc (1899–1963) who composed the song for the dialogue. The composer created his 'Colloque pour soprano et baryton avec accompagnement de piano' (FP 108) in December 1940 which was performed for the first time at the Théâtre des Mathurins in Paris on 4 February the following year.

THE CARESS

Composed between early October and early November 1917, the poem, comprising three quatrains of heptasyllables, featured on the lists of titles that Valéry drew up for the *Album de vers anciens* and then *Charmes*. It was published in *Les Écrits nouveaux* 2/8 (June 1918) and included in the 1933 and 1942 editions of *Poésies*.

EQUINOX (*ELEGY*)

Sketched out in July 1918 during his stay at the Château de l'Isle-Manière, the poem was at its inception linked with 'To the Plane Tree', which was begun at the same time in the same notebook ('Charmes II'). The drafts were separated when Valéry transcribed them to a different notebook ('Charmes I') and the poem, briefly entitled 'Pause' then 'Station', appeared on the lists of poems for *Charmes* before being eliminated at the end of 1919. It was published in the 'Pièces diverses' of *Poésies* in 1942.

0.1 *To look...*: consonant with 'Louk', a cryptic dedication to Lucienne Julien Cain (née Meyer), who typed up Valéry's *Notebooks* from 1935. Her husband Julien Cain (1887–1974) was general administrator at the Bibliothèque nationale from 1930 to 1964 and a friend of Valéry.

13 *Psyche*: goddess of the soul.

23 *Persephone . . . Eurydice*: Persephone, daughter of Demeter and Zeus, was carried off to the underworld by Hades until commanded by Zeus that she be released, but she had to spend part of the year with Hades. Orpheus charmed Persephone and Hades with his music while trying to retrieve Eurydice (see the poem 'Orpheus', p. 85).

JOB

This sonnet was written in the manuscript notebook 'Charmes II' in July 1918 while Valéry was working on the collection of new verse. A different version, sold at public auction in March 1989, is reproduced by Florence de Lussy in *'Charmes' d'après les manuscrits de Paul Valéry: Histoire d'une métamorphose*, i (Paris: Lettres modernes, 1990), 266. In the Old Testament, Job was severely tested by Satan but, despite losing his family and wealth, and being afflicted with agonizing sores, remained faithful to God.

SNOW

Sketched out in November 1919 at the same time as 'Silence' in the manuscript notebook 'Charmes II', the poem was reworked in 1921 and early 1922 during which time Valéry undertook twelve different drafts. Having featured on the lists of poems to be included in the *Album de vers anciens* and then *Charmes*, it was subsequently eliminated. It is dedicated to Jacqueline Pasteur Vallery-Radot (1866–1970), wife of the eminent doctor Louis whom Valéry met in 1919. Grandson of Louis Pasteur, he treated Valéry for various complaints from the 1920s on and particularly for recurrent gastric problems towards the end of his life. The poem was published in *Mélange* in 1939, a month after his stay at the country residence of the Vallery-Radots at Marrault in Burgundy (see note to 'A Memory of Marrault', p. 319).

BEGUILER II

The poem was composed in 1924 for Catherine Pozzi in the manuscript note-book 'Charmes II' at the Bibliothèque nationale. It is a supplement to 'The Beguiler', published in *Charmes* in 1922.

SONNET FOR IRENE (BY MONSIEUR DE SAINT AMBROYSE, 1644)

Written in 1924, the Baroque-style sonnet was published in 1939. Valéry creates the effect of the *sonnet galant* through the use of archaic spelling, diction, and imagery, which is reminiscent of the classical verse of François de Malherbe (1555–1628). As in the verse of youth, Valéry signs the poem with his middle name Ambroise (which was originally his first name; he was born Ambroise Paul Toussaint Jules Valéry). The voice is that of the poet expressing his desire to the woman whom he addresses directly in the third and fourth stanzas.

THE CRUEL BIRD

An initial rough draft of six lines was sketched out in the *Notebooks* (*Cahiers*, xviii. 177) in July 1935, and the full sonnet was composed soon after. It appeared for the first time in the 'Pièces diverses' of the 1942 edition of *Poésies*.

AT DAWN

Written in 1935 and similar in tone to the previous poem of the same year, it was published in the 'Pièces diverses' of *Poésies* in 1942. This evocation of dawn is reminiscent of the many prose aubades and matinal psalms of the *Notebooks* which the writer compiled under the heading 'Poems and Short Abstract Poems' (one of the thirty-one rubrics comprising his 'System' of self-science). See Steven Romer's translation in Valéry, *Cahiers/Notebooks*, ed. Stimpson, ii. 343–404.

A SPECIAL SONG

The initial sketch was drafted in the *Notebooks* (*Cahiers*, xxi. 508) on 3 July 1938, and composed in late August. It appeared in the 'Pièces diverses' of *Poésies* in 1942.

'IT IS TRUE, I AM GLOOMY'

This quatrain was published by Octave Nadal in his introductory 'Note' to *Douze poèmes* in 1959.

QUATRAINS AND DEDICATIONS OF ALL PERIODS

VERSE FOR MME DE R——

Dating from 1892, the poem expresses the forlorn obsession that Valéry experienced for Sylvia de Rovira (née Blondel de Roquevaire), a young Catalan widow first glimpsed at the end of 1889, and occasionally mentioned in his letters to Gide. The destructive passion and the resultant emotional turmoil came to a head in Genoa on the night of a violent storm on 4–5 October 1892, which became subsequently known as the 'Night in Genoa'. Henceforth, Valéry abandons poetry for over twenty years, turning his attention instead to rational intellectual analysis and investigation into all areas of human sciences.

AMBROISE, IN THE BOTANIC GARDEN...

Written on 2 October 1917, the poem was sent to Gide, along with 'In Genoa', three weeks later to thank him for the copy of the new edition of *Les Nourritures terrestres* (originally published in 1897). Valéry reminisces here about the evenings which the two young writers spent in the Botanical Garden of Montpellier in May 1891 (Gide and Valéry, *Correspondance 1890–1942*, ed. Fawcett, 456).

1 *Ambroise*: Valéry's middle name (see note for the 'Sonnet for Irene') .

9 *Fruits of the Earth*: the English title for Gide's novel *Les Nourritures terrestres*.

IN GENOA

Written on 2 October 1917, this light humorous poem which Valéry sent to Gide three weeks after (see previous note) features on some of the lists of poems for *Charmes*. Valéry reworked the piece in November and again in January 1919, but finally excluded it. It evokes familiar visual and olfactory sensations experienced during earlier stays with his mother and her niece Gaeta Cabella in Genoa, notably in August 1910 (his first visit since 1895), where he was convalescing from whooping cough. Valéry wrote a similar prose poem in the *Notebooks* (*Cahiers*, iv. 164–5); see *Œuvres*, ed. Jarrety, iii. 442–3.

FOR YOUR 'TOWERING' BEECH TREE

Valéry stayed at the Gides' country residence in Cuverville, Normandy from 20 July to 6 August 1917 and would go for a walk barefoot around the estate set in luxuriant countryside. On 27 July he wrote to Gide, giving notice of his intention to compose a poetic tribute to the magnificent beech trees of the estate:

> I have just gone barefoot to worship the Towering Beech tree. [. . .] it would merit that I add a few lines to the small ode. But these verses have not yet come to me. I neither summon nor rebuff them. [. . .] I limit myself thus, at the foot of the Beech tree, to gazing at it, to feeling it with my mind, without endeavouring to make it speak. It will speak of its own accord, far from here, some day, when it will have found in my substance a ground, an air, a sun non present, less present, and more actual. (Gide and Valéry, *Correspondance 1890–1942*, ed. Fawcett, 764–5)

The poem was composed on 2 November in the notebook 'Charmes I' and sent the same day to Madeleine Gide (ibid. 778) to whom it is dedicated. In a letter to André four days later, Valéry writes:

> The lines of verse that I sent to your wife are not at all what I wanted to write for her. I intended thanking her for her butter which is delicious, and celebrate a little the splendid tree, for the pleasure of it. But it was All Souls' Day and despite the author's aim, the song became solemn; the intimate tone just about stopping it from turning into a lamentation – and countering it, it appears to me, by a certain '*ritenuto*'. I sent it hot off the press – on the evening of the day I began it. I need to touch it up. (ibid. 780)

There are six versions—mostly identical—of the poem, comprising seven octosyllabic quatrains which featured on the lists of pieces to be included in *Charmes* before being eliminated in October 1918 and replaced by 'To the Plane Tree'. Valéry included the poem, along with 'The Caress', in the 1933 version of *Poésies*.

27 *Verdun*: the longest and bloodiest battle of the Great War. It was fought between 21 February and 18 December 1916 during which the French, under the command of General Pétain, repulsed a major German offensive directed by Erich von Falkenhayn.

QUATRAIN FOR ADRIENNE MONNIER (1917)

Written in 1917 and published in *Paul Valéry vivant*, 158. Valéry was a regular visitor to Monnier's renowned bookshop, the Maison des Amis des Livres on the rue de l'Odéon. She published the *Album of Old Verse* in 1920.

DEDICATION TO LÉON-PAUL FARGUE

The dedication is dated 17 April 1917 and written on a copy of *The Young Fate* which Valéry offered to poet and essayist Léon-Paul Fargue (1876–1947). The latter had the idea of organizing a reading of the poem at the home of Arthur Fontaine to mark its publication. Following a rehearsal on 21 April where Fargue read the poem in the presence of Gallimard, a formal presentation and a reading, again by Fargue before an audience of friends, took place eight days later. The dedication appeared in various texts such as the *Cahiers du Sud* and in Paul Rauhut's *Paul Valéry, Geist und Mythos* (Munich: Max Hueber, 1930).

Fargue frequented Mallarmé's salon at the rue de Rome where he met Valéry in the early 1890s.

  5 *Beneath the helm, she takes to the open sea*: in the French text, Valéry replaces 'largue' (itself a nautical term: *larguer*—to cast off) for 'large' (open sea) to rhyme with Fargue.

VERSES FOR MISS NATALIE CLIFFORD BARNEY

Natalie Clifford Barney (1876–1972), American playwright and literary figure, moved to Paris in 1909 after inheriting a fortune. Valéry made her acquaintance at a reading of *The Young Fate* at the residence of Élisabeth de Gramont, Duchesse de Clermont-Tonnerre on 24 June 1917. Dated 30 December 1917, these verses appeared along with the poem 'Dawn' and the manuscript of 'The Beguiler' in her volume of reminiscence, *Aventures de l'esprit* (Paris: Éditions Émile-Paul Frères, 1929), 130–2.

  1 *the road of the Vineyards*: Clifford Barney lived for a time on the rue des Vignes in the 16th arrondissement of Paris, the same district as Paul Valéry and Pierre Louÿs who resided at 49 rue Vineuse.

VERSES FOR NATALIE CLIFFORD BARNEY

These lines were included in a letter of 11 August 19 . . . (date incomplete) for Natalie Clifford Barney who, for over sixty years until her death in 1972, held her famous Friday evening salon in a two-storey pavilion (separated from the main house) at 20 rue Jacob in the 6th arrondissement. Valéry became a habitué of the salon which was frequented by the leading writers, painters, and intellectuals of the era (Joyce, Eliot, Stein, Toklas, Pound, Rodin, Capote, Scott Fitzgerald, Isadora Duncan, Nancy Cunard, Peggy Guggenheim).

SONNET FOR MME LUCIEN MÜHLFELD

Lucien Mühlfeld (1875–1953, née Jeanne Meyer) provided financial assistance to Valéry around this time of his career, and he sent the sonnet to her in January 1918 as a New Year's offering. Commonly known by her more familiar appellation 'The Witch' ('La Sorcière'), she lived at 3 rue Georges-Ville in the 16th arrondissement, round the corner from Valéry's home at the rue de Villejust. He frequented her salon daily from 1917, when it was one of the most fashionable gatherings of the literary and artistic elite. Valéry sent the sonnet to Gide (Gide and Valéry, *Correspondance 1890–1942*, ed. Fawcett, 783) with the commentary: 'As for the Neighbour, I sent her this sonnet instead of flowers and chocolates [. . .] I assure you it's not as bad as all that. The end must give you a toothache. With a little more work, we'd have carried it off.'

  6 *Boissier*: celebrated confectionery founded in 1827 by Bélissaire Boissier, a friend of Victor Hugo, who developed a new glazing technique and opened boutiques on the elegant boulevards of Paris. His products are mentioned in works by Zola, Alexandre Dumas *fils*, and the Goncourt brothers.

  7 *Mnemosyne*: the Titan goddess of memory in Greek mythology.

'OLD DIAL OF MINE, I LONG FOR YOUR HOURS'

Sent to André Lebey in June 1919 following Valéry's three-day stay at Pentecost in his friend's house in Hautot-sur-Mer near Dieppe in the Seine-Maritime department. The poem was published in *Valéry-Lebey—au miroir de l'histoire: Choix de lettres 1895–1938*, ed. Micheline Hontebeyrie (Paris: Gallimard, 2004), 371.

2 *Pallas*: allusion to Lebey's dialogue *Isis et Pallas: Dialogue d'Orient et d'Occident*, published in 1927. Pallas Athena, daughter of Zeus, was the goddess of wisdom.

5 *The shaken rose now opens without me*: Lebey's house was named the 'Loge des roses', to which Valéry refers here.

'TIME, THIS VILE ENEMY'

Written on 24 December 1919 and sent to the novelist and diplomat Paul Morand (1888–1976) for Christmas, it was published for the first time forty years later in the weekly magazine *Arts*, 754 (24–9 December 1959), 4. It is reproduced in Valéry, *Œuvres*, ed. Hytier, i. 1693.

9 *my Fate*: reference to Valéry's *The Young Fate*.

QUATRAIN FOR VALÉRY LARBAUD

Written at the end of January 1920 in reply to a postcard from Larbaud (1881–1957) who quoted it in his book *Paul Valéry et la Méditerranée* (Maastricht: A.A.M. Stols, 1926). Novelist, critic, and one of the translators of Joyce's *Ulysses*, Larbaud met Valéry early in the century and became a fervent admirer of his verse, informing him in a letter of the success of *The Young Fate* in Spain.

2 *Viñes*: Ricardo Viñes y Roda (1875–1943), Spanish pianist whom Valéry met in 1910 at the home of the Polish man of letters Cyprien (known as Cipa) Godebski (1875–1937) and his wife Ida, at 22 rue d'Athènes in Paris; their salon was frequented by artists and composers, like their close friend Maurice Ravel.

DEDICATION TO ANNA DE NOAILLES

Anna de Noailles (born Countess Anna-Elisabeth Bibesco-Bassaraba de Brancovan, 1876–1933) was a poet, literary personality of the early century, and friend of Proust, Colette, Cocteau, and Rilke. She was introduced to Valéry in May 1919 at the residence of Mme Lucien Mühlfeld at rue Georges-Ville. He frequented Anna de Noailles's salon and regularly met her in the literary circles of Paris during the 1920s. The dedication is inscribed on a copy of *Charmes* which Valéry sent to her in 1922.

VERSES FOR RENÉE DE BRIMONT

The correspondence between Valéry and Catherine Pozzi which dates from 1920 to 1927 contains various unfinished poems. In an appendix of Pozzi and Valéry, *Correspondance*, 671–4, the editor Lawrence Joseph published the six most complete poems (including 'Silence' published by Nadal in *Douze poèmes*). I have selected the examples below.

'LIGHT SPIRITS CROSSING THE WALLS'

This poem, written in Nice and dated 28 March 1922, is dedicated to Baroness
Renée de Brimont (1880–1943), the poet whose verse *Mirages* was set to music
by Fauré in his song cycle of the same name (Op. 113). Valéry, whom she met in
1919, became a close confidant and thereafter a regular visitor to her salon.
There is no extant copy of the original manuscript but Catherine Pozzi transcribed the poem which was published in Pozzi and Valéry, *Correspondance*, 356.
Jealous of his relationship with Renée, Pozzi satirizes the poem in her *Journal*
in an entry of 31 January 1924: 'The lines of verse are bad, even for a lunatic.
They are to thank her [Renée de Brimont] for a gift of carnations [. . .] I am
"the hand that cannot be grasped, that strikes he whom she knew to choose"'
(ibid. n. 1). On the back of an envelope where she quotes this sonnet, Pozzi
rejects the charge of being the source of Valéry's woes. He first met Pozzi at
a dinner organized by Renée at the Hôtel Plaza Athénée on the Avenue
Montaigne in Paris in June 1920.

'ON THE EDGE OF HEAVEN'

First published in Pozzi and Valéry, *Correspondance*, 672. Béatrice is another of
Valéry's code names for Pozzi.

'THE SPLENDOUR AND SERENITY'

Dated July 1922, this evocation of Catherine Pozzi's country residence with its
large trees at La Graulet in Bergerac, where Valéry stayed in September 1920,
was published in Pozzi and Valéry, *Correspondance*, 672. In March–April, their
tumultuous relationship, then almost two years old, witnessed one of its numerous crises, this time concerning Pozzi's friendship with the painter Jean
Marchand and the jealousy it engendered. A version of the poem appears
in Catherine Pozzi's *Journal* (reproduced ibid. 649) and referred to by Valéry in
a letter dated 21 July (ibid. 462). Valéry wrote a longer unfinished ode on 30 July
(ibid. 468–9). Another poem entitled 'Ode à la Sage' (published ibid. 467),
dates from this same month.

SMALL THINGS

Inscription beneath a Portrait

Written in the *Notebooks* (*Cahiers*, x. 491) in 1924 under the title 'Quatrain for
[a] photo', referring to a photograph offered 'To my friend François Mauriac'.
It was published in *Mélange* in 1939.

ON A FAN

Published in *Mélange* in 1939, the quatrain was offered to Mme de Martel, the
wife of the surgeon Thierry Martel de Janville (1875–1940) who was Jeannie's
gynaecologist from 1909 and operated on her in 1929. Valéry and Martel
remained friends, and were together promoted *grand officier de la Légion d'honneur* in February 1939.

TO JUAN RAMÓN JIMÉNEZ

For having missed Valéry's conference at the Institut français de Madrid on 20 May 1924, Jiménez (1881–1958) sent him a bouquet of roses with the words '6 rosas con silencio' ('6 roses accompanied by silence'). Valéry sent him the two-verse poem the following day. In the collection *Hommage des écrivains étrangers à Paul Valéry* (Bussum: A.A.M. Stols, 1927), Jiménez, poet and future Nobel Laureate (1956), called his tribute to Valéry '6 rosas con silencio'.

VERSES FOR CHARLES-ADOLPHE CANTACUZÈNE

The two poems were written for Charles-Adolphe Cantacuzène (1874–1949), prolific Romanian French-language poet and his country's chargé d'affaires in Paris. He was a friend of Mallarmé through whom he met Valéry in the 1890s. The first piece (originally written in 1918) appeared as an advertisement in the *Mercure de France* (15 April 1926) for the publication of *Identités versicolores—les Phosphores mordorés* (Librairie Perrin).

The second poem, 'Hypotyposis', was written in 1916, the year of the publication of *Hypotyposes, aléas et alinéas* (Librairie Perrin).

6 *Père Lachaise*: largest cemetery in Paris (20th arrondissement) and the burial ground of some celebrated figures. It is named after Louis XIV's confessor who resided in the Jesuit house there.

0.1 *Hypotyposis*: a term in rhetoric, meaning a vivid depiction of visual experience as though it were actually present or visible. Kant introduced the term in his *Critique of Judgement*, distinguishing between schematic and symbolic hypotyposis.

3 *syrinx*: the vocal organ of birds situated at the base of the trachea. In Greek mythology, Syrinx was a naiad (nymph) who was transformed into a river reed to save her from amorous pursuit by Pan who cut the reed into pieces from which he fashioned his musical pipes or syrinx.

QUATRAIN FOR TRISTAN DERÈME

Quatrain addressed to the 'poète fantaisiste' Tristan Derème (pseudonym for Philippe Huc, 1889–1941) and published in A. Berne-Joffroy, *Présence de Valéry* (Paris: Plon, 1944). Although having briefly met each other after the war, Derème and Valéry became formally acquainted in the early 1920s. Derème wrote an article in the literary supplement of *Le Figaro* in August 1923 announcing that Valéry had been awarded the *Légion d'honneur*. Four years later, Valéry presided over the banquet organized at the Palais d'Orsay for Derème who was awarded the same decoration.

4 *Thirtieth October seventy-one*: Valéry's date of birth.

QUATRAIN FOR RENÉE VAUTIER

This quatrain was sent without any accompanying letter to the young sculptress Renée Vautier (1898–1991) at the end of December 1933 on paper headed 'Hotel Nacional Madrid' and published in Paul Valéry, *Lettres à Néère*, ed.

M. Jarrety (Paris: La Cooperative, 2017), 159. Valéry first met 'Néère' (code name and anagram of Renée taken from Tibullus' *Elegies*), who was twenty-seven years his junior, in May 1925. In early 1931, she began sculpting a bust of Valéry who fell passionately in love with her but the feelings were never reciprocated which provoked a profound emotional crisis for the writer. He wrote the preface, entitled 'My Bust' ('Mon Buste'), for the exhibition of her work at the Galerie Charpentier on the rue du Faubourg Saint-Honoré in March 1935, after which time they became estranged.

QUATRAIN FOR MME M.B.

This quatrain was written for Mme M.B. (Marcelle Ballard) on 26 May 1938 and accompanied a drawing by Valéry of his own hand holding a cigarette, which is reproduced in *Paul Valéry vivant*, 136 (plate III). Valéry was introduced in 1932 to her husband Jean Ballard (1893–1973), poet and editor of *Les Cahiers du Sud*, whom he befriended during his subsequent visits to Marseilles in the 1930s and early 1940s.

A MEMORY OF MARRAULT, SEPTEMBER 1939

The poem appeared in *Paul Valéry vivant*, 99, with the essay 'Pages inédites de Paul Valéry parmi quelques souvenirs' written by Louis Pasteur Vallery-Radot to whom Valéry sent it for Christmas in 1939 along with a watercolour of their 'salon' bearing the inscription 'Living room interrupted by the war...'. On 4 August, the doctor brought Valéry by car to his Renaissance-style Château de Marrault, situated in the Yonne department in Burgundy, where he stayed for three weeks, visiting the region as well as nearby Switzerland, and rowing on the lakes of the property. He departed for Paris on 25 August, a week before the outbreak of the Second World War. On the accompanying watercolour, dedicated to Mme Jacqueline Vallery-Radot, Valéry wrote: 'Dear friend, the verses are worthless. The watercolour is dreadful. They are well matched. But my heart is in them. It wishes for you both all that dear and true friends can wish for.' The *Cahiers* (xxii. 483) contain another watercolour of a room in the château painted during the same stay.

INDEX OF TITLES

Titles of French poems are in *italics*; titles of English translations are in roman type.

INDEX OF FIRST LINES

First lines of French poems are in *italics*; first lines of English translations are in roman type.

American Literature

British and Irish Literature

Children's Literature

Classics and Ancient Literature

Colonial Literature

Eastern Literature

European Literature

Gothic Literature

History

Medieval Literature

Oxford English Drama

Philosophy

Poetry

Politics

Religion

The Oxford Shakespeare

A complete list of Oxford World's Classics, including Authors in Context, Oxford English Drama, and the Oxford Shakespeare, is available in the UK from the Marketing Services Department, Oxford University Press, Great Clarendon Street, Oxford OX2 6DP, or visit the website at www.oup.com/uk/worldsclassics.

In the USA, visit www.oup.com/us/owc for a complete title list.

Oxford World's Classics are available from all good bookshops.

French Decadent Tales
Six French Poets of the Nineteenth
Century

HONORÉ DE BALZAC   Cousin Bette
Eugénie Grandet
Père Goriot
The Wild Ass's Skin

CHARLES BAUDELAIRE   The Flowers of Evil
The Prose Poems and Fanfarlo

DENIS DIDEROT   Jacques the Fatalist
The Nun

ALEXANDRE DUMAS (PÈRE)   The Black Tulip
The Count of Monte Cristo
Louise de la Vallière
The Man in the Iron Mask
La Reine Margot
The Three Musketeers
Twenty Years After
The Vicomte de Bragelonne

ALEXANDRE DUMAS (FILS)   La Dame aux Camélias

GUSTAVE FLAUBERT   Madame Bovary
A Sentimental Education
Three Tales

VICTOR HUGO   Notre-Dame de Paris

J.-K. HUYSMANS   Against Nature

PIERRE CHODERLOS DE   Les Liaisons dangereuses
LACLOS

MME DE LAFAYETTE   The Princesse de Clèves

GUILLAUME DU LORRIS   The Romance of the Rose
and JEAN DE MEUN

ÉMILE ZOLA

L'Assommoir
The Belly of Paris
La Bête humaine
The Conquest of Plassans
The Fortune of the Rougons
Germinal
The Kill
The Ladies' Paradise
The Masterpiece
Money
Nana
Pot Luck
Thérèse Raquin